REGULATING
THE
NATIONAL
PASTIME

REGULATING
THE
NATIONAL
PASTIME

Baseball and Antitrust

Jerold J. Duquette

PRAEGER

Westport, Connecticut
London

Library of Congress Cataloging-in-Publication Data

Duquette, Jerold J., 1968–
    Regulating the national pastime : baseball and antitrust / Jerold
J. Duquette.
        p.   cm.
    Includes bibliographical references and index.
    ISBN 0–275–96535–X (alk. paper)
    1. Baseball—Law and legislation—United States.   2. Antitrust
law—United States.   3. Progressivism (United States politics)
I. Title.
KF3989.D87   1999
344.73′099—dc21   99–16060

British Library Cataloguing in Publication Data is available.

Library of Congress Catalog Card Number: 99–16060
ISBN: 0–275–96535–X

First published in 1999

Praeger Publishers, 88 Post Road West, Westport, CT 06881
An imprint of Greenwood Publishing Group, Inc.
www.praeger.com

Printed in the United States of America

The paper used in this book complies with the
Permanent Paper Standard issued by the National
Information Standards Organization (Z39.48–1984).

10 9 8 7 6 5 4 3 2 1

To my Mother, my Wife, and my Daughter,
the women whose love and support sustain me.

Contents

Acknowledgments

No endeavor such as this is accomplished without help. Although many people contributed to this effort in one way or another, the following few made special contributions deserving of acknowledgment. My academic mentor and benefactor, Jerome Mileur, read this manuscript literally dozens of times; each time his criticisms and suggestions improved the work. His counsel and support continue to be vital to my work. To him I owe the greatest debt of gratitude. George Sulzner also contributed comments and suggestions that improved the work. Professors Mileur and Sulzner are dear friends for whom I have great respect and admiration. My good friend Peter Fairman also deserves mention. Peter provided me with tremendous assistance and advice on this project for which I could never repay him. Finally, I must thank my wife Kara, a captain in the U.S. Marine Corps and a lawyer. In addition to her unfailing love and emotional support, Kara financially supported us for the one year I spent writing full-time. Without her, this book would surely not have been possible.

Introduction

It is said that few things in life are certain. Until the summer of 1994 most Americans would probably have said that, in addition to death and taxes, one thing that could be counted on was the World Series. Every fall since 1904 Americans had enjoyed the world championship of baseball. In 1994, this was not to be. This grand tradition was not interrupted by economic depression, world war, or even natural disaster. Nor was the Fall Classic canceled by an arrogant pennant winning manager unwilling to play against inferior talent. The 1994 World Series fell victim to a labor/management dispute. The player strike, baseball's ninth work stoppage since 1970, was the culmination of three decades of unrest in the business of baseball.

The 1994 baseball strike exposed the less wholesome side of our national pastime more vividly than anything before. The business of baseball took a bit of the shine off what most considered a national treasure. Indeed, baseball seemed to be losing its special place in the American psyche. Long separated from discussions of politics and industrial relations, baseball was suddenly at the center of serious public policy debates at the highest levels of government. In this more somber atmosphere, the long dormant issue of baseball's exemption from federal antitrust laws acquired a new life. Disgusted with the failure of the players and owners to come to an agreement, many, inside government and out, began pushing for repeal of the antitrust exemption as a way to pressure owners into an agreement with the players. The popular concern with baseball was reflected in both the appointment of a mediator by the President of the United States to bring baseball's "labor" and management together and by a renewed interest in the exemption by members of Congress.

This study will examine what has come to be known as the "baseball anomaly." Major League Baseball's exemption from federal antitrust laws represents a regulatory paradox in American political development, which has again been brought to the forefront by the most recent unrest in the game. Baseball is set apart from most other industries, including all other professional sports, by its exemption from federal antitrust law. The decisive question animating this book is, "Why?" Why has baseball been granted this immunity from the laws of the land? And, why has this regulatory anomaly been maintained for three-quarters of a century?

Analyses of this phenomenon have heretofore lacked comprehensiveness. They have been too narrow in their methodology and focus. Scholarly inquiries into the baseball anomaly have generally fallen into one of three categories. They are either legal histories, unsystematic cultural studies, or interest group studies. Missing from the literature is a systematic attempt to integrate these approaches and theories into a comprehensive examination of baseball's unregulated monopoly.

Legal analyses chronicle the history of antitrust litigation in baseball, beginning with the 1922 Supreme Court decision that granted baseball its sweeping antitrust exemption. Subsequent challenges to this decision are examined and the exemption's survival is attributed to historical accident, originating with a Supreme Court whose progressive politics and sentimentality for America's national pastime led it to look away from the true commercial nature of the game. Legal analyses of the exemption focus on the power of precedent, or *stare decisis*, and the Court's insistence that the Congress is the appropriate venue for removing the exemption. Such analyses are uncritical in attributing the origin of the exemption to sentimentality and then focus too narrowly on the rules of the judicial branch to explain its long life. This approach fails to systematically address the impact of ideas on the exemption's survival and treats institutional inertia too narrowly, focusing on the judicial branch to the exclusion of the legislative and the executive.[1]

Several studies have traced the cultural significance of baseball, connecting it to larger social and economic trends. None, however, attempts to distinguish the role of baseball's cultural significance in its retention of the antitrust exemption. These studies are useful in explaining baseball's continued unregulated monopoly insofar as they connect baseball's cultural significance to the attitudes of legislators and fans.[2] In this, they integrate cultural ideas and the struggle of interests but fall short of the full explanation due to their lack of attention to institutional contexts and detail.

Political/economic analyses of the anomaly conclude that powerful interests preserve it by applying continuing political pressure on Congress to protect the exemption.[3] This pressure is credited with chastening members of Congress who might support the repeal of baseball's anomalous status. Warren Freedman sums up the logic of the interest group theory approach when he writes, "The history of antitrust application to the business of professional sports is an absorbing tale of sentimentality and of special interests."[4] While the interest-group explanation of the exemption's continuation is not without merit, it also tends to be reductionist and too narrow, as it fails to consider systematically the impact of institutions and ideas on public policy.

The primary objective of this study is an integrated and comprehensive explanation for the persistence of the baseball anomaly. It will explore the institutional and ideological, as well as the political and economic factors, that have contributed to the paradoxical regulatory status of the business of baseball. Building on the work of numerous scholars, this study examines the impact of institutional and ideological structures and environments, as well as the interplay of interests, to provide a more comprehensive explanation of baseball's unusual commercial status.

This study employs an historical institutionalist methodology, which is part of an emerging approach in political science that falls loosely under the heading of "new institutionalism" or "American political development." This newer institutional focus seeks to expand the narrower "scientific" focus of political scientists since the behavioral revolution in the discipline that emerged in the 1940s and 1950s. The new institutionalism aspires to synthesize the behavioralist/pluralist approach with an earlier institutional approach to the study of government, broadening the analytical focus to the interplay of institutions in an historical and developmental context.

The behavioralist/pluralist methodology grew up in reaction to the rigid institutionalism of traditional political science, which was criticized for being descriptive rather than analytical. Behavioral/pluralism was grounded in an understanding of human nature that finds man an economically rational animal. The methodology operates on the assumption that behavior is shaped by rational self interest, not by ideals, values, or institutional constraints. This assumption leads to the conclusion that public policy is the outcome of the competition between rationally defined interests.[5]

New institutionalists charge that behavioral/pluralism has overvalued the explanatory significance of societal forces in its analysis of politics and the making of public policy, with the result that institutions as explanatory variables have been greatly undervalued. Scholars, such as Theda Skocpol, Stephen Krasner, James March, John Olsen, Eric Nordlinger, and Stephen Skowronek to name only a few, argue that behavioral/pluralism fails to account for the role of institutions and ideas in the process of policy formation and political change. March and Olsen deftly catalogue the indictment of behavioral/pluralist political science as follows:

[T]he basic vision that has characterized theories of politics since about 1950 is (a) *contextual*, inclined to see politics as an integral part of society, less inclined to differentiate the polity from the rest of society; (b) *reductionist*, inclined to see political phenomena as the aggregate consequences of individual behavior, less inclined to ascribe the outcomes of politics to organizational structures and rules of appropriate behavior; (c) *utilitarian*, inclined to see action as the product of calculated self interest, less inclined to see political actors as responding to obligations and duties; (d) *functionalist*, inclined to see history as an efficient mechanism for reaching uniquely appropriate equilibria, less concerned with the possibilities for maladaptation and non-uniqueness in historical development; and (e) *instrumentalist*, inclined to define decision making and the allocation of resources as the central concerns of political life, less attentive to the ways political life is organized around the development of meaning through symbols, rituals and ceremonies.[6]

Behavioral/pluralist political science is also charged with being society-centered, an orientation in which institutions, like the state, have no autonomy in the formulation of public policy. The causal arrow goes one way, from society to polity, with the state being merely a neutral referee of societal forces that compete with one another to shape public policy decisions. These decisions are thus understood as allocations of benefits among competing groups. In explaining policy decisions, political scientists focus on societal "inputs" to government and then examine the distributive effects of government policy ("outputs") on societal actors.[7] The government, or the state, is seen as the "black box" that merely processes social interests, which is to say that institutional arrangements in government are accorded no causal role in the making of public policy.[8]

A key difference between the behavioral/pluralist approach and the historical-institutional approach lies in their differing conceptions of the influence of rationality on public policy making. Behavioralism is reductionist and utilitarian. It sees politics as the aggregate consequences of individual behavior, ignoring the effects of organizational structures. Behavioral/pluralism also sees all action as the product of calculated self-interest irrespective of duties, obligations or rules. From this perspective institutions are at best constraints upon exogenously defined self-interests. The goals of actors are *not* defined by institutions.[9]

The historical institutional perspective sees institutions as structuring behavior more completely. Institutions provide more than the context within which rational strategies are formulated. They provide the context that shapes the actual goals and preferences of actors. In other words, historical-institutionalism sees actors' self definitions of their interests as being shaped by institutional arrangements, as well as by rational calculation. From the historical-institutionalist perspective, human action is seen as an attempt to "satisfice" and thereby fulfill expectations that are context specific and deeply embedded in cultural, socioeconomic, and political fields or structures.[10] Individuals do not initiate decision making by asking themselves how to maximize their utility in a given situation. They ask instead, what is the appropriate response to a particular situation given their position and responsibilities? People may make decisions based on a rational calculation of their own or their group self interest, but the calculus is weighted heavily by the historical, institutional, and ideological context in which the decision occurs.[11]

The behavioral/pluralist perspective detaches law, history, and values, as well as institutions, from the study of politics. The assumed universality of rationality effectively diminishes the importance of rules, history, ideas, and values. The historical-institutionalist orientation seeks to reintegrate these variables in a study of politics without simply abandoning the description of American politics offered by the behavioral/pluralist theory of democracy.[12]

In adopting an historical-institutionalist methodology, this study makes particular use of the work of Marc Allen Eisner, whose concept of regulatory regimes provides an historical backdrop for the analysis of baseball's unregulated monopoly. Eisner identifies these regimes as historically specific configurations of policies and institutions which establish certain broad goals that transcend the problems specific to particular industries. Eisner shows how regulatory policy results from the interaction of societal interests, institutional contexts, and the prevailing philosophy of government regulation.[13]

Eisner posits four regulatory regimes in the United States from 1880 to the 1990s. He identifies the first such regime as the "market" regime, which began in 1880 and ended in the 1920s. The market regime was characterized by the implementation of government regulation of the economy with the goal of reproducing market-like results in the Industrial Age. The Progressives dominated the market of ideas. The institutions of the state were struggling to emerge from their nineteenth century underdevelopment. The politics of the era was marked by the struggles of the Progressives to seize power from the political party bosses and urban political machines. Baseball's important place in American society, as well as the game's promotion of progressive values, allowed its peculiar commercial character to escape scrutiny during this period.

This Progressive Era regime was followed by the New Deal Era from the 1920s to the early 1960s, which Eisner calls the "associationalist" regime. He describes this era as a synthesis of "New Nationalist" progressivism and the experience of economic planning in World War I. Cooperative arrangements between government and industry during the 1920s in the form of government-supervised trade associations were designed to foster economic stability. Franklin Roosevelt's New Deal programs would expand these quasi-corporatist arrangements in order to lift the nation out of economic depression. Baseball's unregulated monopoly, with Commissioner Kenesaw Mountain Landis at the helm, thrived in this environment.

This regime was followed in the 1960s and 1970s by the "societal" regime, which was marked by the proliferation of direct government regulation of the economy. This new era of regulation differed from the past in two important respects. It was not governed by the desire to reproduce market results or to stabilize a faltering economy. Government regulation in the 1960s and 1970s was designed to promote social justice. Politics was dominated by rebellion to authority, and baseball was not immune from this larger environment. It was in this era that baseball's unregulated monopoly would face its most severe challenges. Although the game continued to avoid government regulation during this period, it did so by transforming its internal policies significantly.

Finally, the 1980s and 1990s are characterized as the "efficiency" regime. Like its predecessor, this regime was and is largely a reaction to what came before. Conservative economic and political ideology became fashionable in the 1980s. Baseball's monopolists began to find comfort in the shifting consensus on regulatory politics. Although their cartel has lost considerable potency in relation to the players, they continue to stand alone in the enjoyment of the benefits of monopoly control.

This study will trace the evolution of baseball's unregulated monopoly through Eisner's four regimes, identifying the institutional, ideological, and political factors that have shaped the evolution of this regulatory anomaly. Chapter one describes the early history of baseball, its evolution from fraternal recreation to major commercial enterprise, and its place in American society as we entered the twentieth century. The compatibility of baseball's special commercial status with the ideas, institutions, and politics of the Progressive Era's "market" regime is analyzed. Chapter two examines the place of baseball in the New Deal Era. The institutions, ideas, and politics of Eisner's "associationalist" regime are linked to baseball's continued insulation from government regulation during the Depression and World War II years. The stability within baseball created by the commissioner system is contrasted to the turbulent political and economic environment in the country at large.

Chapter three examines the onset of instability within baseball, exploring the effects of shifting political winds from the 1960s to the 1980s. The rise of the baseball players union, as well as unionism across professional sports, is analyzed. The third chapter also looks at the challenges faced by baseball with the emergence of television and the rise of other professional sports to rival the popularity of the national pastime. The effect of these changing technological and political phenomena on baseball has been profound. In a period when old values were questioned and even ridiculed, baseball's special place in American culture was also questioned and possibly lost. The fourth chapter brings the story of baseball's unregulated monopoly up to the present. The impact of the game's most recent and most severe labor strike is analyzed.

The study concludes with an examination of the immediate future of the game's special commercial status. The heightened interest in baseball's antitrust exemption in the last several years by the Congress and the courts has introduced new variables into the analysis of baseball's future. The final chapter will attempt to identify the larger institutional, ideological, and political trends that have determined the fate of baseball's unregulated monopoly for nearly a century. Also examined are the long term future prospects of baseball's antitrust exemption, in light of the current transformation of American society from the industrial age to what is variously called the "information" or "technological" age.

NOTES

1. Legal analyses of baseball's exemption are found only in law reviews or journals. There are no book length studies of this kind. Noteworthy examples include: Rogers, C. Paul, "Judicial Reinterpretation of Statutes: The Example of Baseball and the Antitrust Laws," *Houston Law Review* 14 (1977), p. 611–634; Berger, Robert G., "After the Strikes: A Reexamination of Professional Baseball's Exemption from the Antitrust Laws," *University of Pittsburgh Law Review* 45 (1983), p. 209–226; Irwin, Richard L., "A Historical Review of Litigation in Baseball," *Marquette Sports Law Journal* 1, no. 2 (1991), p. 283–300; and Juarez, Michael H., "Baseball's Antitrust Exemption," *Hastings Communication and Entertainment Law Journal* 17 (1995), p. 737–762.

2. Such studies include: Johnson, Arthur T., "Public Sports Policy," *American Behavioral Scientist* 21, no. 3 (January/February 1978), p. 319–344; Lipsky, Richard E., "Toward a Political Theory of American Sports Symbolism," *American Behavioral Scientist* 21, no. 3 (January/February 1978), p. 345–360; and Johnson, Arthur T., "Congress and Professional Sports: 1951–1978," *Annals of the American Academy of Political and Social Science* 445 (September 1979), p. 102–115.

3. Noteworthy in this regard is Ellig, Jerome R., "Law, Economics, and Organized Baseball: Analysis of a Cooperative Venture," (Ph.D. Dissertation, George Mason University, 1987). Ellig attributes the preservation of Major League Baseball's (MLB) antitrust exemption to the game's vertically integrated governance structure, which enables MLB to utilize the lobbying power of the minor leagues to prevent the legislative repeal of the game's antitrust exemption. This lobbying advantage is not shared by other major professional sports leagues, who either rely on colleges for player development, or have under-developed minor league systems.

4. Freedman, Warren, *Professional Sports and Antitrust* (Westport, CT: Greenwood Press, 1987), p. 31.

5. See Somit, Albert, *The Development of Political Science: From Burgess to Behavioralism* (Boston: Allyn and Bacon Publishing, 1967).

6. March, James G. and Johan P. Olsen, "The New Institutionalism: Organizational Factors in Political Life," *The American Political Science Review* (September 1984), p. 735.

7. See Easton, David, *The Political System: An Inquiry into the State of Political Science* (New York: Knopf Publishing, 1953).

8. Skocpol, Theda, *Bringing the State Back In* (New York: Cambridge University Press, 1985), p. 4.

9. See Schweers Cook, Karen and Margaret Levi, *The Limits of Rationality* (Chicago: University of Chicago Press, 1990).

10. See Simon, Herbert, *Reason in Human Affairs* (Stanford: Stanford University Press, 1983).

11. For a thoughtful critique of New Institutionalism and a defense of behavioralism see Almond, Gabriel, "The Return of the State," *The American Political Science Review*, 82, no. 3 (September, 1988), p. 853–874.

12. March, James and Johan Olsen, *Rediscovering Institutions* (New York: Free Press, 1989).

13. Eisner, Marc Allen, *Regulatory Politics in Transition* (Baltimore: The Johns Hopkins University Press, 1993), p. 1–9.

REGULATING
THE
NATIONAL
PASTIME

1

Progressivism and the Baseball Anomaly

Federal antitrust law is a significant legacy of the politics and the political thought of American progressivism. Antitrust law represents an approach to the regulation of the economy born in the last decades of the nineteenth century in the face of burgeoning industrialization. Baseball was born in Jacksonian America. It was a sport played by fraternal clubs. It was a recreational activity that created camaraderie among neighbors and fellow toilers in the new urban workplace.

By 1890, when the Sherman Antitrust Act became the law of the land, baseball had grown into a professional commercial enterprise. The National League had already replaced the National Association of Professional Baseball Players as organized baseball's dominant institution and the game had already experienced the turmoil of strained labor/management relations that would be commonplace in the Industrial Age.[1] As the new century dawned, American industry flowered in the soil of progressivism's vision of industrial regulation, while baseball's evolution continued unchecked by the laws of commerce. By 1912, when the Clayton Antitrust Act gave further definition to the rules of the game in the realm of interstate commerce, baseball had weathered considerable turmoil in its ranks as a result of player revolts and interleague wars. Despite its highly visible strife, Major League Baseball, unlike any other industry of its scope, would never be forced to fully comply with federal antitrust law, nor would it fall under the jurisdiction of any federal regulatory agency. The celebrated Holmes decision of 1922 would suspend Major League Baseball in a seemingly preindustrial state.

THE EARLY HISTORY OF BASEBALL

What historians call the "baseball fraternity" dates to the early decades of the nineteenth century. Historian Benjamin Rader traces the origins of this fraternity to shared childhood experiences playing various ball games as well as the "peculiarly American penchant for forming voluntary associations."[2] The first fraternal baseball club widely discussed by most historians of baseball was the New York Knickerbockers, founded in 1845 by a bank clerk named Alexander Cartwright. Typical of preprofessional baseball clubs the Knickerbockers were a social as well as athletic club.

These clubs provided a diversion for the workers of the young Industrial Age. Baseball historian Warren Goldstein describes the atmosphere of mid-nineteenth century baseball as "not very far removed from the world and culture of the urban workplaces." He writes of the Eckford Club of Brooklyn, made up of shipbuilders and mechanics from the nearby Eckford shipyards. In Washington, DC, government clerks made up most of the membership of several local clubs.[3]

By the 1850s, baseball was already being touted as America's national sport. Sixteen New York area clubs banned together in 1857 to form the National Association of Base Ball Players (NABBP). By 1861, the NABBP had member clubs in New Haven, Detroit, Philadelphia, Baltimore, and Washington, DC, raising the number of member clubs to sixty-two. The purpose of the NABBP was to create uniform rules of play and to bring organization and order to interclub competition. The association was also intended to cultivate and preserve the fraternal character of the game.[4]

The Civil War is also generally thought to have contributed to the expansion of baseball's popularity nationally. New York area troops are often credited with having introduced men throughout the country to baseball, inspiring them to start their own clubs when they returned home after the war. The contention that the war helped nationalize the game is occasionally supported with unconfirmed stories such as the one about a game played on Christmas day, 1862, by two teams of New York volunteer infantrymen at Hilton Head, South Carolina, which is said to have attracted more than 40,000 spectators.[5]

The NABBP's founding devotion to amateurism and genteel fraternity began to erode even before the war. As competition on the field grew more intense, so too did the desire to win. The dynamic of the baseball fraternity was being transformed. Gradually clubs became less interested in leisure and more interested in competition. The quest for victories for the honor and prestige of the club began to transform most of the club members from players to boosters. Only the most skilled members would comprise the club's nine on game day. The increasing competitiveness of interclub baseball also brought out the commercial potential of the game. Clubs began to charge admission to spectators of the game to be used for club expenses. It was also common for surplus gate receipts to be divided among the players.[6]

By 1859 the competitive rivalry was so intense that the NABBP was forced to adopt a rule prohibiting the practice of luring players from one club to another to gain a competitive edge. The association hoped to curb this tactic, known as "revolving," by requiring all players participating in a game to have been a member of their respective clubs for at least thirty days.[7] The rule was not enough to stem the tide toward professionalism. Other National Association rules of similar intent, such as the prohibition of playing for "money, place, or emolument,"[8] were seldom enforced.

At first, the wealthy backers of club teams would offer good jobs to players with hours and duties that would allow for significant practice time. In New York City, for example, many of the players on the New York Mutuals team were given patronage positions in city government. In 1867, the young Albert Spalding was hired by a Chicago wholesale grocery and paid forty dollars a week with the understanding that his nominal duties would not interfere with his play.[9] This thinly veiled pay for play soon gave way to outright pay for play. As early as 1862 the top players were reportedly receiving cash payments for their services on the diamond. Future sporting goods magnate Al Reach is widely reported to have been one such player. Reach was offered a straight salary by the Athletic Club of Philadelphia in 1863.[10] The embattled National Association gradually caved in to the inevitability of professional baseball. The NABBP, unable to preserve amateurism in the face of declining membership in the National Association and without power to enforce its rules even on its member clubs, finally succumbed to professionalism in 1870.

One year before the NABBP folded its tent the issue of professionalism had shifted so much that the Cincinnati Red Stockings were able to put forth the first admittedly all-salaried professional baseball team. One year after the demise of the NABBP the advocates of professionalism in baseball formed their own organization. The National Association of Professional Base Ball Players (NAPBBP) began operation in 1871. The NAPBBP is considered by most historians as the first professional baseball league and the first organized attempt to structure the business of baseball.[11]

The NAPBBP governed baseball for five years. The association had a ten dollar membership fee for each club, which qualified that club to compete for the "Championship of the United States." The professional association limped through five seasons. Financial ruin had cut the number of teams from twenty-five to fourteen in the first year. By 1875, the association's last season, only four of the original teams remained, and none of these made a profit. In a speech years later about the failure of the association, A. G. Mills remarked:

[E]ach summer's campaign was planned during the preceding winter and the habit was general on the part of clubs to take on obligations in the way of players' salaries that were not justified, as the spring games would inevitably demonstrate that the majority of such clubs could have no hope of winning even a respectable number of games. Moreover, this condition was greatly aggravated by the general practice on the part of the richer clubs, of stripping the weaker ones of their best playing talent. Then would follow the collapse of a number of these clubs in mid-season, leaving their players unpaid, while the winning clubs, owing to the disbandment of the weaker ones, would also frequently fail from inability to arrange a paying number of games.[12]

Mills' description of baseball's dilemma reflected the frustration in and around professional baseball with the difficulty of managing competition between clubs both on the field and in the marketplace. In addition to its financial woes the National Association had allowed baseball to become associated with ungentlemanly conduct such as gambling, drinking, and sundry other unscrupulous behaviors.

In 1876, William A. Hulbert, president of the Chicago Base Ball Club, mindful of the failings of the NAPBBP, convinced the owners of seven eastern professional clubs to break away from the fledgling National Association to create a new professional league. The National League of Professional Baseball Clubs aspired to be the premier major league of baseball. The league would limit the number of teams allowed to join, give each team a territorial monopoly, and honor an interleague agreement not to raid each other's player rosters during the season. The new league's fewer number of teams was intended to reduce demand for players, reduce salaries, and enhance profits.[13] The territorial monopolies and restrictions of mid-season revolving were intended to help stabilize competition between clubs.

Another goal of the creators of the National League was to return respectability to the game. In the years prior to the formation of the National League the sport's popularity with the nation's more sophisticated classes had waned. Hulbert and his fellow National League owners sought to make baseball more compatible with the Victorian sensibilities then ascendant in the United States. In an effort to market the sport to the gentry, the National League enacted strict codes of player conduct. They would no longer play on Sundays. Gambling, drinking, and other ungentlemanly behavior would be prohibited at the ballpark. A standard fifty cent admission price would ensure a more upscale crowd.[14]

The National League was created with two goals in mind: (1) to create stable and profitable professional baseball, and (2) to bring respectability and Victorian sensibilities to the game. Historians are mixed in their assessments of the second goal's achievement, but there is unanimity on the question of economic stability in the first few years. None of the National League clubs showed a profit in 1876, 1877, or 1878, and only one club profited in 1879.[15] The National League's concerted effort to gain respectability forced it to attempt the strict enforcement of its rules, which created considerable turbulence in the league. Of the original eight National League teams, two were expelled for failing to complete their schedules after just one season, three more went out of business due to financial difficulty after the 1877 season, and one was expelled from the league for selling liquor at the ballpark in 1878. By 1882, the only original National League teams still afloat were Boston and Chicago, both of which were helped by very successful teams on the field.[16]

One of the most distinctive features of the National League at its inception was the fact that it was an association of clubs, not players. The effect of this distinction was that the National League was in fact a business with very distinct and separate roles for the players (labor) and the owners (management). In this new industrial atmosphere, which was by then common in many other enterprises, the blame for economic distress was placed by the owners squarely on the backs of the players. The owners believed that it was essential to reign in player salaries in order to make National League teams viable. While the National League had avoided the destructive effects of mid-season movement of players between teams, its rules allowed for the free competition for player talent in the off-season.

The owners' need to reduce salaries led them to enact the first reserve rule, which was put into effect for the 1880 season. The rule allowed each club to reserve five of its players for the following season in order to reduce the number of players on the market each year. The number of players each club could reserve would increase to eleven in 1883, twelve in 1885, fourteen in 1887, and by the 1890s all players were covered by the reserve rule. In addition to the reserve rule, the owners adopted a standard player contract in 1879. The purpose of the standard player contract was to "enforce newly adopted [league] rules giving each club authority to suspend indefinitely any player who was found guilty of drunkenness, insubordination, or dishonorable conduct."[17] These new rules were backed up by the extralegal practices of blacklisting and boycotting. All National League clubs agreed not to hire any player who jumped a National League contract, and the clubs also agreed not to play any team that hired a contract jumper.

The reserve rule did help stem the rising tide of salaries, and the standard contract improved interleague discipline and communication, yet these innovations also opened the door for competing leagues that could entice players away by offering them free contracting.[18] The first successful rival major league was the American Association founded in November 1881. The American Association was organized by financial backers in six cities that were not part of the National League, including Cincinnati, which had a club that had been expelled from the National League for allowing alcohol to be consumed at the ballpark.[19] The American Association was originally comprised of teams from St. Louis, Brooklyn, Philadelphia, Pittsburgh, and Louisville, as well as Cincinnati. Most of the teams that would play in the new league were owned by breweries.

The American Association sought to lure fans from the National League by allowing alcohol to be sold at the ballpark, playing on Sundays, and charging only 25 cents for admission. These measures were intended to attract those fans who had been abandoned by the National League's campaign to instill Victorian values and standards.[20] The Association sought to lure players from the National League by offering free contracting. There was no reserve rule in the American Association. The new league was commercially successful, allowing it to compete with the National League for the best player talent. By 1883, the competition between the two leagues expanded from players to territory. Resigned to the viability of the upstart league, the National League president A. G. Mills decided to negotiate with the American Association in the spring of 1883. The result of these negotiations was the first national agreement. Historians point to this first interleague pact as the birth of organized baseball.

The National Agreement of 1883 extended the reserve rule to the American Association. The new universal reserve rule had the same effect as the old one. One year after the truce between the American Association and the National League a third league began operation without a reserve rule. The thirteen-team Union Association was founded with the backing of railroad magnate Henry Lucas in 1884. However, the Union Association lacked the fan luring innovations of the American Association and also had difficulty competing with the two major leagues for talent. The new league was a commercial failure but it was successful enough to garner its founder, Henry Lucas, a National League franchise. Essentially, Major League Baseball had fended off its first challenge by co-opting its challenger.

In 1885, with no upstart leagues on the horizon, the owners in both leagues got together and announced that they would impose a salary limit of $2,000. The imposition of organized baseball's first salary cap inspired the players to form the National Brotherhood of Professional Baseball Players under the leadership of John Montgomery Ward. A New York player, Ward charged that the owners had abused the reserve rule. The salary cap was merely the straw that broke the camel's back. Among the abuses alleged were the buying and selling of players without their permission, the threat of blacklisting to force players into unfavorable contracts, and the practice of lending players to others clubs without the consent of the players.[21]

Initially, the owners negotiated with and appeased the players organization by agreeing to disregard the salary cap and include a negotiated form of the reserve rule in every standard contract. However, one year later the owners adopted what they called a "salary classification scheme." According to this "scheme" players would receive salaries ranging from $1,500 to $2,500 depending upon their length of service. Despite the owners assurances that the scheme would not apply to current players, the issue sparked a revolt by the players.[22]

On November 6, 1889, Ward's Brotherhood of Professional Baseball Players and a number of financial backers announced the creation of the Players League. With trust-busting rhetoric, the new league announced it would not abide by the national agreement. Desperate to stop the flow of star players to the Players League, organized baseball turned to the courts in an attempt to enforce player contracts. In the case of *Metropolitan Exhibition Co. v. Ward* in 1890, the New York Supreme Court held that the reserve clause was unenforceable due to its lack of definiteness and mutuality. The court also called the reserve clause unconscionable.[23]

Having failed to use the courts to destroy the Players League, Major League Baseball returned to the use of extralegal methods. All clubs in the American Association and National League were prohibited from playing teams in the Players League. Players were induced with large salary offers to renounce the Players League and return to their former employers. National League and American Association games were scheduled at the same times as Players League games so as to compete for attendance.[24] The result of these measures was lost revenue for all concerned. However, most baseball historians agree that the Players League slightly outdrew organized baseball. This conclusion is supported by the fact that after one season the Players League was absorbed into organized baseball with some teams selling out and others being added to the established leagues.[25]

Shortly after the Players League war was concluded tension broke out between the National League and the American Association over the division of players who had jumped to the Players League. The interleague dispute resulted in the withdrawal of the American Association from the national agreement. The nullification of the national agreement resulted in bitter wars for players causing salaries to skyrocket. The fierce unregulated competition for players caused the 1891 season to be a financial disaster for both leagues. Following the 1891 season the National League absorbed the American Association and became the only major league. In 1892, the National League and various minor leagues drew up a new national agreement which included the first player draft as a way of bringing players up to the big league.[26]

The National League monopolized major league baseball for the rest of the century. However, in 1892 Ban Johnson created a minor league called the Western League. During the 1890s Johnson's Western League grew. The National League attempted to co-opt the upstart minor league by allowing Western teams in two of its cities, Cleveland and Chicago. In 1900, Johnson changed the name of his league to the American League and sought further concessions from the National League. The National League's refusal to deal with Johnson touched off yet another baseball war. In 1901, Johnson proclaimed his league to be a major league. His contention was supported by the fact that the American League had lured more than 100 players away from the National League.[27]

One such player was Napoleon Lajoie, the second baseman for the National League's Philadelphia club. The owner of the National League Philadelphia club sued to block Lajoie's attempt to play for the American League Philadelphia club in 1901. The suit was heard by the Court of Common Pleas in Philadelphia with Judge Robert Ralston presiding. Ralston, echoing earlier precedents, found Lajoie's contract lacked mutuality and was unenforceable.[28] The National League owner of the Philadelphia club appealed the lower court's decision to the Pennsylvania Supreme Court and won an injunction against Lajoie, barring him from playing for the American League Philadelphia club. Justice Potter of the Pennsylvania Supreme Court used a partial performance argument in overturning the lower court. He held that the mutuality of Lajoie's contract had been made irrelevant by Lajoie's partial performance. That is, because Lajoie played one season under the terms of the contract and the Phillies had paid him in full for that performance, mutuality was established.[29]

The Supreme Court's decision was muted by a swift maneuver on the part of the owner of the American League club in Philadelphia. He sold Lajoie to the American League's Cleveland team where he was outside the jurisdiction of the Pennsylvania courts. Justice Potter's opinion, however, would have far greater implications. In it, Potter characterized professional baseball as a business with a "peculiar nature and circumstances." Its production processes, distribution techniques, and commercial practices were distinguished from conventional business practices of the day. It was a "game," a "sport," that was deserving of special consideration. Potter's opinion laid the groundwork for Major League Baseball's anomalous treatment in the courts thereafter.[30]

In January 1903, the American League war ended with the signing of a third national agreement. Under the terms of the agreement the American and National Leagues formed the organization of Major League Baseball. The two leagues agreed to recognize each other's reserve clauses and to form a three-man commission to oversee organized baseball. The commission would be made up of the two league presidents and a third member chosen by them. The role of the commission was to arbitrate disputes between the two major leagues and the various minor leagues.[31] The ensuing ten years would see little conflict in Major League Baseball. The only incident of note was a one day walkout by the members of the Detroit Tigers over the suspension of Ty Cobb. The period is also remembered for Albert Spalding's creation of the Doubleday origins myth.

Organized baseball's newfound serenity was disturbed in 1913 when an upstart league called the Federal League declared itself a major league for the 1914 season. In 1913, the new league attracted only a handful of big league talent, but those who went to the Federal League earned huge salaries. In the 1914 and 1915 seasons hundreds of players defected to the Federal League.[32] In 1914, the New York State Supreme Court handed down a ruling with far-reaching implications.

In the case of Hal Chase, a player who defected to the Federal League, the court overturned the *Lajoie* precedent in finding Chase's contract lacked mutuality and was unenforceable. However, the court's language echoed the sentiments of the Pennsylvania court in terms of its treatment of organized baseball as a peculiar and exceptional enterprise. Building on Justice Potter's logic, the Court in the *Chase* case declared that baseball was not a commodity or article of merchandise subject to the regulation of Congress. It was a sport, an amusement, and as such was explicitly outside of the purview of the antitrust laws.[33]

In 1915, the Federal League sued Major League Baseball for restraint of trade in violation of section one of the Sherman Antitrust Act of 1890. The case was heard in the U.S. District Court of Illinois by future baseball commissioner Judge Kenesaw Mountain Landis. Judge Landis made several friendly comments about Major League Baseball from the bench, then encouraged settlement while he took the case under advisement. During the nearly one year wait for Landis' decision a settlement was reached between Major League Baseball and the Federal League.

Not all the teams of the Federal League were content with the settlement, which consisted of either a $50,000 buyout, or absorption into Major League Baseball. The Federal League team from Baltimore refused the buyout offer and filed an antitrust suit against Major League Baseball in 1916. In the restraint of trade suit under sections one and two of the Sherman Antitrust Act, the Baltimore club was awarded treble damages of $240,000 by the Indiana State Supreme Court. In April 1921, this decision was reversed by the District of Columbia Court of Appeals.

In its opinion, the DC Court of Appeals held that Major League Baseball was not subject to federal antitrust laws because it did not constitute interstate commerce. The court's opinion read in part, "the players travel from place to place [is] interstate commerce, but they are not the game [which] is local in its beginning and in its end. The fact that the [owners] produce baseball games as a source of profit, large or small, cannot change the character of the games. They are still sport, not trade."[34] This decision was upheld on May 29, 1922, in the U.S. Supreme Court case of *Federal Baseball Club of Baltimore v. National League*.[35]

While the Federal League controversy occupied the courts Major League Baseball went through a crisis of a different type. The early history of baseball saw numerous league wars and player/management strife. Also, the shadow of impropriety, gambling, and sundry other ungentlemanly pursuits had occasionally darkened the glow of organized baseball. The creation of the National League was, in fact, partially motivated by the desire to clean up the game. But, it was not until the Black Sox Scandal of 1919 that the integrity of the game was truly jeopardized. Eight members of the 1919 Chicago White Sox team conspired to throw the World Series to Cincinnati in return for cash to be paid by gamblers. Despite the fact that all eight players were acquitted of charges stemming from the "big fix," as it became known, the scandal exposed bitter divisions in Major League Baseball as well as the impotency of the National Commission, the governing body of Major League Baseball.[36]

The Black Sox Scandal forced Major League Baseball to get its house in order. In the new National Agreement of 1921, Judge Kenesaw Mountain Landis was named the lone Commissioner of Baseball, replacing the ineffectual National Commission. Landis would rule organized baseball with an iron hand, assisted by Justice Holmes' 1922 decision granting sweeping immunity from federal antitrust law to Major League Baseball.

Major League Baseball came of age in the Progressive Era. However, the preceding history of baseball's economic structure, labor relations, and its legal and economic principles seems drastically out of step with the history of other Progressive Era American industries. Antitrust policy is a creation of progressivism. It is a cornerstone of progressive industrial regulatory policy. In order to examine the compatibility of the baseball anomaly with the spirit of progressivism it is necessary to understand the place of antitrust policy in progressive thought as well as action.

ANTITRUST POLICY AND THE POLITICAL PHILOSOPHY OF THE PROGRESSIVES

Antitrust policy developed after the Civil War in response to developments in business organization. The creation of large business firms produced hostility and fear, especially among the agricultural communities. The first manifestations of these fears took the form of state regulation. Farmers of the south and west, who felt the eastern sponsored railroads had taken advantage of them, formed the Grange movement. These granges became powerful interest groups at the state and local level. They lobbied for the passage of state antimonopoly statutes which protected them from exorbitant railroad rates among other things.

By 1887, the variety of these state regulations had propelled the issue to the federal level. The railroads themselves were eager for federal regulation as a means of bringing uniformity to the various state requirements. The Interstate Commerce Commission Act of 1887, directed at the railroads, became the first attempt by the federal government to regulate the national economy.

By 1890, the fear of spreading cartels, the plight of western farmers, the size of eastern banks, and above all the activities of the Standard Oil Company led to the passage of the Sherman Antitrust Act.[37] In addition, the same forces that motivated the enactment of the various state antimonopoly statutes were unquestionably important in the passage of the Sherman

Act. One study supports this view by pointing out that at that time U.S. Senators were elected by state legislatures, and the Sherman Act was introduced in the Senate.[38]

While the passage of the Sherman Act made it clear that the issue of corporate power had a prominent place on the progressive public policy agenda, it was the merger movement around the turn of the century that elevated the issue of unfair corporate combinations to the forefront. Between 1895 and 1904 more than 1800 firms were consolidated into fewer than 160 holding companies. The vast majority of these corporations would control at least 40 percent of their market shares.[39]

Antitrust enforcement was limited prior to 1905, but two Supreme Court decisions during this period would lay the groundwork for vigorous antitrust enforcement in the wake of the merger movement. In 1899, in *Addyston Pipe & Steel Co. v. U.S.*, the Court held that the Sherman Act prohibited all cartel agreements to divide markets or fix prices. This decision meant that federal courts would treat cartels as unlawful conspiracies without regard to arguments of equity or efficiency. In 1904, in the case of *Northern Securities Co. v. U.S.*, the Court's ruling had the effect of conferring upon the federal government the power of corporate divestiture. The Court's holding was based upon the Sherman Act's authorization of the attorney general to seek enforcement through proceedings in equity.[40]

The period between 1906 and 1920 saw vigorous enforcement of antitrust under the Sherman Act. With the notable exception of baseball, no industry was spared scrutiny. The Court's holdings on cartels and its conferral of divestiture power enabled the federal government to challenge the big trusts including Standard Oil, American Tobacco, DuPont, as well as the nation's five leading meatpacking companies. Also during this period, the application of antitrust to labor unions would be clarified by the Clayton Antitrust Act of 1912, which declared that the labor of a human being is not a commodity and therefore is exempt from federal antitrust law. This provision of the Clayton Act would have important implications for the treatment of baseball in the courts.

The regulatory policies of the Progressive Era, manifested in the Sherman and Clayton Acts, as well as in the creation of the Interstate Commerce and Federal Trade Commissions, reflect two strands of political thought as to the role of government in the regulation of an industrial economy. The resulting debate was among the most important between progressive scholars and public officials and produced a mixed public policy response.

The two strands of progressivism came to be known as the "New Nationalism" and the "New Freedom." While these were the slogans of Theodore Roosevelt and Woodrow Wilson in the 1912 presidential campaign, the substance of these programs had been developed years earlier by Herbert Croly and Louis Brandeis. Indeed, the 1912 campaign was a watershed event. Wilson and Roosevelt's alternate visions of the government's role in an industrial economy would define the schizophrenic legacy of progressivism, leading generations of scholars to search in vain for a unified progressive political philosophy. Many have argued that the coming of the New Deal, with its development of the administrative state, signaled the fact that, while Wilson won the election, Roosevelt won the debate.

Wilson's New Freedom was a concerted effort to construct a Jeffersonian concept of individual liberty for the Industrial Age. Wilson recognized that industrialization had created a permanent employee class. No longer could every man compete equally to become his own boss. The advent of corporate combinations had provided tremendous advantages to a few at the expense of the many. Wilson and Brandeis' New Freedom sought to recreate a level playing field for economic competition, giving the small entrepreneur the ability to compete just as he had in the nineteenth century prior to the advent of the corporation. The goal was to restrain corporations from abusing their power without stifling their economic freedom.

Wilson's program was animated by the Jeffersonian suspicion of a centralized state. This sentiment made the use of antitrust policy particularly appealing. By using antitrust law, casting policy as law enforcement rather than direct regulation, market competition was encouraged in a way that fit nicely with the Jeffersonian norms of limited government intervention.[41] The name New Freedom was carefully chosen to indicate that the nineteenth century concept of individual freedom was to be adapted to the Industrial Age by way of the least intrusive means. Antitrust policy was seen as the best method to restore the "conditions in which the freely operating market mechanism, rather than the political mechanism, disinterestedly distributed material wealth and life chances among its participants."[42]

While Wilson campaigned using the powerful and populist rhetoric of "trust-busting," Roosevelt was championing a more radical approach to economic regulation. Inspired by Herbert Croly's *The Promise of American Life*, Roosevelt dubbed his program the New Nationalism and advocated a sharp departure in the direction of American government's role in the economy. Abandoning Jefferson's suspicion of centralized government, Roosevelt championed a strong national government, which would take on the responsibility of regulating the economy.

While the New Freedom aspired to recreate the nineteenth century spirit of competition, Roosevelt's program sought to allow and even welcome the concentration of industry, subjecting it to direct government regulation. The government would utilize the power of these industrial combinations to further the national interest. The creation of a permanent employee class would be mitigated by conferring special benefits on disadvantaged groups.

Roosevelt did not propose to repeal the Sherman Act, although he favored "continuous administrative action" over "necessarily intermittent law suits."[43] He argued that the act should be amended so that only corporate combinations injurious to the public interest would be prohibited, making a distinction between good and bad trusts. Roosevelt proposed giving government supervisory power over businesses engaged in interstate commerce, as well as requiring comprehensive reporting of all business activities to the government. To some degree this was already occurring voluntarily due to the activities of the Bureau of Corporations, which was created by the Roosevelt Administration in 1902.[44]

Roosevelt viewed Wilson's program as a reactionary attempt to reverse the consolidation movement, which meant breaking up the mechanism offering the greatest potential for national collective action. Wilson saw the New Nationalism as too intrusive and as an abandonment of American principles of limited government. Often overlooked is the third candidate in the 1912 presidential election, William Howard Taft.

Unlike Wilson and Roosevelt, Taft's position on the government's role in the economy was not the product of a preconceived program. During the Taft administration a record number of prosecutions were secured under the Sherman Act, despite the President's reported disbelief in the economic soundness of antitrust laws. Ultimately, Taft abandoned the hope of distinguishing between good and bad trusts and became a forceful advocate for the vigorous enforcement of the Sherman Act.

Writing about the Supreme Court's role in constructing the parameters of the Sherman Act, Taft praises the Court for its role in creating a "valuable and workable interpretation [of the Sherman Act] which anyone who gives it sincere attention can understand and can follow in the methods of his business."[45] This endorsement of both the statute and the judicial construction of it meant that Taft's view was ultimately closer to Wilson than to Roosevelt. However, it is also important to note that Taft's position was distinct from Wilson in that he was content with what Roosevelt had called "intermittent law suits."[46] Wilson, on the other hand, advocated the use of the power of the attorney general to enforce the antitrust laws. Although Taft's view of antitrust was quickly obscured out by the antitrust enforcement mechanisms of the Justice Department and the Federal Trade Commission, it may be fair to characterize his perspective as a third strand of progressive thought on antitrust.

Despite their differences on specific means, the New Freedom and the New Nationalism were united in their objectives and ultimately the measure of progressivism's regulatory legacy is in the policies of the era. Marc Allen Eisner has skillfully teased out the unifying themes of the competing visions of regulatory policy in the Progressive Era, subsuming them within what he calls the "market regime." Eisner's market regime contains elements of both Wilson's and Roosevelt's visions.[47]

The market regime (1880–1920) was characterized by the promotion of market governance.[48] This is reflected in Wilsonian support for antitrust law, which attempted to recreate market-like results through administrative means. Roosevelt's vision found realization in the numerous independent regulatory commissions created in the Progressive Era. The goal of both strategies was to ameliorate the harmful conditions brought on by the industrial revolution and the advent of concentrated commercial power, without stunting the nation's economic growth. Both approaches, which were pursued concurrently, sought to prevent monopoly control of markets.

With the fateful 1922 *Federal Baseball* Supreme Court decision, organized baseball found itself the only industry of its size in the United States subject to neither antitrust laws nor any government regulatory agency supervision. Organized baseball had navigated its way through the Progressive Era without being touched by affirmative government intervention. The high profile of Major League Baseball throughout the era, including its frequent labor/management squabbles, makes the absence of government intervention in the business of baseball seem unusual.

Organized baseball's early history seems to be at odds with the spirit of either of progressivism's major strands of political thought regarding the government's role in economic regulation. How did organized baseball slip through the cracks, avoiding the subjection to antitrust law envisioned by Wilson as well as the direct regulation advocated in the New Nationalism?

THE COMPATIBILITY OF THE BASEBALL ANOMALY WITH PROGRESSIVISM

Historians often link the exploding popularity of baseball in the 1880s and 1890s to its synergy with the culture of the Progressive Era, [49] but scant attention has been paid to how this cultural affinity contributed to organized baseball's ability to conduct its business without any government supervision or intervention. In an era when state intervention into the regulation of commerce became the norm, how did the business of professional baseball, with all of its highly publicized difficulties, such as player revolts, league wars, and gambling scandals, escape federal regulation?

Progressivism had many faces. Political scientists tend to concentrate upon that part of the movement which drastically altered the political process. The progressives transformed our politics from a Jacksonian party system of representative democracy and a government of the common man to a system grounded in direct citizen participation in the electoral process and a more rationalized, bureaucratized, and professional governing structure. Legal scholars probe the opinions of the nation's jurists, searching for the ways in which progressive jurisprudence guided and structured the politics and social relations of its day. Historians and sociologists view the progressives differently, studying the broader social movement and changing social and economic relations of which the liberal political reforms were only a part.

This broad social movement, which grew up in reaction to the rapidly changing character of life and community, had a deep and lasting effect on the culture of America in the Industrial Age. Above all, progressives were reformers who sought to guide the country through a transition from its agrarian adolescence into an urban, industrial age. Most profound perhaps was the impact of this period upon American culture. Many historians have argued that baseball provided turn of the century Americans with an escape from the harsh, sterile atmosphere of the urban industrial workplace. The pastoral feel of the game linked Americans to a romanticized, possibly mythical, rural past when life was simpler. The good old days phenomenon seems to find its way into the sentimental lexicon of every generation. In the increasingly modern atmosphere of the Progressive Era, baseball clearly helped fuel romantic sentimentality for a bygone era.

To say that baseball had great cultural significance in the Progressive Era is to say that it held special meaning and significance for individuals, especially for the men who would shape the culture of America in the new century. Historian Ronald Story has argued that the explosion of baseball's popularity as a spectator sport in the 1880s and 1890s resulted from the popularity of playing baseball in the 1850s and 1860s.[50] The young men of this earlier generation would become the parents, teachers, public officials, businessmen and social and political reformers of the Progressive Era. In essence, the opinion makers and cultural trendsetters were men who grew up playing a game that their fathers neither understood nor approved. Their love for the game, forged in the camaraderie and fellowship of the sandlot, would dispose them to protect and spread this game, the cultural significance of which approached that of family traditions and ethnic heritage for their generation.

For the leaders and reformers of the Progressive Era, baseball was a tool of reform not the object of reform. Baseball was a game that would be used by these social reformers to inculcate certain values into American society. Fair play, teamwork, sound minds and bodies; these were the buzzwords of a social movement. Baseball was a prop, a metaphor used in the social gospel of progressivism. The ills of the dawning Industrial Age were in the complexities and intrigues of a changing commercial landscape; baseball was a cultural institution that served as a bulwark of values from a simpler time.

The social and political reformers of the Progressive Era were not the only ones initiated to baseball's cultural significance. The owners and promoters of Major League Baseball were well aware of the sentimental hold the game had on this generation. In a highly organized campaign throughout the era, baseball marketing touted the special nature of the business of baseball. In developing its internal regulatory structure, organized baseball was keenly aware of the need to link its commercial strategies with the prevailing cultural attitudes about the game.[51]

G. Edward White argues that organized baseball exploited the cultural significance of the game for the progressive generation by translating these cultural attitudes into fundamental assumptions about baseball's largest constituency, the fans. These assumptions were: (1) fans appreciate close competition, (2) they get vicarious satisfaction from identifying with a hometown team, and (3) their attachment to a hometown team is enhanced if the identity of the players on the team remains relatively stable.[52]

These cultural assumptions would govern the development of "baseball law" which has ruled Major League Baseball since its inception, with only occasional prodding from external social and political entities. The three fundamental tenets of baseball law are: (1) a universal reserve clause to stabilize rosters and ensure better competition on the field, (2) territorial autonomy for major league clubs, which preserves the economic viability of clubs and enhances the hometown loyalties of fans, and (3) the maintenance of a monopsony, or one buyer market for top player talent.[53] The cultural salience of baseball to the progressive generation allowed organized baseball to preserve its peculiar entrepreneurial character. By constructing its governing assumptions around the cultural expectations of the fans, or the people, Major League Baseball was able to insulate itself from government intervention.

The idea that the experience of playing baseball as children in the 1850s and 1860s contributed to the popularity of baseball as a spectator sport in the 1880s and 1890s must be clarified in order to see its role in linking culture to organized baseball's anomalous commercial development. In the 1880s and 1890s, when professional baseball was weathering severe commercial turbulence in the form of player revolts and interleague wars, political leaders in the states and nation were seeking ways to curb the abuses of corporate combinations that threatened the competitive heart of our free enterprise system. These same leaders, whose generation made baseball the cultural icon it became, saw it not as a business, but as a child's game that could be used to instill proper values in America's youth.[54] The leaders of the Progressive Era were predisposed to see baseball as having special cultural significance. This, combined with Major League Baseball's exploitation of the cultural appeal of the game in creating its internal governing principles and structure, left very few advocates for government intervention into the operation of the sport.

The difference between attitudes within baseball and outside of baseball in the Progressive Era is striking. While the owners, promoters, and players in professional baseball seem to have developed businesslike attitudes as early as the 1870s with the formation of the first professional leagues, the fans of baseball, among them the political leaders of the day, maintained a general ignorance of or indifference to the commercial implications of the game. The concerted marketing campaign of organized baseball combined with a generation's personal experience of playing the game undoubtedly contributed to the preservation of baseball's unique entrepreneurial char-acter. This apparent blindness to the commercial difficulties of organized baseball is most vivid in some of the judicial decisions of the day involving professional baseball.

In the 1902 case of Napoleon Lajoie, the Pennsylvania Supreme Court managed to treat baseball more like other commercial enterprises even as they provided the grounds for future courts to treat baseball differently. In addition to ordering Lajoie to honor his National League contract, Justice William P. Potter's opinion for the court explicitly held that baseball was not to be regarded as a conventional business enterprise. He called it "light hearted" and "more trivial" asserting that the business of baseball was "more culturally significant than other American enterprises."[55]

Justice Potter's conferral of special cultural significance was echoed in the 1914 decision in the *Hal Chase* case. In *Chase*, the court held that Major League Baseball, although clearly a monopoly, was a peculiar and excep-tional enterprise. The court also clarified Justice Potter's opinion holding that baseball is not a commodity or article of commerce subject to regula-tion by Congress. The court took pains to say that baseball was a "sport" and an "amusement," indicating that it was something other than big business.[56]

In the 1915 suit by the Federal League against Major League Baseball, Judge Kenesaw Mountain Landis of the Illinois U.S. District Court declared from the bench that "any blows at . . . baseball would be regarded by this court as a blow to a national institution."[57] Landis added that, "as a result of thirty years of observation, I am shocked because you call playing baseball labor."[58] He then sat on his decision for nearly a year, during which time the suit was settled out of court. Landis' declarations make it clear that he per-ceived baseball as very different from other commercial enterprises.

The court holdings in *Lajoie* and *Chase*, as well as the Landis pronounce-ments set the groundwork for the 1921 District of Columbia Court of Ap-peals decision that overturned the antitrust verdict in the Federal League's suit against Major League Baseball. This court accepted the cultural signifi-cance language of the *Lajoie* case as well as the contention advanced by the court in the *Chase* case that baseball was not a commodity or article of trade subject to federal regulation. Furthermore, the court held, in an opinion written by Chief Justice Constantine Smyth, that the game of baseball "is not susceptible of being transferred."[59]

This apparent denial of the commercial nature of organized baseball would be echoed in the Holmes opinion of 1922. Holmes wrote: "But the fact that in order to give the exhibitions [of baseball] the leagues must in-duce free persons to cross state lines and must arrange and pay for their do-ing so is not enough to change the character of the business." He went on to say, "the transport is a mere incident, not the essential thing. That to which it is incident, the exhibition, although made for money would not be called trade or commerce in the commonly accepted use of those words."[60]

Holmes' reference to the terms "trade" and "commerce" are significant. The cultural grip of baseball on the aforementioned jurists was not the only factor in these seemingly unrealistic appraisals of the enterprise of organized baseball. Progressive Era jurisprudence was shaped in many cases by preindustrial, nineteenth-century legal definitions. These antiquated definitions of terms such as trade and commerce retained their nineteenth century associations into the 1930s.[61]

When Holmes wrote his 1922 opinion for the court the term trade was associated with the buying and selling of products. It was not associated with the buying and selling of personal services. The term commerce was associated with the traffic of goods, but not the goods themselves. Nor was commerce associated with the production or manufacture of goods. These more restrictive definitions were also applied in cases arising out of the Sherman Act unrelated to baseball.[62] The courts did not hold business combinations liable under Sherman if they could show that their business was local or that it involved manufacture, production, or personal effort not related to production. The logic of the Holmes *Federal Baseball* opinion was consistent with Progressive Era jurisprudence regarding the treatment of "incidental" interstate transportation.[63] This consistency has been overlooked by virtually all commentators who examine the opinion.[64] The now accepted notion that Holmes' opinion was mere sentimental folly which gave birth to a historical accident that is the baseball anomaly ignores this consistency between the Holmes opinion and progressive jurisprudence.

Baseball's peculiar commercial development is less peculiar after considering the synergy between baseball and progressive culture, the marketing campaign of organized baseball that exploited that synergy, and the limitations of progressive jurisprudence. Yet the question remains whether the prevailing public policy assumptions on which baseball's virtual self-government rested were consistent with progressive regulatory policy.

At first blush one would be hard-pressed to find consistency between the development of Major League Baseball's apparently unregulated monopoly and either of the two dominant strands of progressive thought regarding economic regulation. Both the New Freedom and the New Nationalism sought to check such abuses with state action. The former would use the government's law enforcement mechanisms via antitrust law, while the latter would empower independent regulatory agencies to regulate the abuses of the trusts directly. In addition, the views of the Progressive Era president and jurist, William Howard Taft, who advocated the judicial construction and enforcement of the antitrust statutes, sheds no light on the situation. Organized baseball's immunity from any of these types of state action, despite its obvious monopolistic nature, seems to indicate that progressive public policy cannot be squared with organized baseball's commercial development.

To examine this question more fully, however, requires that we determine what the goals of progressive regulatory policy were and what the parameters were of state action as the progressives understood them. If state action refers only to the enforcement by the federal government of antitrust law and the creation of independent regulatory commissions, then, indeed, organized baseball's commercial development cannot be squared with progressive public policy. If, however, we can show that Major League Baseball's self-government furthers the attainment of progressive public policy goals and that it does so within the parameters of state action as the progressives understood it, then we can square the commercial development of Major League Baseball with the spirit of progressivism.

Two goals of progressive public policy are well known: (1) it sought to mitigate the harmful social and economic effects of the Industrial Age, and (2) it sought to liberate individuals through political reforms that would bring down the corrupt political party machines, whose pure patronage politics had weakened the moral fabric of the nation. In the economy, trusts and other large commercial combinations threatened the values of the free market, sponsoring instead the incubation of a might makes right mentality. The pursuit of narrow, local, and sectional interests by party machines had effected the same type of depravity in the political arena.

Stephen Skowronek describes the pre-progressive regime as localist, demonstrated by state courts and parties. "These two nationally integrated institutional systems tied together the state's peculiar organizational determinants and established its effective mode of operations."[65] The U.S. Constitution created a fragmented government of checks and balances and institutional conflicts. Soon after the enactment of the Constitution, political parties (not mentioned in the Constitution) were formed as a means of coordinating the operations of this unwieldy arrangement. Political parties allowed the separated institutions of the government to be brought together behind one electorally accountable agenda while the courts gave meaning and effect to the law. The progressives saw the need to create stable government institutions that were not dependent upon electoral coalitions for their continuity. The needs of the Industrial Age were such that a permanent administrative structure was necessary.

Herbert Croly's *Progressive Democracy* makes clear that the hegemony of political parties and powerful commercial combinations has greatly weakened the state's ability to pursue substantive democracy. By destroying the party system and guiding the efforts of large commercial entities, progressive reformers hoped to enhance the collective power of the state to pursue truly national interests.[66] The pursuit of narrow sectional interests, which flourished under the nineteenth century hegemony of the courts and the parties, and which was shrouded in constitutional law and the spirit of Jeffersonian individualism, was a major obstacle to the realization of the progressives' vision of democracy.

Through illegitimate combinations in both politics and the economy, powerful actors pursued their own selfish interests without regard for the national interest. Progressives were agreed on the necessity of state action in the pursuit of the national interest or public good. The question that remained was the nature of the state. For "most of the Progressives, the state is first 'located' in the good citizen who, in *whatever role and location,* spontaneously acts according to consciously held-and shared-ideas of the public good. . . . A good citizen is 'state-oriented' in the sense of seeking to achieve a larger public good in his actions in every sphere of life."[67]

According to this interpretation, the state must be located prior to any external expression in "an internalized idea of membership and shared values."[68] The existence of a state presupposes the existence of a people who share a common vision of the public good and who integrate that vision into their individual purposes. Such a people are said to be governed, both individually and collectively, by a social ethic, which leads to the realization of social justice.[69] In this formulation, the "state" is equated with the pursuit of the public good, which is normatively agreed upon by the people. When individuals act in the pursuit of the public good they are acting as the state. This construction of the "state" implies that nongovernmental entities and individuals can act in a state capacity to the degree that their actions pursue the public good, or national interest. Eldon Eisenach labels such public spirited entities "parastates."[70]

If organized baseball is seen as a parastate, the political question is: has it acted in the national interest, or in accord with the public good, and was it a good citizen in the Progressive Era? In Eisenach's formulation, parastates were private entities that pursued the public good. Included among them were the family, settlement houses, churches, schools, and universities. These institutions in society were parastates because they were "supportive of government both by producing good citizens and by themselves carrying out the substantive ends that would be desired by an ideal state."[71] It is clear that any institution or individual who pursued the progressive vision of democracy was seen by the progressives as an agent of the state. Organized baseball's peculiar commercial development is therefore consistent with progressivism insofar as it sought to produce good progressive citizens and to govern itself according to the substantive ends that would be desired by an ideal progressive state.

Baseball's use by progressive social reformers as a tool of reform is well documented. The ostensibly native American game was used to socialize disparate ethnic traditions. It was instrumental in bringing the Protestant ethic of the reformers to the urban immigrants and other beneficiaries of the party machines that they were attempting to destroy. Baseball's symmetry with the nativist, Protestant culture of the progressive reformers made it a special enterprise.

The substantive goals of Major League Baseball during the Progressive Era were in many ways the mirror image of the substantive goals of progressive reformers. From the formation of the National League with the goal of cleaning up the game to the installation of progressive Republican Kenesaw Mountain Landis as Commissioner of Baseball, organized baseball shared with the progressive reformers the substantive goals of displacing lower-class, ethnic behavior and ways of life with an upper-class, nativist, and Protestant morality in the workplace, the voting booth, and the ballpark.[72]

The progressive reformers sought to promote an enlightened and far-sighted citizenship, which would be ever mindful of the national interest over narrow, sectional interests. Major League Baseball's structure for self-regulation was designed with the same communitarian ethos. The monopoly practices of organized baseball produced, for the most part, internal fairness. In addition, these commercial practices, which were prohibited in other industries, were necessary to produce the kind of baseball that Americans wanted to see and to patronize.

In a open and free baseball market there is no way to control costs or prevent lop-sided competition on the field. In essence, there is no way to enforce in baseball a broader understanding of self-interest that is consistent with the public, or national interest, other than to allow Major League Baseball to regulate itself. The connection between the progressives' campaign for state-minded citizens and Major League Baseball's attention to the greater good in baseball through the enforcement of baseball law is evidenced by the congruity of the progressives' vision of the national interest and Major League Baseball's vision of the interests of baseball.

Major League Baseball's development as a legal monopoly, while inconsistent with the regulatory policies of the Progressive Era national government, was nonetheless wholly consistent with the spirit and substantive goals of the progressive movement. In both the New Nationalism and the New Freedom it is clear that the substantive goal was to curtail the harmful effects of corporate combinations without stifling their ability to engage in collective action that was consistent with the public good or national interest. Baseball's commercial development was anomalous, not because it was out of step with progressivism, but because it was the only industry of its size and scope that was not subjected to regulation by the federal government.

Baseball's birth and early development as a professional spectator sport coincided with and helped fulfill certain cultural needs existent in the decades surrounding the turn of the century. In a time of instability and uncertainty baseball provided continuity and a sense of shared identity to a generation that was charged with ushering the nation through its most profound transition. The transition from an agrarian to an industrial society brought with it explosions of immigrant migration to America's cities and the awkward integration of these disparate immigrant cultures with an American culture that was itself in transition.

Those who controlled Major League Baseball in the Progressive Era, from William Hulbert to Judge Kenesaw Mountain Landis, were vocal advocates of the progressives' social, cultural, and political agenda. The owners and promoters of organized baseball exploited both the cultural significance of the game and the institutional frailties of the federal government in their development of baseball law. Progressive jurisprudence and the cultivated ambiguity of the commercial nature of organized baseball combined to effect the preservation of baseball's unregulated monopoly. Moreover, the harmony of Major League Baseball's substantive goals with those of the progressive reformers overshadowed the inconsistency between the regulatory policies affecting other industries and Major League Baseball's exempted status.

NOTES

1. See Pearson, Daniel M., *Baseball in 1889: Players vs. Owners* (Bowling Green, OH: Bowling Green State University Popular Press, 1993).

2. Rader, Benjamin G., *Baseball: A History of America's Game* (Chicago: University of Illinois Press, 1992), p. 2.

3. Goldstein, Warren, *Playing for Keeps: A History of Early Baseball* (Ithaca: Cornell University Press, 1989), p. 24.

4. Rader, p. 12.

5. Voigt, David Q., *American Baseball: From Gentleman's Sport to the Commissioner System* (Norman: University of Oklahoma Press, 1966), p. 11.

6. See Voigt, p. 14–22.

7. U.S. Congress, House, Committee on the Judiciary, Subcommittee on the Study of Monopoly Power, *Organized Baseball* (H.R. Rept. No. 2002, 82nd Cong., 2d Sess., 1952), p. 16.

8. U.S. Congress, House, Committee on the Judiciary Subcommittee on the Study of Monopoly Power, *Organized Baseball* (H.R. Rept. Number 2002, 82nd Cong., 2d Sess., 1952), p. 17.

9. Rader, p. 22.

10. Voigt, p. 17–18.

11. Goldstein, p. 134.

12. U.S. Congress, House, Committee on the Judiciary, Subcommittee on the Study of Monopoly Power, *Organized Baseball* (H.R. Rept. No. 2002, 82nd Cong., 2d Sess., 1952), p. 18.

13. Zimbalist, Andrew, *Baseball and Billions: A Probing Look Into the Big Business of Our National Pastime* (New York: Basic Books, 1992), p. 3.

14. Voigt, p. 60–80.

15. U.S. Congress, House, Committee on the Judiciary, Subcommittee on the Study of Monopoly Power, *Organized Baseball* (H.R. Rept. No. 2002, 82nd Cong., 2d Sess., 1952), p. 20.

16. U.S. Congress, House, Committee on the Judiciary, Subcommittee on the Study of Monopoly Power, *Organized Baseball* (H.R. Rept. No. 2002, 82nd Cong., 2d Sess., 1952), p. 20.

17. U.S. Congress, House, Committee on the Judiciary, Subcommittee on the Study of Monopoly Power, *Organized Baseball* (H.R. Rept. No. 2002, 82nd Cong., 2d Sess., 1952), p. 24.

18. Zimbalist, p. 4.

19. Zimbalist, p. 4.

20. Rader, p. 47.

21. U.S. Congress, House, Committee on the Judiciary, Subcommittee on the Study of Monopoly Power, *Organized Baseball* (H.R. Rept. No. 2002, 82nd Cong., 2d Sess., 1952), p. 32.

22. U.S. Congress, House, Committee on the Judiciary, Subcommittee on the Study of Monopoly Power, *Organized Baseball* (H.R. Rept. No. 2002, 82nd Cong., 2d Sess., 1952), p. 33.

23. Rogers, C. Paul, "Judicial Reinterpretation of Statutes: The Example of Baseball and the Antitrust Laws," *Houston Law Review* 14, no. 3 (1977), p. 614.

24. U.S. Congress, House, Committee on the Judiciary, Subcommittee on the Study of Monopoly Power, *Organized Baseball* (H.R. Rept. No. 2002, 82nd Cong., 2d Sess., 1952), p. 35.

25. Zimbalist, p. 6.

26. U.S. Congress, House, Committee on the Judiciary, Subcommittee on the Study of Monopoly Power, *Organized Baseball* (H.R. Rept. No. 2002, 82nd Cong., 2d Sess., 1952), p. 36.

27. Zimbalist, p. 7.

28. See *Metropolitan Exhibition Co. v. Ward*, 9 N.Y.S. 779 (1890).

29. White, G. Edward, *Creating the National Pastime: Baseball Transforms Itself (1903–1953)* (Princeton: Princeton University Press, 1996), p. 56–57.

30. White, G. Edward, *Creating the National Pastime: Baseball Transforms Itself (1903–1953)* (Princeton: Princeton University Press, 1996), p. 58.

31. Rader, p. 81.

32. Zimbalist, p. 9.

33. Markham, Jesse W. and Paul Teplitz, *Baseball Economics and Public Policy* (Lexington, MA: D.C. Heath and Co., 1981), p. 7.

34. Quoted in Zimbalist, p. 10.

35. Holmes' decision will be fully discussed and analyzed in chapter 2.

36. Rader, p. 100–110.

37. Dewey, Donald, *The Antitrust Experiment in America* (New York: Columbia University Press, 1990), p. 4.

38. Boudreaux, Donald, Thomas DiLorenzo, and Steven Parker, "Antitrust before the Sherman Act," in McChesney, Fred S. and William F. Shughart II, *The Causes and Consequences of Antitrust* (Chicago: University of Chicago Press, 1995), p. 256.

39. Keller, Morton, *Regulating a New Economy: Public Policy and Economic Change in America, 1900–1933* (Cambridge, MA: Harvard University Press, 1990), p. 24.

40. Dewey, p. 6.

41. Eisner, Marc Allen, *Antitrust and the Triumph of Economics* (Chapel Hill: University of North Carolina Press, 1991), p. 1.

42. Abrams, Richard, (ed.), *The Issue of Federal Regulation in the Progressive Era* (Chicago: Rand McNally & Co., 1989), p. 25.

43. Keller, p. 28.

44. Abrams, p. 23.

45. Taft, William Howard, *The Antitrust Act and the Supreme Court* (New York: Harper & Bros. Publishing, 1914), p. 5.

46. Keller, p. 28.

47. See Eisner, Marc Allen, *Regulatory Politics in Transition* (Baltimore: The Johns Hopkins University Press, 1993).

48. The exact years of the Progressive Era are a matter of scholarly debate. Some bracket the first two decades of this century. Others locate progressivism more broadly in the four decades from 1880 to 1920. This study finds the latter interpretation more instructive and useful. Studies using the broader period include Marc Allen Eisner's *Regulatory Politics in Transition* (Baltimore: The Johns Hopkins University Press, 1993); and Eldon J. Eisenach's *The Lost Promise of Progressivism* (Lawrence: University Press of Kansas, 1994).

49. See Riess, Stephen, *Touching Base: Professional Baseball and American Culture in the Progressive Era* (Westport, CT: Greenwood Press, 1980).

50. See Story, Ronald, "The Country of the Young: The Meaning of Baseball in Early American Culture," in Hall, Alvin (ed.), *Cooperstown Symposium on Baseball and American Culture* (Westport, CT: Meckler Publishing, 1991).

51. Many historians have made a big deal of the partnership between the sports press and organized baseball, arguing that the press and baseball had a quid pro quo type arrangement that facilitated the highly effective baseball marketing that was instrumental in preserving the peculiar nature of the business of baseball.

52. White, p. 59.

53. White, p. 66–82.

54. Story, p. 325.

55. White, p. 58.

56. White, p. 56–58.

57. Rader, p. 109.

58. Zimbalist, p. 10.

59. White, p. 73.

60. Waller, Spencer W., Neil B. Cohen, and Paul Finkelman, (eds.), *Baseball and the American Legal Mind* (New York: Garland Publishing, Inc., 1995), p. 208–209.

61. Justice Holmes relied on the very limited understanding of "commerce" set forth in *Hooper v. California*, 155 U.S. 648 (1895).

62. See *Paul v. Virginia*, 8 Wall. 168 (1869), *Hooper v. California*, 155 U.S. 648 (1894) and *U.S. v. E.C. Knight*, 156 U.S. (1895).

63. White, p. 74–75.

64. A noteworthy exception to this is G. Edward White's *Creating the National Pastime: Baseball Transforms Itself, 1903–1955* (Princeton: Princeton University Press, 1996).

65. Skowronek, Stephen, *Building a New American State: The Expansion of National Administrative Capacities, 1877–1920* (New York: Cambridge University Press, 1982), p. 24–35.

66. See Croly, Herbert, *Progressive Democracy* (New York: Macmillan Publishing, 1914).

67. Eisenach, Eldon, *The Lost Promise of Progressivism* (Lawrence: University Press of Kansas, 1994), p. 132.

68. Eisenach, Eldon, *The Lost Promise of Progressivism* (Lawrence: University Press of Kansas, 1994), p. 132.

69. Eisenach, Eldon, *The Lost Promise of Progressivism* (Lawrence: University Press of Kansas, 1994), p. 132–133.

70. Eisenach, Eldon, *The Lost Promise of Progressivism* (Lawrence: University Press of Kansas, 1994), p. 131.

71. Eisenach, Eldon, *The Lost Promise of Progressivism* (Lawrence: University Press of Kansas, 1994), p. 135.

72. It is noteworthy that the creation of the commissioner system in baseball was similar to the efforts of the Hays Commission in Hollywood. The Hays Commission was created to clean up the content of movies during the 1920s, bringing them more into line with progressive sensibilities. Will H. Hays became the czar of the movie business in much the same way that Landis became the czar of baseball.

_____ 2 _____

The New Deal Era
and the Baseball Anomaly

Organized baseball's peculiar entrepreneurial character was forged in the interests, institutions, and ideas of the Progressive Era. In the decades around the turn of the century organized baseball preserved its unique entrepreneurial character by exploiting the ideas of the progressives' social gospel as well as the limited institutional capacities of the federal government. With the onset of the Depression, American regulatory politics was transformed. Instead of ameliorating the harmful effects of corporate combinations, the goal of New Deal regulatory policy in the wake of market collapse, was recovery. In these highly volatile economic conditions stability was valued over all else.

The Progressive Era regulatory regime, designed to preserve market conditions amidst the growth of corporate power, gave way to a new regulatory regime in the wake of the Depression. Marc Allen Eisner calls the regulatory regime of the New Deal Era the "associational" regime. This regime is rooted in a synthesis of New Nationalist progressivism and the experience of economic planning during World War I. While the Wilsonian, or New Freedom, strand of progressivism sought to recreate the fair market conditions of the preindustrial age, Theodore Roosevelt's New Nationalist progressivism sought to use the institutions of the state to guide and manage the economy through cooperative arrangements between government and industry. The quasi-corporatist arrangements envisioned by Croly and Roosevelt would become a prominent feature of Franklin Roosevelt's New Deal recovery program, and they would also provide philosophical justification for the continuation of baseball's unregulated monopoly.

The consistency between the public policy goals of the Progressive Era and baseball law, which spawned baseball's unregulated monopoly, would be extended to the New Deal Era. While other industries were increasingly becoming subject to government regulation in an effort to stabilize and improve the economy, Major League Baseball was seen as a model of stability, effectively coping with economic hard times while at the same time carving out a special niche in American culture and society. The turmoil of economic depression and world war overshadowed baseball's anomalous commercial development. The unprecedented internal stability of Major League Baseball combined with the game's self-conscious role in uplifting the spirits of a troubled nation during this era contributed to Major League Baseball's ability to avoid government regulation.

While the politics of the nation was undergoing its most profound upheaval since the Civil War, Major League Baseball was enjoying what might be called a golden age of stability.[1] From January 1921, to his death in 1944, Judge Kenesaw Mountain Landis presided over a sport that saw no player revolts and no challenges from outlaw leagues. Prior to Landis, baseball had hardly enjoyed a single decade without having to cope with an outlaw league or disgruntled players. Landis presided over the game through the roaring '20s, the depressed '30s, and the Second World War of the early '40s without so much as a whisper about government intervention in the governance of the baseball.

With the close of the Landis era and the end of World War II, baseball began to experience adversity. The national pastime, which had served as a window to better times during the nation's most troubling decades, begin to reflect the ills of society rather than provide a pristine escape from them. Having just fought a war for freedom, Americans began to grapple with oppression at home. A new activism among minority Americans would find expression in the triumphs of Jackie Robinson and the integration of baseball. The ugliness that greeted Robinson in the big leagues ended forever the days when baseball evoked only the joys of a child's game. As the postwar economy picked up, professional baseball players began to realize that they deserved a bigger slice of the pie. Eventually it would be the players' pursuit of workers' rights that would erode the pillars of baseball law and threaten the game's unregulated monopoly.

THE GOLDEN AGE OF STABILITY: THE LANDIS YEARS

From 1903 to 1920, baseball was governed by the National Commission made up of the National and American League presidents and a third member chosen by them. The National Commission enjoyed about ten years of stability before it began to falter with the Federal League war. While many historians charge that the National Commission was dissolved as a result of the Black Sox Scandal, historian Harold Seymour disagrees. He argues that the commission would have been replaced in any event.[2]

In its later years, the National Commission was weakened by scandal. In 1918, the National League President, John K. Tener, was forced to resign amidst charges of corruption. The members of the commission were often accused of allowing their financial interests to interfere with their duties on the commission. In the summer of 1920, the commission's chairman, August Herrmann, resigned under pressure, leaving the commission without a chairman for the remainder of its existence.[3]

Organized baseball foresaw the end of the National Commission. The so-called Lasker plan for a governing structure in baseball was circulating a full year before the Black Sox Scandal. Albert D. Lasker, a Chicago advertising executive and prominent member of the Republican party, was part owner of the Chicago Cubs. His plan was to create a commissioner of baseball and two associate commissioners in whom total authority would be vested to govern the game. These commissioners would be prominent men who had no financial interest in the game. The idea was that the owners should not and could not govern themselves. They needed an impartial governor. The owners were not attracted to this plan for obvious reasons; however, the Black Sox Scandal made it much more palatable.[4]

On November 12, 1920, the owners of the 16 major league clubs met at the Congress Hotel in Chicago, where they created the governing structure of baseball that continues to this day. With the Lasker plan as a benchmark, the owners unanimously chose to have a single commissioner. They dropped the associate commissioners, fearing that they would dilute the authority of the commissioner. They also chose to make the commissioner a virtual czar of baseball, vesting him with absolute authority to rule in the interests of the game in the hope that his strong hand could restore the integrity of baseball in its time of profound crisis. The confidence of the American people in the incorruptibility of baseball was badly shaken and was thought to require swift, decisive action.

The commissioner's post was officially created in the new National Agreement adopted on January 12, 1921, and Judge Kenesaw Mountain Landis was named to the position. Chosen over such notables as former President William Howard Taft, General John J. Pershing, and Senator Hiram Johnson, Landis had illustrated his affinity for the game as a federal district court judge. In 1915, Landis hastened the settlement of the original Federal League challenge by delaying his decision from the bench and encouraging an out-of-court settlement.

Baseball's first commissioner was born in Millville, Ohio, in 1866, the son of Doctor Abraham Landis, who had served as a Union Army surgeon in the Civil War. Landis got his distinctive name from the battle of Kennesaw Mountain, which his father had experienced only two years earlier. Landis was appointed to the federal bench by his idol and family friend,

President Theodore Roosevelt. As a jurist, Landis was not shy about impos-
ing his progressive values. He distinguished himself as a trustbuster in
1907 by fining Standard Oil company $29,240,000 in what would become
the most famous antitrust decision of the era. His widely acknowledged
love of baseball combined with his storied resolve in the face of the mighty
trusts made Landis appear to be the perfect choice for the job of restoring
baseball's image and preserving the game's unregulated monopoly.

The owners created a quasi-public post by constructing the office of
commissioner much like the independent regulatory commissions of government. By empowering Landis to rule in the best interests of baseball free
from the influence of the owners, organized baseball had effectively regulated itself in a manner consistent with the New Nationalism principles
that would animate regulatory politics in the New Deal Era. One of the
terms of the National Agreement of 1921, which created the commissioner's position, was that in the event of the commissioner's death or incapac-
ity, the President of the United States would choose a new commissioner of
baseball.[5] This provision illustrates the owners' conscious attempt to make
the governance of the game consistent with the regulatory philosophy of
the day.[6]

The commissioner would be the final judge in all disputes. The owners
and the leagues surrendered their rights to appeal rulings of the commissioner to the courts.[7] Landis quickly exercised his sweeping power by banning the eight Chicago Black Sox players from baseball for life, despite the
fact that they were acquitted of wrongdoing in a court of law. This established both his authority and his authoritarian style. Even the appearance
of impropriety would not be tolerated. Landis would impose his progressive sensibilities and values on the game for a quarter of a century.

Baseball historian David Voigt describes the chagrin of the majority of
owners when they realized what they had done in the face of the Black Sox
Scandal. Their fear of losing the game's status as the national pastime
caused them to appoint a dictator. But once the guilty season was past, they
realized that they had left it to the dictator to decide what was and was not
detrimental to the game. Voigt writes:

Landis quickly consolidated his power. His best weapon was his own image as the
personification of baseball integrity. He used publicity masterfully and kept himself
in the news along with the swashbuckling Babe Ruth. Each in his own style grabbed
headlines, and together they epitomized the baseball revolution that produced the
new golden age.[8]

Voigt goes on to describe Landis and Ruth as "two poles of attraction" for
Americans, with Ruth representing "the nation's faith in skill and power"
as well as "the yearning for unrestricted pleasure," while Landis epitomized "lingering Protestant values" and served as "the antidote to Ruthian
excess."[9] Baseball historians are mixed on the question of who saved base-

ball in the wake of the Black Sox Scandal. Some argue that it was the hard line discipline of Landis; others contend that the Sultan of Swat simply made everyone forget about the past. Undoubtedly, both men contributed to the rehabilitation of baseball's image in the 1920s.

Landis' job was to restore the good name of baseball. He was not involved in creating or changing the rules of the game, unless there was a conflict, in which case he acted as arbitrator. First and foremost, Landis was charged with putting the shadow of the Black Sox Scandal behind and forging a new wholesome image for the game. To accomplish this, Landis imposed the severest punishments, often quite disproportionate to the offense.

In his first year of 1921, Landis banned more than a dozen players from baseball, including the infamous eight. Upon banning the eight Black Sox players Landis announced: "Regardless of the verdicts of juries, no player who throws a ball game, no player that sits in conference with a bunch of crooked players and gamblers where the ways and means of throwing a game are discussed and does not promptly tell his club about it, will ever play professional baseball."[10] Among the other players banned in 1921 were Hal Chase and Ben Kauff. Chase was repeatedly linked to gamblers, and Kauff was banned for consorting with car thieves.[11] In addition, Landis suspended three Yankees, including Babe Ruth, for barnstorming in the off-season, and also ordered Charles Stoneham and John McGraw of the New York Giants to divest themselves of their interests in race tracks in New York and Cuba.[12]

On May 29, 1922, the Supreme Court, ruling on a case lingering from the Federal League challenge gave baseball an exemption from the federal antitrust laws. This gave government sanction to what some have called baseball's private self-government, with Landis as an independent and chief executive.[13] In his opinion for the Court, Justice Oliver Wendell Holmes argued that baseball was not engaged in interstate commerce and was therefore beyond the reach of federal antitrust law. Based on the logic that the actual playing of a game was within one state, Holmes held baseball to be a "purely state affair." He held further that the interstate travel necessary for games was "mere incident, not the essential thing."[14]

With this, baseball was officially special. Many commentators argue that the Holmes decision does not say that baseball is special, or that it has special cultural significance as our national pastime. One year after the *Federal Baseball* decision, however, in the case of *Hart v. Keith Vaudeville Exchange* Holmes ruled that traveling vaudeville shows were engaged in interstate commerce.[15] By ruling that traveling vaudeville shows were engaged in interstate commerce, despite the fact that the shows appeared to be purely state affairs for which interstate travel was merely incident, Holmes inadvertently signaled that baseball was indeed special.

In the *Federal Baseball* decision, Holmes took pains to mention in his opinion that the appeals court "went to the root of the case" and "got it

right."[16] This endorsement of the appeals court decision is important because, in addition to holding that baseball was in effect not a matter of interstate commerce, the lower court held specifically that the reserve clause
was not an unreasonable restraint of trade and that baseball was sport, and
not trade. By endorsing the appeals court decision, Holmes was therefore
endorsing the entire decision, including its specific language about baseball's reserve system as well as its distinction between sport and trade.

With the blessing of the highest court in the land, Landis ruled baseball's
private self-government without regard for trifling concepts such as due
process. Landis fined, suspended and banned anyone who, in his estima-
tion, endangered the image of the national pastime. At the same time, Landis' ability to gauge public opinion enabled him to temper his wrath when
the situation called for greater subtlety. In 1927, two of the game's living
legends—Ty Cobb and Tris Speaker—were linked to fixing games in the
1919 season. Landis chose not to expel these popular players. Instead, he
chose merely to move them to other teams and justified this lenient punish-
ment on the fact that the alleged infraction occurred before he took office.
Most baseball historians agree that Landis' mercy was motivated by his desire to protect two baseball legends from a scandal that would have reflected badly on baseball as a whole.[17]

David Voigt argues that the Cobb/Speaker decision marked a shift in
Landis' tactics. Because the public was beginning to forget the Black Sox
Scandal, Landis transformed himself from stern disciplinarian to "efficient
priest."[18] Landis' rulings during the remainder of his tenure were no less
arbitrary, but they were less harsh.

The 1920s was a decade of prosperity in the nation and in organized
baseball. The Age of Babe Ruth brought renewed popularity to the game.
The American economy was growing and the standard of living in the nation was rising precipitously. National prosperity was matched by economic prosperity in baseball. Average attendance at major league games
rose fifty percent in the 1920s.[19] Baseball's economic prosperity was also
helped by the rapid growth of urban areas in the 1920s as well as the explosion of industry. Factory production almost doubled in the 1920s.[20] Indeed,
the roaring '20s brought prosperity to a growing nation and provided an
excellent environment for refurbishing baseball's tarnished image. It was
easy to forget the troubled past amidst the rosy present.

The most lively debates in baseball in the 1920s may have been about the
minor leagues. Before reaching a stabilizing agreement in 1931, the issue of
the minor league draft was hotly debated. On one side were minor league
owners who saw the draft as antithetical to their property rights. They
wanted to buy and sell players at will. On the other side, Commissioner
Landis and the big league owners advocated a universal draft wherein any
minor league player could be taken by a major league club. After several

patchwork compromises during the 1920s the Landis position won out in 1931.[21]

Another minor league controversy in the 1920s revolved around the St. Louis Cardinals President Branch Rickey's farm system. Rickey's team owned and operated minor league clubs and thus in effect controlled large numbers of minor league players from the outset of their careers. Commissioner Landis opposed farm systems arguing, like a good progressive, that they created monopolies of talent inimical to free and fair competition for players. They were, he insisted, a perversion of the reserve rule, which left player fortunes in the hands of a single club instead of a free market or player draft.

Throughout his tenure Landis fought farm systems. Unable to outlaw the practice, he attempted to utilize his power to discourage them and to scuttle their use when they were in clear violation of the spirit of free competition. Landis repeatedly chastised the owners for their covert support of the practice of farming.[22] In 1921, Landis got wind of four players being purchased by big league clubs and sent to minor league teams with whom gentleman's agreements were struck to return the players to the majors at the end of the season. Landis immediately condemned the clubs involved for having failed "to obtain waivers from other clubs or use option agreements, the only recognized and carefully restricted exception to the no-farming rule."[23] Landis declared the players free agents able to sign with any team they pleased. Despite the commissioner's persistent and active opposition to farm systems, the practice continued. In 1932, the major league owners officially rejected Landis' position by voting unanimously to adopt a rule that specifically permitted farm systems.[24]

The rosy days of the 1920s would lose their bloom with the onset of the Depression. Although big league attendance maintained its high level through the 1930 season, it declined precipitously thereafter, not returning to pre-Depression levels until the 1940s. In 1933, the national economy was at its lowest point. All the economic indicators were down. Unemployment hit record levels. Throughout the decade baseball struggled to get by. While attitudes in politics were shifting toward support for cooperative recovery measures, baseball remained consistent with its more laissez faire attitudes. Historian Benjamin Rader quotes Yankee owner Jacob Ruppert as saying, "I found out a long time ago that there is no charity in baseball."[25] Shielded from government interference, organized baseball was able to resist the effects of the burgeoning welfare state. Perhaps most telling is the fact that, throughout the 1930s, ticket prices never went down.

In baseball, the richer clubs like the Yankees and Giants were able to make ends meet, while the poorer clubs became caught in a vicious cycle. Because attendance was down, poorer clubs, such as Connie Mack's Philadelphia Athletics, were forced to generate revenue by selling off players, which meant ability to win on the field declined, in turn causing a further drop in fan interest and attendance. In other words, the rich got richer and better, while the poor got poorer and worse. While this situation was not new, the depressed economy made it particularly egregious in the 1930s. Numerous proposals for profit sharing arrangements to help alleviate this cycle and improve competition on the field were scuttled by the richer clubs. Nevertheless, baseball limped on, managing to survive the worst of times.[26]

Baseball in the 1930s was an important tool for boosting the morale of a dejected nation. Franklin Roosevelt recognized the utility of the national pastime as a way to provide hope amidst despair and as a way to promote positive thinking and wholesome values. Dizzy Dean's biographer, Robert Gregory, captures this theme by quoting Roosevelt upon throwing out the first ball of the 1933 season. The president said, "Baseball has done as much as anything to keep up the spirits of the people."[27] The president's remarks made it clear that the spirit of the game would be instrumental in seeing the country through hard times. Politicians of the day routinely invoked the spirit of the game. Baseball metaphors were conspicuous in the political rhetoric of the Depression.

While not immune from the hard economic times of the 1930s, baseball was nonetheless enjoying relative stability. There were no attempts to unionize by players, no interleague wars and no franchises were lost to financial ruin. Ironically, the economic challenges of the decade contributed to this stability. Player revolts, which surely would have occurred given the across the board salary reductions of the decade, were never launched. Because of the abject poverty rampant in the nation such a revolt would surely have met with overwhelming public disapproval.

When Babe Ruth complained about a salary cut of 33%, he was excoriated in the press. Even Judge Landis was forced to take a pay cut in order to show his willingness to shoulder some of the burden of getting the game through financial hard times. Baseball may have been exempt from the legal regulation of antitrust statutes, but it was not immune to the regulating influence of public opinion. Outlaw and upstart leagues were likewise discouraged by economic conditions as much or more than by baseball's legal monopoly or by its strong commissioner.

This stability was not seamless. Major League Baseball did face internal controversies in the 1930s. Controversy over salary cuts was joined by debates over night baseball and radio broadcasts of ball games. Night baseball had been banned in the big leagues until 1934, when the Cincinnati Reds began to play under the lights. Radio broadcasts were generally thought to be bad for attendance. Ironically, the Chicago Cubs were the last team to play night games at home but the first team to broadcast games regularly on the radio.[28]

Night games were an attempt to increase revenue during the Depression. The theory was that attendance would be boosted because those who were working could attend games after work. Commissioner Landis opposed night baseball, arguing, again like a good progressive, that it detracted from the wholesome character of the game by putting it on a par with the less savory activities common to the night. Financial necessity, however, superseded progressive values, and the commissioner acquiesced to a limited number of night games.

While the economic exigencies of the Depression worked in favor of night baseball, they had the opposite effect on radio broadcasts of games in the 1930s. Club owners feared that, if games were on the radio, financially strapped fans would stay home and listen to the games rather than come to the ballpark. The prevalence of this attitude is evident in the ban on radio broadcasts agreed to by all three New York clubs. This ban remained in effect through the 1939 season.[29]

Baseball entered the 1940s down, but not out. As the economy began to recover due to the economic effects of war, baseball's fortunes rebounded. Just as it had been during the ravages of economic depression, baseball was an important symbol of American values during World War II. In a letter from President Roosevelt to Commissioner Landis dated January 15, 1942, the president expressed his desire for baseball to continue on during the war. He wrote that baseball would provide crucial opportunities for recreation in a time when an overburdened people desperately needed such diversion. The president expressed confidence that despite its depleted ranks during the war, the popularity of the game would not suffer. Roosevelt also urged Landis to permit additional night games so that day shift workers could see a game occasionally.[30] Though long an opponent of night baseball, Landis permitted an expansion of night games during the war.

Major League Baseball accepted its special role in the war effort. In 1941, the owners purchased $25,000 worth of bats and balls for use by the military. The proceeds from each of the all-star games during the war were donated to the cause. Large numbers of big leaguers entered military service. Admission to most ballparks was free to military personnel, and in many other ways baseball sought to pull its weight for the war effort.[31] Despite drops in attendance during the war years, Major League Baseball failed to earn a combined profit only once, in 1943, and in that year twelve of baseball's sixteen teams were individually profitable.[32]

In his nearly twenty-five years at the helm of professional baseball, Judge Landis presided over a stable, if not serene, industry. In the final analysis, it was this stability that made government intervention seem unnecessary. While the most palpable shield from external involvement in the business of baseball may have been the antitrust exemption granted in 1922, baseball was also left to its own devices during the reign of Landis because of the commissioner's vigorous defense of and advocacy for free market conditions within the game itself.

The free market values of the Progressive Era had a voice inside of baseball in Commissioner Landis. His support for a universal draft for minor
leaguers and his opposition to farm systems exemplified his commitment
to free market principles.[33] Furthermore, the nation's policymakers had far
more important fish to fry. Economic depression and world war distracted
policymakers from the baseball anomaly and, at the same time, enabled
Major League Baseball to contribute to the national weal in its own unique
way.

THE POLITICS OF THE DEPRESSION AND
THE NEW DEAL

During the Landis years in baseball, national politics was being transformed. The regulatory environment went from its Progressive Era focus
on the market to the New Deal Era emphasis on what Eisner calls "associationalism." This regulatory regime change was but a part of a much larger
change in American politics as the nation moved further away from its
nineteenth-century state of "courts and parties" to the full blown "administrative state" of the mid-twentieth century. Politics was becoming more national, moving from its locus in decentralized political parties and state
courts to one in the federal executive branch. This transition would require
a major shift in political values as well as federal jurisprudence in order to
be completed. The tension within progressivism between Jeffersonian
democratic values and Hamiltonian concepts of nationalism, as expressed
in debates between the New Freedom and the New Nationalism, would
continue to shape American politics. As the nation's politics moved toward
greater involvement of the government in the regulation of the economy,
the pressure on baseball's private self-government increased.

Marc Allen Eisner locates the genesis of the associational regime in the
experience of war mobilization during World War I. In an effort to organize
the mobilization effort, the federal government created the War Industries
Board (WIB), which was made up of fifty-seven sections covering virtually
every conceivable industry. Each section of the board solicited the input of
business rivals on the maintenance of price stability, the establishment of
production priorities, and the promotion of rapid response to military
needs. The WIB succeeded in forging a closer relationship between the government and industry representatives like the U.S. Chamber of Commerce.
The experience of the WIB also showed the potential benefits of quasi-
corporatist schemes of industrial planning.[34]

The 1920s saw a tremendous proliferation of trade associations. These
associations, made up of industry rivals, shared consumer statistics, credit
information, cost formulas, and other important industrial information.
The ostensible purpose of these associations was to curb unfair market
practices, but they defined fair and unfair price policies in ways that in ef-

fect reduced competition. In this way, these associations dampened competition with one hand while embracing the strictures of the Sherman Act with the other.[35] In the 1920s, when trade associations flourished with the blessing of the federal government, baseball's unregulated monopoly seemed much less an anomaly. It was distinct only in that no government agency facilitated the cooperation of the baseball owners.

Secretary of commerce and later president, Herbert Hoover was very impressed with these trade associations to the degree that they performed their designed purpose. To Hoover, these associations represented an extension of the experience of wartime mobilization. Hoover believed "that a network of cooperative associations facilitated by the national government could serve to coordinate and rationalize production." What Eisner calls Hoover's vision of "associational self-regulation" was designed to "provide a means of directing economic development, eliminat[e] damaging competition, and ensur[e] that firms producing comparable goods would agree to meet specific standards."[36] During the 1920s the Commerce Department and the Federal Trade Commission pursued many of these types of industry-friendly associationalist initiatives. Major League Baseball under Commissioner Landis approximated this "associational self-regulation" quite well despite the absence of federal oversight. Additionally, the game was seen in the 1920s as just that, a game, not an industry. To the degree that anyone perceived a need to regulate baseball, the creation of an independent commissioner to be replaced by presidential appointment, was considered more than sufficient.

The stock market crash of 1929 drastically and unalterably transformed perceptions of economic stability and growth. The previous decade saw a nation ruminating over ways to expand and build on its economic prosperity. The associationalism of the 1920s was undertaken, not out of grave necessity, but as a way to help stabilize and expand commercial success. The collapse of the economy in the aftermath of the stock market crash completely changed the tenor of such initiatives. Just as world war had required a nationally coordinated mobilization effort, the collapse of the economy would require a nationally coordinated economic recovery effort.

Despite his associationalist tendencies as secretary of commerce, President Hoover refused to expand the concept in order to defeat this enemy, economic depression. His efforts to create cooperative arrangements among industry competitors with the help of the state had always been animated by his strong belief in a free market. When presented with a proposal that would have required the suspension of antitrust laws and the creation of a regulatory agency with broad powers to coerce commercial entities into complying with its recommendations, President Hoover rejected it as a plan that would create destructive monopolies and extend government intervention in the economy beyond its constitutional limits. Contrary to Hoover's reluctance, there was a general feeling among industry representatives that the present crisis required the suspension of antitrust laws as well as some manner of government supervised trade agreements. These measures were seen as necessary to restore stability to a highly volatile and unstable economy.[37]

The mood of the country was shifting rapidly in 1930 and 1931 toward greater receptivity of government involvement in the economy. Hoover resisted this political trend. In the belief that the stock market crash was just a "paper debacle that could be checked by intelligent cooperation at the top," Hoover encouraged industry representatives to increase spending voluntarily to spur the economy. He acted as public cheerleader for the "self-recuperative power and socially cooperative spirit of [American] business." Hoover's optimism and faith proved futile, and his attempts to instill a "keep the faith" attitude would become fodder for the satire of a generation.[38] Historian Dixon Wecter captures Hoover's intransigence:

Hoover believed that the obligation for relief and reemployment began with the individual. Failing there, the effort might then call upon private organizations like the Red Cross, thence turn to municipal and state governments and, finally, as a last resort to the federal government—whose succor, in this ultimate extremity, should take the form of loans rather than gifts. Slowly and reluctantly Hoover was driven back trench after trench in what he conceived to be his defense of the public treasury.[39]

Although historians are quick to point out that the presidential campaign of 1932 was not waged between opposing visions of economic regulation, it is fair to say that Hoover's inability to stem the tide of economic despair led to Franklin Roosevelt's landslide victory. Roosevelt's campaign rhetoric was bold, but inconsistent. Having concluded that the American political spectrum ranged from those who doggedly adhered to Jeffersonian laissez faire principles to those who supported the bold New Nationalism of the previous President Roosevelt, FDR used rhetoric that included something for everyone. Under FDR, a new approach to economic regulation would eventually be blessed by both public opinion and the Supreme Court.

Just as the political atmosphere of the previous decade was shaped by the conservative values of Presidents Harding, Coolidge, and Hoover, the politics of at least the next forty years would be shaped by the values of Roosevelt's New Deal. The seeming inconsistency of his campaign rhetoric reflected more than his uncanny ability to forge winning coalitions in politics, it represented the tensions within his own mind about American politics.

The most popular interpretation of the New Deal holds that it was a series of ad hoc responses to the economic crises of the Depression brokered by a highly skilled politician whose talent for coalition building was aided by his decided lack of a coherent political philosophy.[40] Marc Allen Eisner probes deeper and enriches our understanding of the New Deal, arguing that its transformation of state–society relations was the combined result of experience with war mobilization and the New Nationalist strand of progressivism.[41] While Eisner's thesis is compelling and accurate, the work of Sidney Milkis better illustrates how FDR transformed the political landscape. Milkis argues that "FDR consciously patterned his leadership after that of Woodrow Wilson and Theodore Roosevelt, seeking to reconcile the strengths of these leaders."[42]

FDR was drawn to Wilson's attempt to preserve the nineteenth-century spirit of individual liberty, but he was also conscious of the pathological effects of advocating a Jeffersonian individualism in an age when the barriers to freedom were more often erected by economic elites than by government interference. The president's heralded "brain trust" was headed by two men whose ideas were the product of the two strands of progressive thought. Adolph Berle used his influence to push the president toward Theodore Roosevelt's New Nationalist program, while Felix Frankfurter exercised his prerogative as one of the president's top advisors to support the ideas of Wilson and Brandeis, who preferred political deliberation and choice to the imposition of administrative power.

To bridge the gap between Wilson and Roosevelt, indeed between Jefferson and Hamilton, FDR laid out his philosophy in what has come to be known as the manifesto of the New Deal, the Commonwealth Club Address, delivered during the 1932 campaign. In the speech, written by Adolph Berle and inspired by the work of John Dewey, Roosevelt redefined liberalism for the Industrial Age. This new liberalism sought to recognize an understanding of individualism that was consistent with the realities of industrial society. The new liberalism would get around Americans' Jeffersonian distrust of centralized administration by convincing Americans that such arrangements were necessary for the realization of individual liberty in an Industrial Age. In essence, FDR, like Dewey, was adapting eighteenth- and nineteenth-century values of Jeffersonian individualism to twentieth-century conditions. He was redefining individualism and liberty in the context of the social and economic realities of the Industrial Age. By cloaking his advocacy for an expansion of the federal government in the liberal constitutional language of individual rights, Roosevelt was able to give legitimacy to progressive ideals in a way that Wilson and Theodore Roosevelt were never able to achieve. In so doing, he moved decisively toward nationalizing American politics.[43]

Franklin Roosevelt's new liberalism was successful in changing the mood of the nation in a way that the progressives were unable to do. Although FDR's new liberalism was rhetorically compelling, the harsh conditions of economic depression no doubt helped Americans to understand the exigencies and changed context of an industrial society. Roosevelt's success in turning the philosophical corner from Jefferson to Hamilton was not merely accomplished in word. The programs of the New Deal were practical, tangible political manifestations of the transition to a nationalized politics.

Two particular pieces of legislation are often cited in regard to the spirit of the New Deal. The National Industrial Recovery Act (NIRA) and the Agricultural Adjustment Act (AAA), both passed in the early Summer of 1933, provide excellent examples of the nationalistic goals and quasi-corporatist methods of the New Deal. In addition, they illustrate the difficulty and the staccato rhythm of regime change.

The NIRA set up trade associations in the various sectors of industry. Much like the War Industries Board of World War I, the NIRA created government/industry committees to devise codes of fair conduct, which were to be exempt from antitrust law. Final approval of these codes was left to the president. The statute created a system run by representatives of corporations, but there was also a specific provision guaranteeing a place at the table for organized labor. The act's protection of collective bargaining was crucial for the support of labor, without which the legislation would not have passed. Marc Allen Eisner contrasts the NIRA to initiatives of the Progressive Era, showing that this law represents a clear departure from the free market ethos of the progressives' market regime. The NIRA's virtual suspension of antitrust law and creation of government supervised cartels represents the realization of the Theodore Roosevelt and Herbert Croly New Nationalist vision. The AAA was cut from the same cloth as the NIRA. It consisted of the establishment of government supervised cartels in agriculture.[44]

These early bold initiatives of the New Deal represent the political conversion of the nation to a nationalized politics. They were an affront to traditional political and constitutional values. The Supreme Court, which had acquiesced to constitutional experimentation in the face of civil war and world war, was not willing to allow these initiatives to bury the doctrine of laissez faire constitutionalism without a fight. As difficult as regime change is in politics, it is even more difficult in law. In May 1935, in *Schecter v. United States* the Supreme Court struck down the NIRA, holding that it had required an unconstitutional delegation of legislative authority by the Congress to the president.[45]

The NIRA had authorized the creation of codes of conduct by groups formed by the president. These codes, which had the force of law, would thus be made, passed, and entirely enforced within the executive branch. The case produced a clarification of the constitutional doctrine of nondelegation. The so-called Schecter rule states that the Congress cannot delegate legislative power to the executive branch without clear standards and guidelines.

In January 1936, the Supreme Court applied the Schecter rule in striking down the Agricultural Adjustment Act in the case of *United States v. Butler*.

Despite these judicial setbacks, the Roosevelt administration and Congress continued to pass sweeping new initiatives that expanded the regulatory reach of the federal government. The continuing New Deal initiatives despite the Court's resistance illustrates the power of the changed political mood. The Supreme Court was widely and harshly criticized for what most Americans thought was its failure to understand the Constitution in its modern context, and the continuing legislative assault effectively pressured the Court into a fundamental jurisprudential shift.

The Supreme Court finally aligned itself with the political environment in the Spring of 1937. In *West Coast Hotel Co. v. Parrish*, the Court ruled 5–4 in favor of a federal minimum wage law. Justice Owen Roberts had reversed his position. Many commentators argue that Justice Roberts was influenced by FDR's threatened court packing plan as well as by the political mood of the day. In any case, this decision became known as "the switch in time that saved nine." After the *Parrish* decision, the Court regularly upheld New Deal initiatives.[46]

In the remainder of 1937, the Court would give the constitutional seal of approval to both the National Labor Relations Act and the Social Security Act. The new liberal majority was solidified by a series of appointments to the Supreme Court. In 1937, FDR appointed Alabama Senator Hugo Black to replace the resigning Justice Willis Van Devanter. In 1938, with the death of Justice Benjamin Cardozo and the resignation of Justice George Sutherland, FDR appointed fellow New Dealers Stanley Reed and Felix Frankfurter to the Court. In 1939, Justice Louis Brandeis resigned and Justice Pierce Butler died. The former was replaced by William O. Douglass and the latter by Frank Murphy. The last remaining holdout from the conservative court, Justice James McReynolds, retired in 1941, allowing Roosevelt to complete his total redesign of the Court with the appointment of his attorney general, Robert Jackson.[47]

FDR appointed more members of the Supreme Court than any president before or since. His overwhelmingly liberal and activist Court would dramatically impact the nation's politics for the next half century. Interestingly, the Court's role as inhibitor in the regime change from the Progressive Era to the New Deal Era—from the market to the associational regime—would not be replicated in the next regime shift precisely because of its Rooseveltian makeup. Indeed, the Court would be a leader in the shift from an associational regime to what Eisner calls the "societal regime."

Its conversion to New Deal liberalism reversed a half century of the Court defending corporate property rights in the face of attempts to expand state and federal regulatory power. Throughout the Progressive Era the Court staved off legislative assaults on traditional Jeffersonian concepts of individual rights that it felt would have unconstitutionally expanded the regulatory power of the federal government. The conservative jurisprudence of the Progressive Era Court was certainly a factor in the failure of progressives to achieve their more far reaching, New Nationalist objectives and, as discussed in chapter one, it played a part in upholding baseball's unregulated monopoly. It also provides insight into the dominance of less intrusive progressive initiatives like antitrust law and the rhetorical victory of the New Freedom over the New Nationalism.

The New Deal's response to the Depression represents the realization of New Nationalist Progressivism. The pressure created by the exigencies of economic depression provided the impetus for a political, and eventually jurisprudential, revolution. The Supreme Court's acquiescence to the expansion of the federal government's regulatory power did not, however, unleash wholesale corporatism on the nation. The intervention of World War II revitalized the American economy effectively reducing the crisis mentality that had spawned the more far reaching New Deal experiments such as the NIRA.

The noninterference of the federal government in baseball's private self-government in the 1920s was due in part to the posture of the Supreme Court and the Antitrust Division of the Justice Department with respect to corporate combinations. During the 1920s the courts not only failed to dissolve a single corporate merger, they handed down numerous decisions favorable to firms that controlled as much as 90 percent of their markets. Despite Herbert Hoover's ostensible support of antitrust enforcement as both secretary of commerce and as president, the 1920s saw a considerable drop in antitrust prosecutions and convictions. Of the Antitrust Division of the Justice Department in the 1920s, historian Morton Keller writes that it "never met a trust it didn't like."[48]

The associationalism of the 1920s manifest in the proliferation of trade associations, had the effect of dampening enthusiasm for antitrust enforcement and encouraging cooperative relations among industry rivals. Major League Baseball's cartel, led by the strong hand of Judge Landis, did not raise an eyebrow in the 1920s. Major League Baseball's continued freedom from government interference is hardly surprising given that antitrust was the primary means of progressive regulation of the economy and that enforcement was repeatedly discouraged by the Supreme Court and an industry friendly Antitrust Division of the Justice Department. There was in the federal government a general acceptance of apparently benign corporate combinations such as trade associations, among them baseball.

Major League Baseball's private self-government weathered, even exploited, the political and economic upheaval of the 1930s and early 1940s. In the wake of the stock market crash, baseball's monopolistic cartel was hardly a prime target of policy makers, whose overriding goal in the 1930s was the recovery and stabilization of a national economy. These dire circumstances, combined with baseball's relative internal stability, allowed the game not only to avoid government regulation, but also to solidify its special status in American culture.

Political leaders, like FDR, used baseball as a way to rally an anxious nation. In the Depression, the game exemplified America's best traditions and values, a role fully exploited by Major League Baseball to keep the game on a cultural pedestal. Baseball's morale boosting role was extended with the onset of World War II. By the mid-1940s baseball's private self-government was shielded by the fact that the game had captured the hearts and minds of the nation and because, between the Depression and World War II, there were simply more urgent matters before the nation. During the quarter century in which baseball was ruled by Commissioner Landis, the stability inside the game together with the instability outside of it both secured Major League Baseball's standing as the national pastime and insulated it from government interference. Having seen the nation through hard times, baseball had become a cultural icon.

STABILITY IN BASEBALL BEGINS TO UNRAVEL

With victory in Europe and the Pacific, Americans returned to the ballparks in droves. The wartime drops in attendance were quickly erased from 1946 to 1949 as major league attendance doubled its prewar levels and major league profits were in the millions of dollars. But Major League Baseball entered this era of postwar prosperity with a new man at the helm. Judge Landis died in 1944, and organized baseball appointed a U.S. senator from Kentucky, A. B. "Happy" Chandler, as the game's second commissioner. As economic stability and peace returned to the nation, conflict returned to baseball. In the late 1940s and 1950s the game would grapple with a new outlaw league, racial integration, numerous rumblings of player discontent, and its first brushes with federal legislative interference into its governance.

Ironically, the level of cultural significance attained by baseball in the 1930s and 1940s encouraged congressional interference. The careful and successful campaign by organized baseball to convince Americans that the interests of baseball were the interests of America did help to legitimize baseball law and internal self-government. But, it also made Americans feel that the game belonged to them and not to the owners. Much to the owners' chagrin, this view was heralded by their own handpicked successor to Judge Landis. Not long after his appointment, Commissioner Chandler chastised the owners saying, "You don't own the game . . . the game belongs to the American people."[49]

Baseball historians agree that Chandler was chosen by the owners because they felt he was a far cry from the irascible, uncompromising Judge Landis. Chandler was a politician and, as such, the owners expected the former U.S. senator to "play ball." He did not comply with their expectations. The owners were less than thrilled with Chandler's support of Branch Rickey's attempts to end racial segregation in the game.[50] Although he was a thorn in their sides on many issues, the owners could at least count on Judge Landis to protect the complexion of the game. Ultimately Chandler's independence from the owners contributed to his contract not being renewed in 1951.

Chandler had little time to learn or enjoy his new job, as the stability of the Landis years ended shortly after World War II. One year into his term, baseball was faced with the first attempt to create a players union since before the Landis years. In 1946, a labor lawyer with the Congress of Industrial Organizations (CIO) attempted to form a new players union, the American Baseball Guild. With the onset of postwar prosperity players began to feel more comfortable about demanding their fair share. Quickly recognizing the fertile environment for such ventures, the owners formed a committee headed by Yankees part-owner Larry MacPhail to improve relations with the players and alleviate any perceived need for a union. The committee fulfilled its mandate by granting several concessions to the players. The committee agreed to provide each player with a $25 a week stipend during spring training, a raise in the minimum salary to $5,000, a pension plan for the players, and player representation on a committee of club owners and league presidents.[51] The MacPhail committee had fended off the first, but hardly the last, attempt to form a players union in baseball.

Chandler also faced a more serious challenge at the outset of his tenure. The so-called "Mexican League War" broke out as a result of raids on major league rosters by Mexican League President Don Jorge Pasqual. In the winter of 1946, eighteen big leaguers either jumped their reserve clauses or jumped their contracts outright to play in the Mexican League that spring. Responding to the threat of the Mexican League, which enticed such notable players as the Brooklyn Dodgers' catcher Mickey Owen and St. Louis Browns' shortstop, Vern Stephens to play south of the border, Commissioner Chandler suspended all but one of the league jumpers. Before handing down blanket five-year suspensions, the commissioner offered amnesty to any player who agreed to return immediately to his major league club. Stephens took the commissioner up on his offer.

Chandler's harsh penalty was unprecedented for the commissioner of baseball. Even during the Federal League war the penalties were less harsh. Commissioner Landis, well known for his tough brand of justice, never faced the threat of an outlaw league and therefore had not been tested under such circumstances. After Chandler handed down the suspension, and despite its unprecedented severity, the owners ratified the commissioner's action.

At a joint meeting of the major leagues on August 28, 1946, the Chicago Cubs general manager proposed an amendment to the leagues' rules which would sanction the penalty of a five-year suspension for league jumpers. The proposal, meant to support Chandler's action, was agreed to unanimously. A congressional report later quoted Mr. Gallagher of the Cubs at that meeting as saying that "[t]he sight of Mickey Owen sitting on his farm or starting the races at the Springfield Fair will do a lot more to discourage Stan Musial from going to Mexico next winter than any suits we may file on the reserve clause."[52]

Musial, all-star outfielder for the St. Louis Cardinals, had been tempted with a lucrative contract to jump to the Mexican League with the others. Gallagher's comments are illustrative of the attitude within organized baseball. Throughout the game's history it was the extralegal maneuvers such as blacklisting and boycotts which quelled unrest and the owners expected this trend to continue. Unfortunately for them it was quickly apparent that the postwar world would be much more complicated than the old days.

In a report to the league committees received the day before the joint meeting of 1946, Commissioner Chandler warned of the legal vulnerability of current baseball law. The reserve clause, a principle component of baseball law, was in jeopardy of being nullified by the courts. Chandler writes in the report that "the present reserve clause could not be enforced in an equity court in a suit for specific performance, nor as the basis for a restraining order to prevent a player from playing elsewhere, or to prevent outsiders from inducing a player to breach his contract."[53]

The implications of the commissioner's warning in the aftermath of the Mexican League War were clear. Without modification, the reserve clause would not hold up and the players who sought to return to Major League Baseball after being dissatisfied with the Mexican League might prevail in court, effectively negating the power of the commissioner to punish those who violated the reserve clause.[54]

Although some of the players who jumped to the Mexican League had actually jumped newly signed contracts, others, including Danny Gardella, had merely jumped their reserve clause. Gardella, who had left the New York Giants to play one season in Mexico before deciding to return, filed an antitrust suit in federal court against the commissioner and the league presidents as representatives of organized baseball. Gardella's restraint of trade suit relied on both the Sherman and Clayton antitrust laws. The Federal District Court of New York City dismissed Gardella's suit for want of jurisdiction. In his opinion for the court, Judge Goddard stated that, despite the "clear trend toward a broader conception of what constitutes interstate commerce," the court was bound by the precedent set in the Supreme Court's *Federal Baseball* decision.[55]

On appeal this decision was reversed and the case was remanded for trial on the grounds that the issue of baseball's interstate character was sufficiently unclear to warrant a trial. Before Gardella's trial was scheduled to take place another federal court refused to grant injunctions reinstating Gardella and other players who were suing Major League Baseball. The court ruled that the plaintiffs' rights to reinstatement depended on questions of law and fact that were in dispute.

Only days after the circuit court of appeals declined to reinstate Gardella and the others, Commissioner Chandler offered to reinstate all the players who had jumped to the Mexican League.[56] Chandler justified his change of heart by saying that the court's refusal to reinstate the blacklisted players was a victory for the authority of the commissioner of baseball and that as such it had made clear to future would-be violators of baseball law that the penalty will be harsh, and more importantly, it will hold up in court. In fact, Chandler's mercy was motivated by the desire to salvage baseball's antitrust exemption which could have been seriously jeopardized by an appeals court's ruling in the Gardella case.

The Second Circuit Court of Appeals overruled a lower court judgment against Gardella, holding that the existence of television and radio broadcasts of baseball had made the game a matter of interstate commerce, thus bringing it within reach of the Sherman Act. Major League Baseball responded to this apparently deadly strike to their exemption by appealing the decision. In the interim, Gardella, surely convinced that organized baseball would tie him up in court forever, settled the case for $60,000 and a trade from the New York Giants to the St. Louis Cardinals.[57] The settlement left the legal status of baseball's exemption up in the air. Would *Federal Baseball* continue to rule, or would the Gardella verdict take precedence? The matter would not be clarified by the Court until 1953.

While organized baseball was quietly suppressing attempts to unionize players and fighting the legal battles of the Mexican League War, the Brooklyn Dodgers' Branch Rickey was breaking the twentieth-century color barrier in Major League Baseball. In 1946, Jackie Robinson was chosen by Rickey to test the informal color barrier in the big leagues. Rickey picked Robinson not only for his superior playing ability, but also for his character. A four sport star at UCLA and a World War II veteran, Robinson was seen by Rickey as capable of handling the tremendous pressure and harsh treatment that would befall the first black player in the major leagues.[58]

Jackie Robinson's accomplishment, while certainly controversial, stands apart from other controversies in baseball. Interleague wars and player revolts are festering problems to which organized baseball responds. Moreover, baseball's great social experiment did not contribute to the game's efforts to maintain its independence from external regulation and may indeed have fueled significant antibaseball sentiment.

The internal stability of baseball continued to be fragile as the 1940s turned into the 1950s. The players' pension plan, created by the MacPhail committee, was a source of continuing controversy. Some baseball historians argue that Commissioner Chandler's sympathy with the players on the issue of funding the pension plan with media receipts hastened his removal from office by the owners in 1951. Chandler was replaced with former sportswriter and National League President, Ford Frick.

With the changing of the guard in the commissioner's office in 1951–1952 and with the legal status of baseball's exemption uncertain, the United States Congress began to take a closer look at the game of baseball. The cases of Danny Gardella and other Mexican League jumpers had cast a shadow, however faint, over baseball. As early as 1949, sensing the growing vulnerability of the game's special status as a result of damaging litigation, "friends of baseball" in the Congress were proposing legislation to validate baseball's judicially created antitrust exemption by statute.

Congressmen Wilbur Mills (D–AK) and A. S. Herlong (D–FL) proposed legislation that would provide legislative sanction to baseball's immunity from antitrust laws. Their proposals sought to utilize analogous language in the Clayton Antitrust Act and the Webb-Pomerene Act to craft a statutory exemption for Major League Baseball. The Clayton Act specifically declared that the "labor of a human being" is not a "commodity or article of commerce."[59] The act had been construed to give antitrust exemptions to labor unions, and some nonprofit agricultural organizations. The Webb-Pomerene Act specifically exempts export trade associations and any of their activities which do not "artificially or intentionally enhance or depress prices within the United States of commodities of the class exported by such associations, or which substantially lessen competition within the United States or otherwise restrain trade therein."[60]

A confidential internal memo sent to Commissioner Chandler in the fall of 1949 discusses the strategy of Major League Baseball in seeking legislative protection of its anomalous status. The memo illustrates the increasing organizational sophistication of organized baseball's efforts to preserve its governance structure. In the memo, Major League Baseball attorney, John Lord O'Brien, explains that the Mills and Herlong bills, using ostensibly analogous provisions of Clayton and Webb-Pomerene, were on the right track. Mills and Herlong were proposing to amend the Communications Act of 1934, not the Sherman Act. This tactic would serve to circumvent a serious obstacle. Because the interstate nature of television and radio broadcasts of baseball were increasingly threatening to jeopardize baseball's exemption created in *Federal Baseball*, these bills proposed to limit antitrust applicability to broadcast rights, thus preserving the core of the exemption while jettisoning the most potent arrows being shot at the *Federal Baseball* decision.[61]

Although these first proposals died in committee, they opened the congressional door to others. By 1951, the number of legislative proposals calling for a statutory exemption from antitrust for baseball had grown to four, three in the House of Representatives and one in the Senate. Mills and Herlong were joined in the House by Congressman Melvin Price (D–IL) and in the Senate by Edwin Johnson (D–CO).

In 1951, three pending House bills seeking complete exemption from antitrust laws for all organized professional sports enterprises were sent to the House Subcommittee on the Study of Monopoly Power of the Committee on the Judiciary. The Chairman of this subcommittee was New York Rep. Emanuel Celler, a long time advocate of vigorous antitrust enforcement. Chairman Celler ordered a thorough investigation into the business of baseball. The subcommittee held hearings on the matter in the fall of 1951. Witnesses were questioned on nearly every aspect of the game. Of specific interest were the nature and operation of the reserve clause, which had been the focus of numerous lawsuits. Every witness supported and defended the reserve clause, be they player or owner.

The hearings produced no smoking gun and in the end the subcommittee considered five options:

1. to outlaw the reserve clause, forcing baseball to operate in a free market for player talent;
2. to provide baseball with complete immunity from antitrust law;
3. to create a federal agency to regulate Major League Baseball;
4. to create a limited statutory exemption for baseball's reserve clause;
5. to avoid influencing pending litigation and refrain from anticipating judicial action by declining to take any legislative action at that time.[62]

The subcommittee chose the fifth option, thus passing the buck to the judiciary. The option of outlawing the reserve clause was never seriously considered. The testimony in the hearings, as well as public opinion, unanimously supported some form of a reserve rule to maintain competitive parity on the field. Discomfort with a complete exemption as well as with creating a new regulatory agency eliminated these options. The option of creating a partial exemption was seriously considered but action was deferred pending new pronouncements from the courts.[63]

Ultimately, the subcommittee felt that, while baseball's private self-government was problematic, they were not capable of addressing the problems. The committee felt that while many aspects of professional sports leagues were indeed unique, the differentiation of essential and nonessential practices in professional sports was a job best left to the courts. With this decision baseball was off the hook, for the time being. However, the Supreme Court would pick up where Congress left off. In *Toolson v. New York Yankees, Inc.*, the Court returned the legislature's favor.

George Toolson was a player on a New York Yankee farm team who refused to honor his reserve clause. Toolson filed a restraint of trade suit under the Sherman Act against the Yankees. The trial court dismissed the case for lack of jurisdiction based on the precedent set in *Federal Baseball*. The case came before the Supreme Court in 1953. The Court surprised organized baseball by ruling that since the Congress had addressed the issue of baseball and its antitrust exemption in 1951 and chosen to let the *Federal Baseball* holding continue to rule, it would honor the wishes of the legislature by reaffirming the lower court's judgment in *Toolson*. Furthermore, the Court held that since baseball had developed for 30 years under the assumption that it was exempt from antitrust law, the task of reversing that assumption was purely political and thus a legislative prerogative.[64]

Several rulings by the Supreme Court over the next few years made it clear that baseball's exemption was special and would not be extended by the courts to other sports. In 1955, in *United States v. Shubert*, the Court held that traveling theatrical companies were engaged in interstate commerce and did fall within the strictures of the Sherman Act. The Court also held in 1955 that boxing promoted and broadcast on radio and television in several states was indeed interstate commerce subject to the Sherman Act.[65] In 1957, the Court would solidify its position even more in the case of *Radovich v. National Football League*.

William Radovich was an All-Pro offensive guard with the Detroit Lions who was offered a job as player/ manager of a minor league club in San Francisco. The Lions threatened the minor league club with punitive action. The minor league club subsequently withdrew its offer. Radovich filed a restraint of trade suit under the Sherman Act. The Court's holding in *Radovich* read in part: "In Toolson we continue to hold the umbrella over baseball that was placed there some 31 years earlier by *Federal Baseball*. . . . Vast efforts had gone into the development and organization of baseball since that decision and enormous capital had been invested in reliance on its permanence. . . ."[66] The Court reasserted that it had washed its hands of baseball and the antitrust laws, deferring to the legislature. In the case at hand, the Court ruled against the NFL holding it accountable under the Sherman Act.

The disparate treatment enjoyed by Major League Baseball, as well as the issue of television broadcasting in all major professional sports, spurred more action on Capitol Hill throughout the 1950s and early 1960s. Major League Baseball exploited the game of hot potato being played by the Court and the Congress, actively assuring both branches that it was within the purview of the other branch to alter baseball's status.[67]

In 1957, following the *Radovich* decision, seven legislative proposals were introduced in the U.S. Congress to deal with baseball's exclusive right to engage in monopoly practices. None of the proposals was proffered or advocated by Major League Baseball. This legislative assault was mounted by the "friends" of professional football, basketball, and hockey. One of these proposals sought to extend baseball's immunity to all professional team sports. Two proposals sought the explicit subjection of all sports, including baseball, to the full measure of the antitrust laws. The remaining four bills called for partial exemptions for all professional team sports, in order to protect the types of collective arrangements that leagues require in order to maintain competition on the field.[68]

The seven bills were sent to Chairman Celler's subcommittee, which undertook its second thorough investigation of professional sports and antitrust. Since Celler's last investigation the Court had muddied the waters by creating disparate policies for different sports. The subcommittee was now charged with examining all sports in an effort to standardize policy. Hearings were conducted with witnesses from all the major sports. The hearings were largely inconclusive, although it was clear to the committee that the options of a blanket exemption or blanket subjection of all major team sports to antitrust law was unacceptable. The committee's report concluded that the most feasible option was some type of partial exemption for these sports, allowing them to undertake those practices required by the unusual nature of the business as well as the need to maintain competition on the field. They reported a bill which took a middle course. The report stated:

It is the intent of the committee in this bill to permit each of these sports in general to continue the types of self-regulation that it has developed historically. . . . The committee has concluded that this course is preferable to, in the alternative, the imposition on these businesses of the widespread direct controls by Government officials that customarily accompanies exemption from, or relaxation of, the requirements of the antitrust laws. The bill, however, assures that the courts under the antitrust laws will be able to proscribe activities that are not essential for continuation of the sports involved.[69]

The bill contained controversial language that would ultimately preclude its passage into law. In language supported by Chairman Celler, it called for the antitrust laws to be applied to all professional sports, exempting only those practices which were "reasonably necessary" to accomplish four conditions. Those conditions were: (1) competition on the field, (2) the right to operate in specific geographic areas, (3) preservation of the integrity of the sport, and (4) regulation of telecasting and other broadcast rights.[70]

There was strong opposition to the phrase "reasonably necessary." It was argued that such vague language would open the floodgates to nuisance litigation. Opponents charged that the "reasonably necessary" clause was so vague as to expose professional sports leagues to the full force of the antitrust laws, which would jeopardize their ability to maintain competitive balance on the field. An alternative to the Celler bill was proposed by fellow New Yorker, Republican Rep. Kenneth Keating. The Walter-Keating bill removed the reasonably necessary clause and spelled out the practices which would be exempt. It was believed that this would accomplish the goals of the Celler bill without creating opportunities for unreasonable litigation.[71]

The House passed the Walter-Keating bill over the strenuous objections of Chairman Celler and with the considerable help of representatives of all the major sports leagues who descended on Capitol Hill like locusts. The bill then went to the Senate where it would be scrutinized by Senator Estes Kefauver's Subcommittee on Antitrust and Monopoly. Like Chairman Celler, Kefauver was a committed advocate of vigorous antitrust enforcement.[72]

Kefauver's subcommittee held hearings that made up for lack of productivity with some very entertaining testimony. New York Yankees' manager, Casey Stengel, and player, Mickey Mantle, testified together providing the senators with great amusement. Mr. Stengel was well respected by the senators who listened patiently to his fumbling double talk, unable to make any sense of it. In hopes of more lucid comments the senators turned to Mantle asking his impressions of the matter. To the delight of all assembled Mantle responded, "My views are just about the same as Casey's."[73]

The senators were persuaded by the testimony of Chairman Celler, who vigorously opposed the Walter-Keating bill. He convinced the senators that the bill was too broad, virtually granting complete immunity from antitrust laws. Celler also told the senators that such legislation in the absence of a regulatory agency with jurisdiction over baseball would constitute an unprecedented departure from past regulatory policy.[74] The 85th Congress closed without Senate action on the bill.

As baseball entered the 1960s the legislative stalemate continued. The changing demographics of the country as well as the expanded importance of television and radio to professional sports were the primary obstacles in the way of maintaining baseball's private self-government. The nation's population was shifting south and west. Even in the cities of the northeast, people were moving to the suburbs in record numbers. These new population centers were increasingly watching their sports on television, and increasingly they were tuning into football and basketball, as well as baseball. Congressional scrutiny throughout the 1950s had not produced government regulation of baseball, but it did play a part, along with competition from other sports and changing demographics, in forcing expansion on Major League Baseball. Members of Congress such as California Republican Pat Hillings relentlessly urged organized baseball to expand to the West Coast or in the alternative to elevate the Pacific Coast League to major league status.[75]

The economic pressures created by competition from other sports as well as the continuing political pressure from members of Congress forced Major League Baseball to face the hard issues presented by expansion. The refusal to expand had been motivated by the desire to maintain the value of current clubs, the need to manage competition for player talent, and the issue of territorial rights. With its back against the wall organized baseball, according to baseball historian James Miller, had four options:

First, the major leagues could give the Pacific Coast League (PCL) a special classification, suspend the draft, and permit it to build up its talents to major league levels.
A second possibility would be to form a special classification league out of PCL and
other minor league teams in major cities and grant this new league freedom from
the draft until it was competitive. A third alternative was to add two or more teams
to each of the existing major leagues. Finally, Organized Baseball could achieve the
goal of increasing the number of cities with major league teams by moving some of
its financially weaker franchises out of cities that already had two teams.[76]

The first three options were unpopular with owners because they would
reduce the value of existing franchises. The last option was the least injurious to present owners. In 1952, both the American and National Leagues
modified their rules to make it easier for financially strapped teams to relocate. The new rules were quickly exploited by the Boston Braves, the St.
Louis Browns, and the Philadelphia Athletics. Less than one month before
the 1953 season, the Braves moved to Milwaukee. Also in 1953, the Browns
became the Baltimore Orioles. The following year the Philadelphia Athletics moved to Kansas City.[77]

The migration of the Giants and Dodgers to California at the end of the
1957 season was the next major change. Brooklyn Dodgers' owner, Walter
O'Malley, decided to make the move out west. The major obstacle to moving west was that there were no other teams to play on the West Coast. The
other major league teams would have a financial disincentive to travel to
the West Coast to play just one team. With this in mind O'Malley convinced
the owner of the financially struggling New York Giants, Horace Stoneham, to move west with him. By moving two teams to California O'Malley
increased the economic viability of such a move. Additionally, the move of
the Dodgers and Giants greatly reduced the political pressure coming from
members of Congress such as Los Angeles Representative Pat Hillings.[78]

While the Dodgers' and Giants' migration may have quelled pressure
from western members of Congress, it also created bad feelings in New York.
In Congressman Celler's second investigation into baseball in 1957–1958 the
migration issue was examined. In hearings before Celler's subcommittee in
the aftermath of the move, the chairman angrily chastised the National
League owners for allowing O'Malley to move to the West Coast. Celler denounced the pure profit motive of the move implying that if decisions in
baseball would mirror those in other businesses, then baseball's antitrust
obligations should too.[79]

Unable to prevent the loss of the Dodgers and Giants to the West Coast,
the Mayor of New York City, Robert Wagner, began courting other National
League teams. Failing to attract a new National League club to New York,
the mayor encouraged New York lawyer William Shea to organize a third
major league, placing a franchise in the city. Baseball's commissioner, Ford
Frick, had throughout the 1950s been publicly supportive of the creation of
a third league; however, he never took any action to encourage such a

league. Under pressure from Shea's attempt to start a third league organized baseball modified its rules in 1958 to allow for a second major league team in cities with over two million people. Organized baseball in the person of Commissioner Frick made it clear, however, that expansion would require settlement of the current major league map as well as a total reorganization of the minor leagues.[80]

On May 21, 1959, Major League Baseball announced that it would welcome a third league. Shea, who had hired an elderly Branch Rickey to head up the new league and who had the support of key members of Congress who begrudged organized baseball its monopoly, accepted the offer. However, it was made clear that if organized baseball was trying to draw out or stall the process, Shea's backers in Congress, such as Chairman Celler and Senator Kefauver, were prepared to push through legislation creating a third league.[81]

With this, Branch Rickey's Continental League came into being. Negotiations surrounding the Continental League were strained, and, in 1960, Senator Kefauver called for hearings regarding the creation of the Continental League, hoping to pressure organized baseball into expediting the formation of the new league. In the Spring of 1960, the new league was at odds with Major League Baseball over Rickey's attempt to establish a new minor league. In response to Major League Baseball's refusal to sanction the new minor league, Rickey threatened to raid major league rosters. After some wrangling in Congress with Major League Baseball allies getting the best of the Continental League supporters, organized baseball did what it had always done in the face of challenges to its monopoly. They co-opted the upstart league. Voting to expand the National and American Leagues, Major League Baseball effectively absorbed the Continental League.[82]

In 1961, with the issue of expansion settled for the moment, congressional interest shifted. With the encouragement of lobbyists from all the major sports leagues, the Congress began to focus on the specific issue of television contracts. Senator Estes Kefauver had been sponsoring bills in each of the last two Congresses that would subject professional sports teams to the strictures of antitrust laws, exempting only those activities which were deemed essential for the commercial viability of the sports. Among the provisions in Kefauver's bills was a provision to give league television contracts an antitrust exemption.[83]

Friends of baseball, as well as of all the other professional sports, in Congress were able to separate this specific exemption making it a stand-alone bill. With the help of serious lobbying by the major professional sport leagues, congressional allies of sports exemptions were able to push through this limited exemption. Public Law 87–331 would allow professional football, basketball, hockey, and baseball leagues to enter into certain television contracts. The opposition of the major television networks, as well as congressional antitrust advocates like Celler and Kefauver, was blunted by the fact that there was consensus on the need for such an exemption. The fact that it was a provision in Kefauver's more comprehensive bill made it difficult for antitrust advocates to fight.

This was a major victory for organized baseball. More often than not during the 1950s baseball had stood alone in defending its special status. The other sports had backed off early on from a strategy of seeking a blanket exemption for all sports. Unfavorable court decisions and a clear unwillingness on the part of Congress to enact such an exemption forced professional football, basketball, and hockey to take a fallback position, which put them at odds with organized baseball. The other major sports leagues began advocating that all sports be subjected equally to the antitrust laws and that all sports be granted limited exemptions.

When the issue came up of exempting television contracting by leagues, all the professional sports leagues supported it. Television revenue was an increasingly important aspect of the business of professional sports. Indeed, professional football, basketball, and hockey only began to rival baseball as a commercial enterprise with the advent of televised sporting events. Baseball, however, would benefit disproportionately by this limited exemption. For the other major sports the exemption provided the potential for greater television revenue and control. For organized baseball, it also short circuited one of the most dangerous threats to its private self-government. Media contracts had been one of the most controversial aspects of professional sports in the 1950s and 1960s. It had been the onset of television that made baseball's interstate commercial character so clear. Team revenues from television broadcasts had by 1961 become almost as important as attendance. By resolving the contentious issue of television contracting the Congress greatly reduced the political pressure on organized baseball, leaving only the question of baseball's disparate treatment with regard to antitrust law. This issue was not new and by cutting television out of the equation Congress effectively eliminated a major source of pressure for eliminating baseball's privileged position.

With the expansion following the Continental League challenge and the apparent legislative settlement of the high stakes matter of media regulation, baseball's special status once again receded from the spotlight. Although legislative proposals regarding professional sports and antitrust laws would re-emerge in 1964–1965, baseball's special commercial status would be eclipsed in the minds of the American people by greater political and social issues in the 1960s. Baseball's anomalous legal status would face threats from within its ranks in the coming years.

Baseball in the immediate postwar era was transformed from an exalted position as the nation's national pastime and as a source of tremendous cultural pride to a position of one among many. The explosion of mass media technology, the changing demography of the nation, and the increased popularity of other professional sports all combined to alter drastically the environment in which baseball operated. Despite their successful efforts to protect baseball's special legal status in the courts and in Congress, organized baseball took some lumps during the administrations of Commissioners Chandler, Frick, and William Eckert (1945–1965).

Judge Landis' successors would not have the unlimited power of baseball's first commissioner, nor would their game be unrivaled in the national consciousness. As the position of commissioner became increasingly an arm of management through the 1950s and 1960s, the position of the players, or labor, evolved in turn. Controversy over the funding of the players pension fund in 1953 has spurred the creation of the Major League Baseball Players Association (MLBPA), which at the time was merely an information clearinghouse for players. However, this organization would evolve into a full-fledged union by 1966. Also, competition from other sports such as basketball, football, and hockey would become significant in the 1950s and 1960s with the advent of television, which lent itself to these faster, time-bound sports.

The MLBPA led by Marvin Miller would transform baseball's antiquated labor/management relations into a much more conventional industrial arrangement. The business of baseball, by the late 1960s, would increasingly be conducted like a business, not an enterprise with special cultural significance. Baseball's united front in defending its anomalous status would be irreparably fractured by the development of the players union. The threat to baseball's private self-government would in the future come as much from within as from without.

Baseball's evolution into a more conventional industry, with the conventional adversarial relationship between labor and management, would greatly threaten the pillars of its private self-government. The ability of players in other sports to operate without undue restrictions caused baseball players to increase the pressure on organized baseball to dismantle the cornerstone of baseball law, the reserve clause.

NOTES

1. A more complete and detailed treatment of the politics of the New Deal Era will be undertaken later in this chapter.

2. Seymour, Harold, *Baseball: The Golden Age* (New York: Oxford University Press, 1971), p. 311–312.

3. U.S. Congress, House, Committee on the Judiciary, Subcommittee on the Study of Monopoly Power, *Organized Baseball* (H.R. Rept. No. 2002, 82nd Cong., 2d Sess., 1952), p. 57–59.

4. Seymour, p. 311–312.

5. Voigt, David Q., *American Baseball, Vol. II* (Norman: University of Oklahoma Press, 1970), p. 140.

6. The provision for presidential appointment of the next commissioner was dropped after Landis' first seven-year term.

7. U.S. Congress, House, Committee on the Judiciary, Subcommittee on the Study of Monopoly Power, *Organized Baseball* (H.R. Rept. No. 2002, 82nd Cong., 2d Sess., 1952), p. 59.

8. Voigt, p. 140.

9. Voigt, p. 140.

10. White, G. Edward, *Creating the National Pastime: Baseball Transforms Itself (1903–1953)* (Princeton: Princeton University Press, 1996), p. 104–105.

11. Voigt, p. 144.

12. Rader, Benjamin G., *Baseball: A History of America's Game* (Chicago: University of Illinois Press, 1992), p. 109–110.

13. Rader, p. 111.

14. See *Federal Baseball Club of Baltimore, Inc. v. National League*, 259 U.S. 200 (1922).

15. See *Hart v. Keith Vaudeville Exchange*, 262 U.S. 271 (1923).

16. White, p. 77.

17. Spink, J. G. Taylor, *Judge Landis and Twenty-five Years of Baseball* (New York: Thomas Y. Crowell Co., 1947), p. 154–163.

18. Spink, p. 154–163.

19. Seymour, p. 343.

20. Seymour, p. 343.

21. White, p. 278–284.

22. Spink, p. 190–192.

23. U.S. Congress, House, Committee on the Judiciary, Subcommittee on the Study of Monopoly Power, *Organized Baseball* (H.R. Rept. No. 2002, 82nd Cong., 2d Sess., 1952), p. 64.

24. U.S. Congress, House, Committee on the Judiciary, Subcommittee on the Study of Monopoly Power, *Organized Baseball* (H.R. Rept. No. 2002, 82nd Cong., 2d Sess., 1952), p. 71–72.

25. Rader, p. 137.

26. Rader, p. 137.

27. Gregory, Robert, *Diz: The Story of Dizzy Dean and Baseball During the Great Depression* (New York: Penguin Books USA, Inc., 1992), p. 95.

28. Rader, p. 137.

29. Rader, p. 137.

30. Letter from President Franklin Delano Roosevelt to Commissioner Landis, on file at the National Baseball Hall of Fame Library, Cooperstown, NY.

31. Voigt, p. 256–257.

32. Zimbalist, Andrew, *Baseball and Billions: A Probing Look Into the Big Business of Our National Pastime* (New York: Basic Books, 1992), p. 12.

33. Ironically, Landis had opposed what the owners called the "single entity theory" in their support for farm systems. A variant of this same concept would be used by Major League Baseball to defend its exemption from antitrust law.

34. Eisner, Marc Allen, *Regulatory Politics in Transition* (Baltimore: The Johns Hopkins University Press, 1993), p. 75.

35. Wecter, Dixon, *The Age of the Great Depression: 1929–1941* (New York: The Macmillan Co., 1948), p. 22.

36. Eisner, p. 76.

37. Eisner, p. 77–78.

38. Wecter, p. 43.

39. Wecter, p. 46.

40. See James MacGregor Burns, *Roosevelt: The Lion and the Fox* (New York: Harcourt Brace Publishers, 1956).

41. See Eisner.

42. Milkis, Sidney, *The President and the Parties: The Transformation of the American Party System Since the New Deal* (New York: Oxford University Press, 1993), p. 38.

43. Milkis, p. 39–41.

44. Eisner, p. 82–87.

45. Kelly, Alfred, Winfred Harbison, and Herman Belz, *The American Constitution: Its Origins and Development* (New York: W. W. Norton & Co., 1991), p. 476–477.

46. Kelly et al., p. 487–488.

47. Kelly et al., p. 489.

48. Keller, Morton, *Regulating a New Economy: Public Policy and Economic Change in America (1900–1933)* (Cambridge: Harvard University Press, 1990), p. 36.

49. Quoted in Rader, p. 187.

50. Rader, p. 187.

51. Rader, p. 187–188.

52. U.S. Congress, House. Committee on the Judiciary, Subcommittee on the Study of Monopoly Power, *Organized Baseball* (H.R. Rept. No. 2002, 82nd Cong., 2d Sess., 1952), p. 78.

53. Chandler, A. B., "Commissioner's Report to the Major League Committee" (August 27, 1946), p. 10.

54. The modifications to the reserve rule recommended by Chandler were adopted by Major League Baseball in 1946. The modified reserve clause was less harsh than its predecessor.

55. See *Gardella v. Chandler*, 79 Fed. Supp. 260, 263 (D.C.S.D.N.Y., July 13, 1948).

56. U.S. Congress, House, Committee on the Judiciary, Subcommittee on the Study of Monopoly Power, *Organized Baseball* (H.R. Rept. No. 2002, 82nd Cong., 2d Sess., 1952), p. 83.

57. Zimbalist, p. 13.

58. Falkner, David, *Great Time Coming: The Life of Jackie Robinson From Baseball to Birmingham* (New York: Simon & Schuster Publishers, 1995), p. 106–108.

59. The Clayton Antitrust Act (1912).

60. The Webb-Pomerance Act (1918).

61. Confidential memorandum titled "Proposed Legislative Program" sent to Commissioner of Baseball, A. B. Chandler. The memo was dated November 30, 1949 and signed by John Lord O'Brien.

62. U.S. Congress, House, Committee on the Judiciary, Subcommittee on the Study of Monopoly Power, *Organized Baseball* (H.R. Rept. No. 2002, 82nd Cong., 2d Sess., 1952), p. 228–232.

63. U.S. Congress, House. Committee on the Judiciary, Subcommittee on the Study of Monopoly Power, *Organized Baseball* (H.R. Rept. No. 2002, 82nd Cong., 2d Sess., 1952), p. 228–232.

64. Berger, Robert G., "After the Strikes: A Reexamination of Professional Baseball's Exemption From The Antitrust Laws," *University of Pittsburgh Law Review* 45 (1983), p. 209–226.

65. See *United States v. Shubert* 348 U.S. 222 (1955) and *United States v. International Boxing Club of New York, Inc.* 348 U.S. 236 (1955).

66. See *Radovich v. National Football League* 352 U.S. 445 (1957).

67. Lowenfish, Lee and Tony Lupien, *The Imperfect Diamond* (New York: Stein & Day Publishers, 1980), p. 181.

68. U.S. Congress, Senate, Committee on the Judiciary, *Applicability of the Antitrust Laws to Certain Aspects of Designated Organized Professional Team Sports* (S. Rept. No. 1303, 88th Cong., 2d Sess.,1964), p. 3.

69. U.S. Congress, House, Committee on the Judiciary, *Applicability of Antitrust Laws to Organized Professional Team Sports* (H.R. Rept. No. 1720, 85th Cong., 2d Sess., 1958), p. 5.

70. H.R. 10378, 85th Cong., 2d Sess. (1957).

71. H.R. 12990, 85th Cong., 2d Sess. (1957).

72. Kefauver's support for antitrust enforcement was spelled out in detail in his book, *In a Few Hands: Monopoly Power in America* (New York: Pantheon Books, 1965).

73. U.S. Congress, Senate, Committee on the Judiciary, Subcommittee on Antitrust and Monopoly Power, *Organized Professional Team Sports, Hearings* (85th Cong., 2nd Sess., 1958), p. 24.

74. U.S. Congress, Senate, Committee on the Judiciary, Subcommittee on Antitrust and Monopoly Power, *Organized Professional Team Sports, Hearings* (85th Cong., 2nd Sess., 1958), p. 375–376.

75. Miller, James E., *The Baseball Business: Pursuing Pennants and Profits in Baltimore* (Chapel Hill: The University of North Carolina Press, 1990), p. 6.

76. Miller, p. 14–15.

77. Miller, p. 79.

78. Miller, p. 79–80.

79. U.S. Congress, House, Committee on the Judiciary, Subcommittee on Antitrust, *Organized Professional Sports Teams, Hearings* (85th Cong., 1st Sess., 1957), p. 1359–1370.

80. U.S. Congress, House, Committee on the Judiciary, Subcommittee on Antitrust, *Organized Professional Sports Teams, Hearings* (85th Cong., 1st Sess., 1957), p. 127.

81. Miller, p. 81.

82. Zimbalist, p. 16–17.

83. U.S. Congress, Senate, Committee on the Judiciary, *Applicability of the Antitrust Laws to Certain Aspects of Designated Organized Professional Team Sports* (S. Rept. No. 1303, 88th Cong., 2d Sess., 1964), p. 4–5.

3

The New Politics of the Old Ball Game

Baseball's unregulated monopoly survived the Progressive Era because it shared the values and goals of the progressives and because the regulatory institutions of the state were not yet mature enough to bring affirmative regulation to baseball. As the state's institutions grew, the nation moved into what Eisner calls the associationalist regulatory regime. This quasi-corporatist regime, in which the regulated community was incorporated into the regulatory decision-making apparatus, was preoccupied with the imperatives of economic depression and world war. Organized baseball preserved its anomaly by providing comfort to a troubled nation and not raising any eyebrows. Internal stability in the game, as well as its role in boosting public morale, camouflaged baseball's private self-government during a time when government regulators had more urgent matters with which to deal.

Although it is commonly seen as the genesis of the welfare state, the New Deal actually created what sociologist John Wilson calls a "franchise state" in which regulatory decisions were largely delegated to the regulated community.[1] The real welfare state, in which there was a shift to predominately direct regulation of industry, is more accurately associated with Eisner's societal regime, which he sees as existing in the 1960s and 1970s. Its origins trace to President Lyndon Johnson's Great Society programs in the mid-1960s. It was during the societal regime that baseball's unregulated monopoly would come under its most severe attack.

THE REGULATORY REGIME OF THE 1960s AND 1970s

Eisner's societal regime, "like the Progressive Era and the era of the New Deal, was characterized by the formation and mobilization of new interests demanding a new role for the state in the economy."[2] The result of the emergent interests was the creation of public policy and institutional change shaped by a new administrative philosophy and a new conception of political economy. With the dawn of Keynesian economic stabilization policy in the 1930s the harsh fluctuations in the nation's economy were gradually tamed. By the post-World War II years the roller coaster that was the business cycle had been transformed into a merry-go-round. Eisner sums up the distinction between the old regimes and the societal regime:

Owing to active macro-economic management, the fluctuations in the business cycle during the first two decades after World War II were mild by comparison with those during the previous half-century; and thus, during this later period, unlike the earlier ones, structural transformations in the economy did not drive group mobilization. In addition, the new regime differed with respect to the kinds of policies initiated. Whereas earlier regimes had focused on questions of economic regulation, the new regime concentrated on new social regulations.[3]

Because the structural economy had been stabilized, in that the nation was essentially insulated from extreme economic depression, regulatory focus shifted to social problems, particularly those resulting from the capitalist production process.

The late 1960s and 1970s witnessed the creation of numerous public interest groups, which sought to address the negative externalities of the capitalist production process. These public interest groups were animated by the political and economic philosophy of the so-called "New Left."[4] Their substantive purpose was to "improve the quality of the goods and services that are produced, and the by-products of the industrial economy which threaten human health and life, and the environment."[5] These public interest groups of the societal regime[6] were dominated by the belief that the New Deal had devolved into an "impersonal, bureaucratic, centralized form of governance that was dehumanizing American society."[7] The New Left charged that the quasi-corporatist policy making procedures of the administrative state were controlled by big business interests whose lust for profit crowded out the public interest. The destruction of the environment, the manipulation of consumers, and the endangerment of workers were said to be the result of the capture of the government's regulatory agencies by big business interests. In baseball, this translates to the capture of the commissioner by the owners' interests.

These public-interest groups, which proliferated at an extreme rate between 1965–1975, sought to open up the regulatory decision making process to average citizens and consumers. Staffed by veterans of the civil rights and antiwar movements of the 1960s, public interest groups sought to democratize legislative and administrative politics by introducing public participation into regulatory policymaking. Armed with the New Left critique of both big business and big government, public interest groups and New Left political activists shepherded dramatic reforms in the regulatory process. Participatory reforms included extensive congressional reforms ushered in by the policy entrepreneurs of the "Class of '74" as well as significant amendments to the Administrative Procedures Act, which governs executive branch agency rule-making.[8]

The public-interest group movement was made up of people who hold what sociologist, Ronald Inglehart, calls "post-industrial values."[9] Inglehart, whose work is premised on the validity of Abraham Maslow's hierarchy of human needs, hypothesizes that people who enjoy high levels of economic and physical security in their formative years develop distinct political and social values. In this view, the generation that grew up in the economic and physical security of the postwar years had fulfilled its lower order needs and thus shifted its focus to higher order needs.[10] Based on Maslow's hierarchy, people who no longer need to strive for food, shelter, and clothing (i.e., materialist ends) are able to strive for the higher order needs of love, esteem, and self actualization (i.e., postmaterialist values).[11] These higher order or postmaterialist values shaped the social and political perceptions of the generation that came of age in the 1960s and 1970s, which in turn shaped the ideology, institutions, and even the interests of the societal regime.

While the associational regime was characterized by the need to bring about economic stability, the societal regime took economic stability for granted and instead focused on the goal of improving social justice and the quality of life in America. New agencies created in furtherance of social regulatory goals included among others the Equal Employment Opportunity Commission (1965), the Environmental Protection Agency (1970), the National Highway Traffic Safety Administration (1970), the Occupational Safety and Health Administration (1970), the National Oceanic and Aeronautic Administration (1970), the Consumer Product Safety Administration (1972), and the Mine Safety and Health Administration (1973).

These agencies, unlike their New Deal Era predecessors, were not focused on the management of economic competition within industries. They were, in fact, focused on the amelioration of negative externalities produced by unregulated production processes. These agencies would impose broad regulations affecting numerous industries. The harmful effects of these new social regulations upon economic efficiency and competition were deemed inconsequential compared to their social and environmental benefits. These social regulations would impose high compliance costs on industrial firms that would cut into profits. The regulatory initiatives of the societal regime destroyed the harmonious relationship between the regulators and the regulated, forged in the regulatory regime of the New Deal, and replaced it with a much more adversarial one.

The societal regime of the 1960s and 1970s saw a shift in the political, institutional, and social environments toward consumers, workers, and individuals, and away from concentrated economic or political power. The new politics of baseball, characterized by a players union that negotiates from a power position of virtual parity with the owners, is also a product of the political and regulatory environment of the 1960s and 1970s. Just as the institutions, interests, and values of the Progressive Era and the New Deal had been instrumental in determining the fate of baseball's private self-government, so too would the regulatory regime of the 1960s and 1970s affect the game's anomalous status.

During the 1960s and 1970s there was a partial erosion of baseball law. Because of the emergence of a powerful players association, whose pressure tactics brought collective bargaining to the game, baseball law has increasingly become subject to public regulation. Television and mass sports marketing removed any doubts that the game was indeed a matter of interstate commerce. The political atmosphere of the societal regime made it easier for players to turn to the state for relief and protection from the tyranny of the owners. The political climate of the 1960s provided legitimacy and public support for the players' attempts to claim full citizenship in baseball. The players were not fighting simply for more money. They were fighting for rights—workers' rights. In this way, they can be seen as animated by postmaterialist values.

Most useful to the players' cause were laws created during the New Deal that sought to protect workers' rights.[12] The most significant of these was the National Labor Relations Act of 1935. This act created the National Labor Relations Board (NLRB), which would have regulatory jurisdiction over labor/management relations in all industries engaged in or affecting interstate commerce.[13] The first opportunity for this law to affect baseball was in 1946 when the ill-fated players union, the American Baseball Guild, sought redress from the NLRB over its claim that the owners had engaged in unfair labor practices. The NLRB declined to investigate the matter on jurisdictional grounds. Echoing the courts, the NLRB ruled that baseball was not a matter of interstate commerce, and therefore fell outside the jurisdiction of the board.[14]

The posture of the NLRB would not change until the late 1960s. In 1969, the NLRB reversed its 1946 position on baseball by claiming jurisdiction in a case involving an attempt by American League Umpires to unionize. In *American League of Professional Baseball Clubs and Association of National Baseball League Umpires*, the board held that recently the courts had found that baseball was a matter of interstate commerce, despite their failure to lift the exemption created in *Federal Baseball*. Accordingly, the board ruled that "professional baseball is an industry in or affecting commerce, and as such is subject to Board jurisdiction under the Act."[15]

The board spelled out four factors that mitigated in favor of their assertion of jurisdiction. First, the board found that organized baseball's system of "internal self-regulation," which relies upon the commissioner to resolve labor disputes, "appears to have been designed almost entirely by employers and owners." The board found this arrangement to be unlikely "either to prevent labor disputes from arising in the future, or, having once arisen, to resolve them in a manner susceptible or conducive to voluntary compliance by all parties involved." The second factor was the board's finding that the Umpires Union was indeed a labor union within the meaning of the National Labor Relations Act. The third factor was baseball's undisputed interstate character. Fourth, the board rejected the owners' contention that the umpires were supervisors and thus did not meet the definition of labor contained in the Act.[16]

This 1969 NLRB decision guaranteed the players association the right to engage in collective bargaining. The players union would marshal this state endorsement of its collective bargaining rights with great effect. The threat of NLRB action stood behind all of the gains of the players association in the 1970s. The emasculation of the century old reserve clause could not have been accomplished without the state's protection of the players' right to bargain collectively.

The development of the Major League Baseball Players Association (MLBPA) into a full-fledged, and very powerful, union was the byproduct of the regulatory climate of the 1960s. While the legislative and administrative initiatives of the societal regime were not directly related to unions, they did create an atmosphere that was amenable to the empowerment of the disenfranchised. In baseball that meant the players. The spectacle of public-interest groups, and activists like Ralph Nader, speaking out for the rights of consumers and citizens to participate in regulatory decision making, as well as the emergence of postmaterialist values across society, contributed to the efforts of the MLBPA to claim participatory rights for the locked out citizens of baseball, the players. The players union's goal was to inject the players into the governance of baseball in the same way that Ralph Nader and others were attempting to inject consumers into the production process.

The New Left critique of a closed system of governance, dominated by corporate interests would surely not sound foreign to baseball players in the 1960s. The New Left's attempt to correct the defects of pluralism by securing a place at the policymaking table for the public interest was not unlike the players union's attempt to attain a role for the players in the policymaking process of Major League Baseball.

MARVIN MILLER AND THE MLBPA

The onset of conventional labor/management relations in organized baseball in the mid-1960s transformed the sport. While baseball had been a big money business since at least the turn of the century, it had never resembled a conventional industry. The evolution of the MLBPA from an information clearinghouse into a full fledged labor union was the catalyst for major reform in organized baseball's private self-government. The MLBPA would become a powerful player in the struggle over baseball's unregulated monopoly. The primary target of the players association would be the century-old reserve clause.

The union would become an effective counterbalance to the owners' unhindered control of the game. The post of commissioner of baseball, which was originally designed to act as a disinterested arbitrator, had by the late 1960s become increasingly sympathetic to the owners. Since the death of Landis, the baseball owners gradually weakened the power of the commissioner, subjecting the post to more control by the owners. Without a truly independent commissioner to protect their interests, the players turned to the union.[17]

Unionization was not popular with owners or players in the 1950s. The MLBPA, created in 1953, had been intended to perform the limited duty of administering the pension fund. The organizers of the association were careful to rebut fears that a union was being formed. Player representative Allie Reynolds tried to calm these fears by telling *The Sporting News* that he had "nothing against unions in industry. But if I had any suspicion that we in baseball were moving towards a union, I would not have anything to do with the enterprise."[18] Reynolds and fellow player representative, Ralph Kiner, had raised the fears of unionization by their efforts to secure various concessions from the owners in the summer of 1953. They gave the owners a list of demands, which included matters such as a raise in the minimum salary as well as the issue of funding the players pension fund. When the owners rejected their demands the players hired lawyer J. Norman Lewis to advise them. The owners, who initially acquiesced to Lewis' attendance at player/management talks, suddenly barred the attorney from talks on the pension fund in December, 1953.[19]

The pension fund matter was settled without Lewis, and the newly formed MLBPA was relegated to the role of assisting in the administration of the fund. Sentiment throughout the game remained staunchly antiunion well into the 1960s. The MLBPA's first president, Bob Feller, was a strong opponent of collective bargaining. In 1963, Bob Friend, the National League player representative for the MLBPA, wrote an article in *The Sporting News* that sharply denounced calls to unionize Major League Baseball players. He argued that "the reserve clause is an absolute must for the survival of baseball" and that the players did not need a union at all. He concluded that a baseball union would be bad for the game because it would betray the special cultural significance of the national pastime. He claimed that possible player strikes would threaten baseball's image and that the "spectacle of someone like Stan Musial picketing the ballpark" would destroy the game.[20]

The MLBPA's antiunion sentiments were also made clear by the appointment of Robert Cannon as the association's legal advisor replacing Lewis in 1960. Cannon, a Milwaukee circuit court judge, was widely known to be interested in the job of commissioner of baseball. Historian James Miller characterizes Cannon's management of the players' affairs as being "in the interests of labor peace and the owners' pocketbooks."[21] Several commentators have quoted Cannon's testimony in a 1964 Senate committee hearing on baseball and antitrust issues in which he praises the reserve clause and claims on behalf of the players that "we have it so good we don't know what to ask for next."[22] Marvin Miller would later write that Cannon "never met an owner he didn't like."[23]

By 1966, the players were ready to appoint a full-time executive director for the MLBPA. Still not comfortable with the idea of a labor union, the players offered the job to Judge Cannon, who surprisingly refused it. The issue of creating a permanent director, an office, and a staff for the association created tension between the players and owners. The owners feared that a permanent executive director would move the organization toward a more adversarial relationship with management in order to legitimate his own position.[24] The selection of Marvin Miller by the MLBPA executive committee contributed to those fears.

Miller was a recognized labor law expert. He had earned his reputation as the chief economist with the Steelworkers Union. The members of the players association executive committee knew that Miller would bring a more adversarial perspective to labor/management relations. By 1966, players were beginning to feel that they were being exploited. Complaints about playing conditions, minimum salary levels, inadequate pensions, large bonuses to amateur players, and even racial discrimination were common.

After his selection by the executive committee of the MLBPA, Miller's appointment would have to be ratified by the players. Miller spent the spring of 1966 going from team to team, explaining to the players how a strong independent organization could protect and forward their interests. The owners tried to paint him as a labor agitator and a thug. His critics accused him of brainwashing players and called him a Svengali.[25]

The players' apprehensions about unions, however, would be overridden by a general atmosphere of discontent in the nation, as well as specific grievances that made a union seem palatable. The players saw salaries rising rapidly in professional football, the expansion of their own sport, and the huge amounts of money that television broadcasts were bringing to the game. These factors combined to make players feel that they were not getting their fair share. In addition, the players' appetite for collective action was wetted by the example of the Dodgers Sandy Koufax and Don Drysdale.[26]

Prior to the 1966 season, as Miller was campaigning for the players vote of confidence, Koufax and Drysdale teamed up in an effort to gain increases in their salaries. Combining their interests, they hired a lawyer to negotiate their 1966 salaries. The Dodger management was forced to negotiate with the two star players who staged a collective holdout until they were offered an acceptable salary increase. In April 1966, the players ratified the appointment of Miller.

The owners reacted to Miller's appointment by reneging on their promise to fund the MLBPA permanent office with proceeds from the all-star game. In addition, according to historian James Miller, the owners vented their anger by blacklisting veteran pitcher Robin Roberts, who, as a member of the MLBPA executive committee, had been instrumental in selecting Miller.[27] The seemingly punitive nature of the owners' refusal to fund Miller's office, as well as the successful collective bargaining of Drysdale and Koufax, provided the new executive director with the opportunity to win over players who had been reluctant to create a labor organization.

The owners claimed that funding the office would constitute a violation of the Taft-Hartley Act, which prohibits employers from paying money to employee organizations. The owners' tactics would have several unintended consequences. Not only would the episode solidify player support for Miller and a strong union type organization, it also opened up a Pandora's box of legal vulnerabilities for organized baseball. By invoking Taft-Hartley the owners exposed baseball's labor-management relations to legal challenges.[28]

Using the threat of such challenges Miller negotiated a player friendly settlement with the owners. The settlement included a raise in the owners' contribution to the pension fund and the elimination of the requirement for the players' regular contribution. Essentially, the owners were forced to assume responsibility for funding the entire pension plan in order to wiggle out of their ill-considered decision to renege on funding Miller's office.

Prior to the 1967 season, Miller announced that he would pursue negotiations with management on a contract covering all aspects of labor/management relations. Any hopes the owners might have harbored about the players association not becoming a full-fledged union were crushed by Miller's declarations. The owners, however, did not believe that Miller would be able to hold the players together under pressure. The negotiations were bogged down by continued management stalling tactics designed to test the players' unity. Finally, in January 1968, Miller and the owners' recently hired professional negotiator, John Gaherin, made a deal. Baseball's first "Basic Agreement" was acceded to by the owners in the face of threats by Miller to bring in federal mediators. The agreement was a two-year contract that increased the minimum salary from $7,000 to

$10,000, gave players the explicit right to hire professional agents, and established a grievance procedure whereby the commissioner arbitrated contract disputes for players who had at least three years in the league. The agreement also set up a joint study group on the reserve clause.[29]

The following year, Miller moved on the issue of increasing the owners contribution to the pension fund. Given the huge profits being garnered by television contracts, Miller sought to obtain a percentage of those profits for the pension fund. The owners were indignant about Miller's proposal. They claimed that the players had no right to television revenues. In response to the owners' unwillingness to link their pension contribution to television revenues, Miller asked the players to refuse to sign their 1969 contracts.

The resulting holdouts left spring training camps without the majority of their veteran players. When the holdout threatened the regular season the television networks threatened not to pay to televise games played without the veteran players. Historian Benjamin Rader quotes an NBC executive as saying that his network would not "pay major league prices for minor league games."[30] The pressure from the television networks hastened a settlement of the dispute. Because Commissioner Eckert had been fired by the owners earlier that year, National League lawyer, Bowie Kuhn, was called on to broker an agreement between the owners and the union. In the settlement the owners would agree to increase their contribution to the pension plan but not to contribute a percentage of the television revenues. Shortly after this settlement, Kuhn was appointed commissioner of baseball.

In the winter of 1969, the new commissioner, Bowie Kuhn, received a letter from a player. Curt Flood was a thirty-two-year-old outfielder with the St. Louis Cardinals, a team with which he had spent his entire eleven-year career. He was writing to the commissioner to complain about having been traded suddenly to the Philadelphia Phillies without his consent. Flood asked Kuhn to intercede on his behalf, arguing that his tenure in the league had earned him the right to determine his own destiny. The commissioner refused to assist Flood. In January 1970, with the backing of the players association, Flood filed an antitrust suit against Major League Baseball.[31]

MLBPA executive director Marvin Miller orchestrated Flood's challenge of baseball's storied exemption. Miller convinced the association to finance Flood's lawsuit. Miller also personally recruited former Supreme Court Justice Arthur Goldberg to represent Flood. Despite the financial backing of the players union, Flood received no significant public support from any major league players. In his autobiography, Miller laments that the association made little effort to organize big name players in support of Flood. He speculates that the players were not yet solidly united as a union and that if the case had come up after the 1972 players' strike, there might have been a greater show of support from the players. The only support offered by fellow players came in the form of court testimony from Jackie Robinson, Hank Greenberg, Jim Brosnan, and Bill Veeck.[32] It may be argued, however, that the silence of the players during the *Flood* case represents an improvement compared to the dozens of active players who were compelled to testify in support of the reserve rule during congressional hearings in the 1950s.

Flood's lawsuit was heard in federal district court by Judge Irving Ben Cooper. Judge Cooper heard the case without a jury, weighing more than 2,000 pages of testimony and dozens of evidentiary documents as well as the arguments of the litigants.[33] The trial judge ruled against Flood, upholding the *Federal Baseball* decision as a matter of stare decisis. In his opinion for the court, Judge Cooper revealed his understanding of baseball's significance when he wrote, "Baseball's status in the life of the nation is so pervasive that it would not strain credulity to say that the court can take judicial notice that baseball is everybody's business.... The game is on higher ground; it behooves everyone to keep it there."[34]

The second circuit court of appeals also rejected Flood's assault on baseball's treasured immunity. In its decision the court held, "If baseball is to be damaged by statutory regulation, let the congressman face his constituents the next November and also face the consequences of his baseball voting record."[35] The appeals court opinion, like that of the trial court, was littered with praise of baseball's cultural significance. In his concurring opinion for the Second Circuit Court of Appeals, Judge Moore recounted the heroes of baseball's past claiming that baseball's most notable players "were probably better known to a greater number of our populace than many of our statesmen; and their exploits better remembered than some of our outstanding public figures."[36]

In the summer of 1972, the Supreme Court received the *Flood* case and thus was faced with the antitrust exemption question once again. Once more, the Court refused to tamper with its *Federal Baseball* decision, holding that while baseball indeed was a matter of interstate commerce, the game's long standing reliance on the *Federal Baseball* precedent made it necessary for the legislature to address the anomaly. In *Flood v. Kuhn*, the Supreme Court opinion, written by Harry Blackmun, reads like a testimonial to the cultural significance of baseball in America. Blackmun's ode to baseball was even more extravagant than that of the lower courts. Throughout the legal odyssey of *Flood*, from the trial court to the Supreme Court, one message is repeatedly affirmed: Baseball is special![37] Despite the instability in baseball since the end of World War II, the reverence for the game was alive and well in 1972.

The Supreme Court decision in *Flood v. Kuhn* served to focus the efforts of the players association on the collective bargaining process as the way to effect reform of the reserve clause. After half a century and numerous court challenges, it was clear that the judicially created exemption was not going to be corrected by the courts. Moreover, the court opinions in the *Flood* case illustrated the continuing reverence for the game and any practices deemed necessary for its stability. Even Marvin Miller himself had doubts about the wisdom of repealing *Federal Baseball*. In an interview in the spring of 1969 Miller told a reporter that "a chaotic situation could exist if a lawsuit overthrew the legality of the reserve clause." He went on to recommend that a "substitute arrangement" should be made that "would be fair to both the club and the player and that would stand up in court."[38]

Even before the outcome of *Flood*, the players association set its sights on the collective bargaining process to achieve its goals. The Second Basic Agreement of 1970 included another raise of the minimum salary and a reduction in the maximum salary cut. Impasse in negotiations over the funding of the pension fund would set off the first regular season, industry-wide players strike in April, 1972. Historian Benjamin Rader describes the issues surrounding baseball's first real strike.

Ostensibly, the strike revolved around how the players' pension fund would be financed, but in the background hovered the general agreement that would be negotiated in 1973 and the status of the reserve clause that was being argued before the Supreme Court. Even though the owners had just negotiated a new television contract with NBC for $70 million, they initially rejected any increase in the share going to the player pension fund. A powerful minority of the owners wanted to seize the opportunity to break the union.[39]

Baseball's first industry-wide strike lasted only nine days into the 1972 regular season. The settlement of the strike garnered the players a $500,000 increase in the owners' contribution to the pension fund. It cost them $600,000 in lost wages. For the players, however, the real benefit of the strike would be reaped later. The unity of the players in 1972 contrasted sharply with the disunity of the owners. The strike had cost the owners much more than the players. The players demonstrated their willingness to suffer short-term losses for long-term gains and in so doing greatly increased their bargaining power in an increasingly adversarial relationship with management.

The resolve demonstrated by the players in 1972 would benefit them in negotiations over the Third Basic Agreement in 1973. Although the reserve clause was left intact, the players were granted the right to impartial arbitration of contract disputes. Instead of the commissioner settling salary disputes, any player with at least two years in the league could submit his case to a three-member arbitration board. The board would consist of one member chosen by the owners, one member chosen by the players, and one independent member. The board was charged with accepting either the player's salary request or the owner's proposed salary, with the decision binding on both parties.[40] Salary arbitration would become one of the most significant achievements of the players association and would lead to the virtual dismantling of the century-old reserve clause.

In the winter of 1975, the new arbitration procedure bore its most significant fruit. Two National League players, the Los Angeles Dodgers pitcher Andy Messersmith and the Montreal Expos pitcher Dave McNally, petitioned for free agent status. They argued that the reserve clause was a one-year option clause and that by playing the 1975 season without a contract, they had fulfilled their obligations.[41] Independent arbitrator Peter Seitz ruled in favor of the players.[42] The owners responded by firing Seitz and appealing his ruling to the courts. U.S. district court judge John Olver ruled that the Seitz decision should stand. The Eighth U.S. Circuit Court of Appeals also upheld Seitz's ruling, holding that the collective bargaining agreement between the players and owners gave Seitz the exclusive jurisdiction to decide the grievances of Messersmith and McNally. The court, however, was careful to note that it was not ruling on the reserve clause itself, but rather on the specific case at hand. Furthermore, the appeals court echoed the sentiments of previous courts in saying that baseball is not a matter for the courts.[43]

In July 1976, when baseball's Fourth Basic Agreement went into effect, the reserve clause had been emasculated. A fifteen-day lockout during spring training had prompted both sides to make major concessions. Free agency had come to America's national pastime. Under the reformulated reserve clause, players were no longer tied indefinitely to one team. For contracts signed prior to August 9, 1976, the team could renew for one year after the expiration of the contract. If the player remained unsigned through this option year, he automatically became a free agent. For contracts signed after August 9, 1976, players with six or more years in the major leagues at the end of their contracts could become free agents simply by giving notice to the players association.[44]

In 1977, the first free agent market in baseball produced significantly higher player salaries and a pronounced increase in multiyear contracts. Commissioner Bowie Kuhn released a report showing that the average player's salary rose from $51,501 in 1976 to $76,349 in 1977. The explosion in the number of multiyear contracts began as soon as the Seitz decision was rendered. Recognizing what the decision would mean for the reserve clause, many clubs signed players to multiyear contracts before the 1976 season. "[I]n all 57 players signed such pacts, 36 hitters and 21 pitchers. Of these 57 contracts, 26 were for two years, 18 for three years, 7 for four years, and 6 for five years."[45] In 1977, 281 players signed multiyear contracts. The breakdown that year was 111 contracts for two years, 105 for three years, 21 for four years, 33 for five years, 10 for six years, and one for ten years.

Despite the apparent advances in reforming baseball's private self-government with regard to labor/management relations, pressure for government regulation again increased in the mid-1970s. In May 1976, the U.S.

House of Representatives created the Select Committee on Professional Sports under the chairmanship of California Democrat, B. F. Sisk. The purpose of the Sisk Committee was to investigate the stability of America's professional sports leagues and to recommend any legislation thought necessary. One of the main issues on the committee's agenda was to determine whether organized baseball should continue to enjoy an exemption from the nation's antitrust laws. The recent failure of the ABA and NBA merger, franchise relocations in football and baseball, several lawsuits and findings of unfair labor practices by the NLRB were all regular stories on America's sports pages. The introduction to a study prepared for the use of the select committee chronicles the woes of professional sports and concludes, "[i]t is rare that the formation of a special investigative committee receives such instant justification for its existence."[46]

The committee held extensive hearings in which they heard from a wide array of witnesses from all the major sports. Baseball representation at the hearings was heavily weighted in the owners favor. Testimony was heard from Commissioner Kuhn, New York Mets Chairman, Grant Donald, National League President Charles Feeney, and American League President, Lee MacPhail. Each spoke to the committee about baseball's storied tradition and its tireless efforts to operate in the public interest. Each assured the committee that baseball's exemption was crucial to the sports continuing commitment to the public interest. The arguments advanced for the exemption were already well known to the committee. Nonetheless, the baseball men reiterated the need for the exemption to control franchise migration, manage competition between clubs, and avoid costly and destructive litigation. Most potent, however, were their veiled promises of expansion. Members of the committee were assured that Major League Baseball intended to expand and that their states were certainly in the running.[47]

These overtures from Major League Baseball were countered by the impassioned testimony of Marvin Miller, as well as testimony from several noted scholars who argued for the repeal of baseball's exemption. Economist Roger Noll and Lawyer Steven Rivkin, both contributors to a 1972 study entitled *Government and the Sports Business*, testified that baseball's exemption created an unequal and destructive tension between the major professional sports and that the Congress should consider legislation to eradicate the anomaly.[48] After balancing the competing interests and arguments of those who testified the committee chose a compromise recommendation.

The final report of the Sisk Committee states:

Based upon the information available to it, the Committee has concluded that adequate justification does not exist for baseball's special exemption from the antitrust laws and that its exemption should be removed in the context of overall sports antitrust reform.[49]

Despite the Sisk committee's conclusion that baseball's exemption should be lifted, it recommended no such legislation. The extensive investigation produced an encyclopedic report, but no legislation. The committee did, however, recommend that its successor committee undertake an extensive study of sports antitrust law. The proposed sports oversight committee was never convened, but a study was prepared and published in 1981.[50]

At the time, it was widely acknowledged in the press that Sisk's committee was the result of his failed attempt to convince organized baseball to locate an expansion team in Washington, DC. Sisk and fellow Congressman Frank Horton (R–NY) had fought for a new team in the nation's capital since 1971 when the Senators left town for a second time. Other members of Congress had been rattling their sabers at organized baseball as well. Rep. Gillis Long (D–LA), who wanted a major league team for New Orleans, sponsored legislation to strip organized baseball of its exemption. In a widely reported tirade during a hearing in which NBA Commissioner Larry O'Brien was testifying, Rep. Long interrupted to announce his bill to strip Major League Baseball of its "favorite son treatment" because, he said, baseball "is beginning to respond to such treatment as many favorite sons do—as a prodigal son."[51] Long's bill, supported by other members whose cities sought major league teams, died in committee.

Baseball's owners went into negotiations over the Fifth Basic Agreement in 1980 determined to roll back some of the players association's advances. The owners sought to end salary arbitration and to modify the free agency rules. Unable to come to terms in 1980, it was decided to postpone negotiations until a joint player–owner committee could study the issues at hand. The 1980 season was played without an agreement.

During the 1980 season the owners took steps to deflect injury from an expected strike in 1981. They used a percentage of gate receipts as a strike fund and they took out strike insurance with Lloyds of London. The 1981 season opened without an agreement. Negotiations broke down on June 10 and the next day a fifty-day player strike began. During the protracted dispute the players charged the owners with bargaining in bad faith. The NLRB sought injunctive relief for the players, then began unfair labor practices proceedings against the owners. The parties finally came to agreement on August 1, the day after the owners strike insurance ran out.[52] The settlement left salary arbitration unchanged and created a complicated formula for compensating teams who lost free agents.

In the 1980s, the impetus for change was shifting from the players, who were making great strides against their "indentured servitude," to the fans. It was during the mid-1980s that baseball's place as an American cultural icon eroded. The rise of the players union to a position of virtual parity with the owners in terms of bargaining power contributed to the changing public mood. As organized baseball moved into the 1980s the public's perception of the relationship between the players and the owners began to change. During the 1970s the players association achieved numerous victories over the owners with the general support of the American public, but in the aftermath of the 1981 strike the fans were disgusted with both sides.[53]

The Fifth Basic Agreement expired in 1984 and once again negotiations were strained. It had become almost routine for the expiration of each Basic Agreement to set off a highly contentious negotiation over a new contract. The 1985 season was no different. A two-day strike in August was settled when the players agreed to a three-year major league tenure requirement for any player seeking salary arbitration. In addition, the free agency compensation rules were modified so as to limit teams that lost players to compensation through amateur draft choices.[54]

The concessions made by the players association in the 1985 Basic Agreement were indicative of the changing mood in the nation regarding baseball. Particularly telling was the players' agreement to a reduction in their share of television receipts from thirty-three to eighteen percent.[55] Baseball scholar James Quirk writes that, from the players perspective, "the mid-1970s to early-1980s were 'Star Wars,' and the mid-1980s looked more like 'The Empire Strikes Back.' "[56] The owners were beginning to win the public relations war. Their cries of poverty were having a positive effect on negotiations with the players. In 1984, the owners complained that they were losing $100 million a year. An independent auditor, appointed by the owners in compliance with NLRB rules, estimated that the owners were losing between $25 million and $35 million a year by 1985.

After the 1985 season it became apparent that the owners intended to strike back. Commissioner Peter Ubberoth laid the groundwork for the owners revenge when he reported to the owners the results of a cost/benefit analysis of free agency. The statistical study concluded that the benefit of signing free agents was outweighed by their cost. Sixty-two players filed for free agency; none was offered a contract by teams other than the team with which they were already playing.[57] The MLBPA charged the owners with collusion and sought redress through the grievance procedure. After two years of what became known as the "collusion hearings" in baseball, an independent arbitrator ruled against the owners' finding that there was owner collusion in the free agent market. Owners were exchanging information about their salary bids for free agents. It was not until 1990, however, that the arbitrator fined the owners $280 million for their collusion. In the 1990 Basic Agreement the players preserved both the arbitration system and free agency, as well as a provision that provided for triple damages to the union if the owners were again found guilty of collusion.

After the collusion decision, the players regained some leverage against the owners, and the new politics of baseball were once again near equilibrium. The outside environment, however, was poisoned by the travails of what had become the baseball industry. The price of labor equity in baseball was not insignificant. The rancorous battles between the players and the owners brought the national pastime into the 1990s looking much different than it had in the 1960s. Baseball had lost its status as a cultural icon. By the 1990s Americans had grown cynical about the game, seeing it more as a nasty business than a national treasure.

OTHER SPORTS: IS BASEBALL UNIQUE OR ONE AMONG MANY?

Organized baseball was the national pastime and a highly profitable industry before the advent of television or the coming of age of professional football and basketball. With the postwar explosion of mass media technology these other sports slowly began to rival baseball's popularity. As television became an important part of the American lifestyle in the 1960s and 1970s, the nation was also undergoing profound demographic change. On the one hand, there was a movement of population from the northeast and midwest to the sun belt and the west. On the other hand, all regions of the country were experiencing sizable migrations from urban centers to outlying areas, the suburbs. The changing demography of the nation and the appearance of television in every living room across the country changed the habits of American sports fans dramatically.

In a younger and more mobile population, the sports best for TV—basketball, football, and even hockey, with their combination of faster action combined with set time limits—drew increasing audiences. Prior to the advent of television, baseball ruled among spectator sports. Going to the ballpark to see a major league game was an experience unrivaled by other professional sports. Gradually, however, especially with the advent of television, the other professional sports cut into baseball's popularity, reducing it to one among many.

The development of football and basketball as professional sports, both of which came of age in the 1950s and 1960s largely through television, had an impact on baseball's private self-government. The fate of these other sports since the 1950s has provided Major League Baseball with the knowledge of what might have been. These other sports dealt with the empowerment of players unions, the explosion of television revenues, and the transformation of professional sports markets without a pre-existing immunity from federal antitrust laws. Their development, despite subjection to antitrust laws, exposed baseball's private self-government. The baseball anomaly, which had gone largely unnoticed until the 1950s, would be repeatedly besieged in the era of television. The perception that baseball was no different than other professional sports, yet it received special treatment, would constantly fuel antagonism with baseball's exemption. As these other sports dealt with antitrust issues, baseball's anomaly was increasingly a target for the press, the public, and the policymakers on Capitol Hill.

Professional football experienced a markedly different path of development from that of baseball in terms of labor/management relations and es-

pecially in its relation to federal antitrust statutes. Football in America can
be traced to the 1870s, when colleges began intercollegiate play. In 1920, the
American Professional Football Association was created, featuring the
legendary college football star Jim Thorpe. In 1921, this league became the
National Football League (NFL), which enjoyed moderate success until its
rise to big time status in the 1960s when it was rivaled, and then joined, by
the newly formed American Football League (AFL).

Professional football's first brush with antitrust law came in 1953 when a
Pennsylvania federal district court ruled that the NFL's sale of pooled television contracts constituted a violation of antitrust law. The decision, which
came in the same year the Supreme Court in *Toolson* upheld baseball's exemption from antitrust, stated explicitly that the court considered football
to be interstate commerce by virtue of its commercial broadcast on radio
and television.[58] This decision fueled ongoing sentiment in the halls of Congress that baseball's special legal status among sports must be remedied.

In 1957, in *Radovich v. National Football League*, the Supreme Court echoed
the 1953 decision of the federal district court, finding that professional football is indeed subject to federal antitrust laws.[59] This decision put to rest
any expectation or speculation that football was exempt from antitrust because of the Court's decision in *Toolson*. The *Radovich* decision also had a
profound effect upon the players union movement in football. Like baseball, professional football had a reserve clause in all standard player contracts which bound players to the team that originally drafted them for the
duration of their careers or until their team sold, traded, or released them.[60]

The National Football League Players Association (NFLPA), formed a
year before the *Radovich* decision, had failed to make any headway with the
owners in 1956 on the issue of the reserve clause or any other player grievances. The 1957 Supreme Court decision, however, greatly improved the
bargaining position of the players. By threatening the football owners with
a multimillion dollar antitrust suit, the football players association, headed
by attorney and former player, Creighton Miller, was able to secure important concessions from the owners. The minimum salary for players was increased to $5,000; players were guaranteed $50 for each exhibition game
played and won the inclusion of an injury clause in their contracts, that
would continue salaries and pay for medical care after an injury; and they
also won a pension plan for the players that began in 1959.[61] At the same
time the fledgling baseball players association continued to languish in a
position of virtual powerlessness vis-à-vis the baseball owners.

In 1961, a federal district court, citing the 1953 Pennsylvania federal appeals decision, struck down the validity of a $9.3 million television contract
between the NFL and CBS on the grounds that it was in violation of antitrust law.[62] Just months after this decision, Congress granted professional
baseball, football, basketball, and hockey an antitrust exemption that
would nullify the court's decision and allow leagues to enter into television

broadcasting contracts as a single entity, rather than requiring each team to make its own broadcasting deals. The practice of leagues entering into television contracts as a unit greatly increased television revenues. The statutory exemption granted by Congress was vigorously opposed by the television networks.[63] While this exemption allowed professional football, basketball, and hockey to increase television revenue dramatically, it was much more significant for organized baseball.

By removing the issue of television revenues, Congress had taken away the most potent weapon in the struggle to repeal the *Federal Baseball* exemption. Television was the most significant factor in exposing Major League Baseball's interstate character as well as its special treatment. Professional football, basketball and hockey only caught on with American sports fans when television brought them into everyone's living room. Television transformed American spectator sports. It leveled the playing field as far as fan interest in sports. Television made baseball just one among many and it revealed baseball's unfair legal advantage over the other sports. The *Sports Broadcasting Act of 1961* eliminated the most potent argument for repealing baseball's exemption and gave new life to the baseball anomaly.

In 1962, football's reserve clause was apparently shattered, more than a decade before any significant alteration in baseball's reserve clause. San Francisco player R. C. Owens played out his option year and signed with the Baltimore Colts for the 1963 season. Given the recent judicial declarations that football was subject to antitrust laws, this move seemed to signal the end of peonage for football players. The owners, however, responded the following year with a creativity reminiscent of their baseball counterparts. The so-called "Rozelle Rule," named for then-commissioner Pete Rozelle, was instituted in 1963. By awarding compensation in the form of players, draft choices, or money to be paid by the team hiring the free agent to the team losing one, the Rozelle rule effectively negated the viability of free agency. The amount and type of compensation would be determined by the commissioner of football. This disincentive to signing free agents was so significant that only a handful of free agents were signed between 1963 and 1976.

In 1963, the players of the newly formed AFL created the American Football League Players Association and almost immediately joined their colleagues in the NFL in opposing the merger of the two leagues. The players contended that the merger would reduce their ability to negotiate player salaries. The merger was officially approved by Congress in October 1966. The newly consolidated NFL began unrivaled play in the 1967–1968 season.

Congressional approval of the merger did not come without a fight. Rep. Emanuel Celler of New York, a well-known foe of baseball's exemption, fought hard to scuttle approval of the merger. But the plan was approved by the Senate in what was widely considered a deal wherein key senators traded their votes for the promise of expansion teams. Senate Minority

Leader Everett Dirksen (R–IL) used a parliamentary trick to get the merger past Celler's forces in the House. He attached it to a House-passed anti-inflation bill. The overwhelming support for the anti-inflation bill in the House allowed the Senate to hold it hostage with the merger plan as ransom. Unwilling to jeopardize the anti-inflation bill, House opponents were forced to acquiesce in conference.[64]

The football merger legislation is a good example of how institutions, and institutional contexts, affect public policy outcomes. Pro-merger forces did not have the political clout to get the merger through the House of Representatives, however, by exploiting the rules of the legislative process pro-merger forces were able to get the plan passed despite not having a majority on their side. The regulatory environment at the time of the merger was such that contravening antitrust principles was very unpopular. Had Congressman Celler and the opponents of the merger been prepared for the parliamentary maneuvering of pro-merger legislators, the merger would surely have failed. A decade later Congressman Celler and his allies on Capitol Hill were prepared for parliamentary strategy when the NBA-ABA merger came before the Congress. The failure of that merger better represents the sense of the majority.

While the passage of the *Sports Broadcasting Act of 1961* might seem to indicate a softening of support for antitrust enforcement, in fact it was the result of the pervasive influence of television, not eroding support for the vigorous enforcement of antitrust law. In 1961, only the NFL, as a result of the aforementioned court decisions, was restricted from selling pooled contracts to television networks. Major League Baseball was beyond challenge on this point due to its blanket exemption. The NBA's and NHL's practice of pooling TV contracts had not yet been successfully challenged in court. Even the NFL's rival the American Football Conference (AFC) remained free to pool TV contracts. The desire to bring parity to this situation combined with the pervasive influence of a relatively new mass media enabled advocates of the broadcasting exemption to argue that the rule of reason dictated that pooling TV contracts was not injurious to economic competition.

In 1968, the NFLPA became the first players association to register with the U.S. Department of Labor as a labor union. Football players seemed poised to join baseball players in pressuring for significant reforms through collective bargaining agreements, protected under the NLRB. In contrast to the MLBPA, however, the football players association achieved little in the early 1970s because they were faced with the owners' refusal to recognize them as a legal unit for collective bargaining. Because the NFL union had merged with the AFL union, it was forced to seek recertification from the NLRB. During the complex process of recertification that resulted, the owners were able to ignore the union and go their own way. While advocates of baseball's exemption often point to this disparity between the effectiveness

of the baseball and football players unions, the success of the baseball players cannot easily be linked to the exemption. The football players union cer-
tification problems muddy the comparison, making it a strained analogy at
best.

    After brief preseason strikes by football players in 1968 and 1970 and a
forty-four-day-long strike at the beginning of the 1974 season, which was
undermined by the lack of player solidarity and lackluster public support,
the NFLPA once again looked to the courts for relief. Baltimore Colts tight
end, John Mackey, who was president of the NFLPA, sued the NFL charging that the Rozelle rule violated the Sherman Antitrust Act. In the case of
Mackey v. NFL, a federal district court ruled in favor of Mackey, finding the
Rozelle rule to be in violation of antitrust law.[65] The decision was upheld by
the Eighth U.S. Circuit Court of Appeals in 1976.[66]

    The decision in *Mackey* was among the events sparking attention on
Capitol Hill in 1976. The Sisk committee, or Select Committee on Professional Sports, held hearings in the summer and fall of 1976. Although the
committee recommended no specific legislation, it did endorse the application of antitrust laws to all professional sports indiscriminately.

    Despite the victory in court and a relaxation of the Rozelle rule negoti-
ated in the 1977 Basic Agreement with the NFLPA, the owners continued to
enjoy the benefits of restricted player mobility by employing the age-old
tactic of blacklisting. The NFLPA limped into the 1980s, and in 1982, encouraged by the 1981 baseball players' strike, the football players went on
strike. For the players union, the fifty-seven-day strike was a failure. The
players were, in the end, forced to accept a settlement on management
terms. Adding insult to injury was the fact that several prominent players
who were union representatives found themselves either cut or traded after the 1982 season.[67] The NFL players would strike again in 1987. That
strike ended, after several games in which teams used replacement players,
with little change in player/management relations. The 1980s ended with
the football players union disorganized and dispirited. Despite the strictures of antitrust law, football owners had been far more successful than
their baseball counterparts in controlling the demands of players.

    The contrast between football and baseball on labor/management issues
extended to the issue of franchise migration. In contrast to the success of
football team owners in restraining player demands, the owners had trouble controlling each other. It was franchise movements, not player relations, that caused problems for football. The problems began when Oakland
Raiders owner, Al Davis, moved his club to Los Angeles in 1982, despite the
lack of league approval. Unable to get the required three-fourths vote of the
owners needed to relocate his club, Davis sued the league, arguing that the
voting requirement for relocation violated antitrust law.

    A U.S. district court agreed with Davis, finding the NFL in violation of
the Sherman Act in its efforts to block the Raiders move. Upheld on appeal,

this decision touched off what economist Paul Staudahar calls the "free agency" era of franchise movement in football.[68] In affirming the lower court decision, the Ninth U.S. Court of Appeals stated that the Raiders move to L.A. would promote competition with the Los Angeles Rams, as well as produce lower ticket prices and greater consumer choice. The court, therefore, justified its invocation of antitrust law by arguing that the move would enhance consumer welfare.[69] Despite concerted efforts to gain statutory exemption for the NFL's ability to restrict franchise mobility, numerous clubs have been relocated. Since 1982, the NFL has seen several high profile team relocations that have evoked much controversy. Organized baseball commonly cites the disruptions caused by franchise relocation in football as an argument for preserving its antitrust exemption on the grounds that it serves the public interest.

Basketball's development has resembled football's in some respects; however, the players association in basketball has been much more effective than its football counterpart. The National Basketball Players Association (NBPA) was created in 1954. In 1956, basketball had its first encounter with antitrust law. In the case of *Washington Professional Basketball Corp. v. NBA*,[70] a federal district court ruled in favor of a prospective team owner who had been prevented from entering the ranks of professional basketball by the NBA. The court held that the NBA operates across state lines by virtue of its travel and its sale of broadcast rights and is therefore subject to the strictures of the Sherman Act.

The basketball owners did not recognize the players union until 1967, when competition from the newly formed American Basketball Association (ABA) greatly enhanced the players leverage over the owners. In 1967, the players and owners agreed to the first collective bargaining agreement in basketball. During the next nine years, the players association did not pursue collective bargaining vigorously.

Suffering from escalating salaries the owners in both leagues began to press for a merger in 1969. The players association strongly opposed the merger, which would of course reduce their leverage against the owners. When the two leagues came to terms on a merger agreement, the players association, led by NBPA president Oscar Robertson, filed an antitrust suit to block it, which included challenges to the draft, the uniform contract, and the reserve clause. A federal court issued an injunction preventing the merger until the merits of the case could be determined. The court also rejected an NBA argument that the court lacked jurisdiction in the case and that the NLRB was the appropriate adjudicative venue. This created a situation peculiar to basketball, as it made recourse to the courts for antitrust challenges the weapon of choice in basketball.

That weapon was used by Spencer Haywood, an all-American basketball player from the University of Detroit and member of the 1968 United States Olympic basketball team. Haywood had signed a contract with the

Seattle Supersonics of the NBA. The NBA Commissioner voided the contract because Haywood had not yet been out of high school for four years,
as required by the NBA rule designed to discourage the signing of college
underclassmen. Haywood sued the NBA charging them with an unlawful
conspiracy in restraint of trade. The courts agreed. In the case of *Haywood v.
NBA*, the Supreme Court ruled that the NBA rule was indeed a violation of
the Sherman Act.[71] This decision officially placed basketball in the same
position vis-à-vis antitrust law as football, and it further illuminated the
disparity between baseball and these other sports.

In the meantime, the NBA and ABA sought approval for their merger
plan on Capitol Hill in 1971. The same approval had been obtained by the
NFL and AFL in 1966, but the politics of the basketball merger were different. Unlike the NFLPA, the basketball players were well organized and a
potent lobbying force against the merger. In addition, those in Congress
who opposed the football merger would not be duped by parliamentary
trickery this time. The basketball merger hearings in 1971 were brief and
unremarkable.[72] There was not great support in Congress to contravene the
antitrust laws once again. This combined with the vigorous and well organized opposition of the NBA players association made passage of the merger
unlikely. Seeking the support of the players for the merger the owners offered to ease the reserve clause, bringing it in line with the football reserve
clause at the time, which included the Rozelle rule. The players refused this
offer and managed to block congressional approval of the merger.[73]

In 1975, a federal district court settled the *Robertson* case by striking
down basketball's version of the Rozelle rule, which had acted as a disincentive to signing free agents, the player draft, and the uniform contract,
finding them all illegal under the Sherman Act. The court also ruled that the
NBA–ABA merger would be a violation of antitrust law.[74] In 1976, following the *Robertson* decision the players and owners negotiated a collective
bargaining agreement in which the players acquiesced to the merger plan
in exchange for major concessions.[75] The newly consolidated NBA began
play in 1976–1977 season.

The issue of franchise migration came to the NBA in the person of Donald Sterling, owner of the San Diego Clippers. In 1982, he tried to move his
club to Los Angeles. After two years of litigation, encouraged by the decision in the *Raiders* case, Sterling moved his team without the NBA's permis-
sion. The NBA sued Sterling and, in 1987, a federal appeals court provided
the NBA with some hope by throwing out a lower court's dismissal of the
NBA's suit and ordering a new trial. In its decision the court stated that
leagues can put reasonable restrictions on franchise movement. The NBA
eventually lost the case, but it did create hesitation regarding unrestricted
franchise migration.[76]

The NBA's labor/management relations have been the most litigious,
but also the most productive. Unlike baseball and football, basketball has

not had to endure a major strike or work stoppage. The threat of antitrust action has chastened the basketball owners and provided the players with a powerful weapon in labor/management negotiations. Additionally, franchise migration has not been a controversial issue in the NBA. Unlike football, the history of professional basketball and the antitrust laws indicates that productive labor/management relations and franchise stability can be maintained despite exposure to federal antitrust law.

The impact of the emergence of other professional sports like football and basketball, which are subject to antitrust law, on the baseball anomaly is mixed. On the one hand, these sports were the beneficiaries of the advent of television. As such they became as popular, and in the case of football more popular, than baseball. At the very least, these sports came to be equally as popular as baseball, which had the effect of exposing the inequity of the baseball anomaly for all to see.

On the other hand, television changed the nature of the game. While it certainly made clear the interstate character of the business of baseball, it also facilitated greater understanding of the cooperative nature of sports leagues and in so doing expanded what would be considered reasonable collaboration among members of such leagues. More importantly, by shielding broadcast activity from the antitrust laws, television diluted the case against baseball's exemption. Baseball limped into the 1980s with its private self-government battered but intact, and as the regulatory environment shifted with the Reagan revolution that private self-government began to look more like the emerging norm rather than an outdated anomaly.

THE REGULATORY REGIME OF THE 1980s

The new politics of baseball involve the players association becoming a powerful labor union, which by the mid-1970s would deal with organized baseball's management on a virtually equal basis. That is to say that the fortunes of the players association were aided by the political environment of the day. The societal regulatory regime of the late 1960s and 1970s was animated by the mobilization of popular sentiment against the exploitation of the capitalist production process by big business. This sentiment worked against the baseball owners and facilitated the progress of the players association in the 1970s. But, the player-friendly political environment shifted in the 1980s. The onset of what Eisner calls the "efficiency" regime provided the owners with some relief from negative public opinion, allowing them to stem the tide of player advances in collective bargaining.

The so-called Reagan revolution of the 1980s caused a shift in regulatory policy. Eisner sees the onset of the efficiency regime as a reaction to the expansive regulatory push of the late 1960s and 1970s. He identifies four defining characteristics of the new regime. First, the efficiency regime is characterized by an "unprecedented centralization of regulatory authority in the Office of Management and Budget (OMB) and in White House re-view bodies." Second, regulatory initiatives during the late 1970s and 1980s were subjected to unprecedented amounts of economic analysis prior to promulgation. Third, regulators assessed the need for regulation and de-signed new policies with economic markets as a benchmark. Fourth, the ef-ficiency regime is characterized by an "overwhelming concern with corporate compliance costs" on the part of advocates of regulatory reform and deregulation. The common thread pervading these characteristics is the pursuit of economic efficiency[77]

Eisner's identification of the shift in regulatory policy in late 1970s and 1980s as a new regulatory regime is controversial. Students of regulatory policy, Richard Harris and Sidney Milkis, contend that no coherent consen-sus developed in support of the type of antigovernment, market-based regulatory program that dominated administrative politics during the pe-riod in question. They agree that the regulatory reform and deregulation initiatives of the 1980s were a reaction to the social regulation of the previ-ous decade and a half, but they see the forces of deregulation as achieving parity with, rather than overwhelming, the forces of social regulation and the societal regime.

Although no firm consensus has developed in support of a market-oriented regula-tory regime, the principles of "real economics" pose a strong challenge to the public philosophy that gave impetus to social regulation. . . . Quality-of-life issues and citi-zen activism will be challenged by well organized business interests and advocates of economic theories, who provide a theoretical alternative to the moral imperatives of social reformers. In one sense this suggests a stalemate between two visions of regulatory politics. In another sense, however, it signifies a confirmation of the pub-lic lobby movement.[78]

In contrast to the prevailing continuity of Harris and Milkis' "public lobby regime" Eisner distinguishes the efficiency regime from the societal regime. He argues that the lack of consensus in the electorate regarding the wisdom of regulatory reform and deregulation does not preclude the exis-tence of a new regulatory regime. Eisner locates the origins of the efficiency regime in elite politics, rather than democratic politics. He identifies three contributing factors in the development of the efficiency regime, none of which is directly related to electoral politics. They are: (1) the use of presi-dential initiatives to affect regulatory reform, (2) new administrative prac-tices and changes in staffing in regulatory agencies, and (3) shifting power configurations in the public interest group system.

These factors did not appear suddenly in the late 1970s. They all began to develop in the early 1970s and thus overlapped with the societal regime. The societal and efficiency regulatory regimes overlapped because of their disparate origins. Like its predecessors, the societal regime resulted from mass political mobilization. It was a regime supported by a majority political coalition, by public opinion. The efficiency regime has its origins in elite politics and finds expression in administrative politics and the mobilization of distinctly minority corporate interests.

While the early 1970s were dominated by more populist citizen and consumer advocacy groups, it was only a matter of time before corporations, and Major League Baseball, began marshaling their superior resources in an effort to regain advantage in the new political environment. By 1980, almost three-quarters of the active lobbyists in Washington, DC, represented corporations or trade associations. Big business exploited the institutional reforms of the societal regime to recapture the reigns of regulatory power, despite the absence of pro-business sentiment in the electorate.[79] What Thomas Edsall calls the "politicization of the business community" was undertaken in the face of a reform-minded Democratic Congress with strong ties to the consumer and environmental movements.[80] In many ways Major League Baseball was ahead of the learning curve in this strategy. Major League Baseball's organized lobbying efforts in Washington, DC, go back to the 1950s.

Large corporations and trade associations used vast armies of professional lobbyists to influence both legislative and administrative policymaking. Taking advantage of the 1974 campaign finance reforms, which increased the importance of so-called political action committees (PACs), as well as a 1975 Federal Election Commission (FEC) decision allowing corporations to use corporate funds to create and administer PACs, corporations and trade association lobbyists in the mid-1970s and 1980s dramatically increased their financial support for conservative policies and candidates.[81] The intricacy and complexity of regulatory policy together with the power of corporate money in elections enabled corporate interests to influence even Democratic members of Congress.

Corporate interests also sought to "redefine the terms of the policy debate over state-economy relations" by spending huge amounts of money on corporate advertising and the funding of new conservative "think tanks."[82] The former was designed to soften the antibusiness sentiment of the public at large, while the latter was designed to press the fight among the nation's intelligentsia.

Corporate advertising failed to create a discernible shift in public opinion in the 1970s, but may have contributed to the wave of conservative values in the 1980s. The effort to influence the scholarly debate, however, met with significant success. The list of conservative think tanks created in the 1970s and 1980s includes, among others, the Heritage Foundation; the Hoover Institution on War, Revolution and Peace; the National Bureau of Economic Research; the Center for the Study of American Business; and the American Council for Capital Formation.[83]

These conservative think tanks largely succeeded in changing the terms of the debate from the appropriate level of government intervention in the economy to whether such intervention was appropriate at all. The virtual consensus on the propriety of government regulation of the economy that had animated the associationalist and societal regimes was fractured by the 1980s. The policy debate was transformed into a battle of laissez-faire advocates versus interventionists, devotees of the Chicago school's "new learning" versus defenders of the traditional structure/conduct/performance paradigm, neoconservatives versus neoliberals.[84] Major League Baseball exploited the increasing influence of the Chicago school's view of antitrust policy. Lobbyists for Major League Baseball consciously adopted the economic argument against antitrust policy, adding it to their rhetorical arsenal in their fight to preserve baseball's unregulated monopoly.[85]

The change in the terms of the debate over state–economy relations combined with the regulatory reform and deregulatory initiatives of presidents of both parties constitutes what Eisner calls the "triumph of economics."[86] By the 1980s, the economic cost of regulation was a prominent feature of the regulatory decisionmaking process. The Reagan administration, claiming a mandate for the drastic reduction of the size and role of government, marshaled all of its resources and power to give effect to its conservative, laissez-faire economic ideology, which constituted an all-out assault on the Keynesian consensus that characterized the previous fifty years of American economic policy.[87]

One of the cornerstones of twentieth-century American economic policy has been antitrust law. As discussed in chapter one, antitrust policy became a principle means of regulating the industrial economy because it was compatible with both the liberal tradition of limited government intervention and the developing institutional capacities of the state. Falling short of the direct regulation envisioned by the New Nationalists of the Progressive Era, antitrust policy, cast as law enforcement, was a means of regulating an expansive industrial economy without abandoning the limited government traditions of America's founders. Antitrust policy was seen by its creators and proponents as a way to preserve the fairness of the preindustrial free market, as a means of protecting the individual property rights and economic opportunities of Americans that the industrial economy might endanger.

The Reagan administration's assault on established economic policy, animated by the economic ideology of the so-called "Chicago school," included a virtual one-hundred-and-eighty-degree turn in antitrust policy.[88] Chicagoans believe in the superior efficiency of the market as well as the superiority of self-regulating market forces. They condemn state regulation of markets as wasteful and corrupt. Their view of antitrust law effectively condemns the economic policies of the United States for the last half-century. The Reagan administration's influence, both institutional and political, as well as the ascendance of the Chicago school's view of antitrust policy, created an environment in which legislative assaults on baseball's private self-government were very difficult.

One of its widely recognized adherents, Judge Robert Bork, identifies the two primary characteristics of the Chicago school's view of antitrust policy. First is the belief that the singular and exclusive goal of antitrust law is to maximize consumer welfare. The second requires the application of rigorous economic analysis to justify antitrust policy. For an application of antitrust law to be legitimate, it must produce greater economic benefits than costs to consumers. The pursuit of maximum consumer welfare via rigorous cost/benefit analysis translates into the preservation of maximum business efficiency, which in turn allows for lower prices to consumers.[89]

Wider definitions of consumer welfare as well as the goals of preserving small businesses and a decentralized economy are considered by mainstream scholars to be among the primary goals of the antitrust statutes.[90] The Chicagoans, however, reject the possibility of political or social goals for antitrust policy. They claim that the legislative history of antitrust supports their conclusion that business efficiency, in pursuit of maximum consumer welfare, is the singular goal of antitrust policy.[91]

The 1970s and 1980s saw virtual equilibrium in the struggle between labor and management. These decades also witnessed the achievement of near parity in the public policy debate over state-economy relations between advocates of the laissez-faire economics of the Chicago school and proponents of the more interventionist philosophy that had dominated regulatory politics since at least the 1930s. The advances made by the players to elevate themselves from virtual peonage ran their course; and, although the central pillar of baseball law which concerned the players had been drastically reformed, the owners' private self-government continued. The ideology of the efficiency regime may not have achieved a coherent consensus in the electorate, but the landslide victory of Ronald Reagan preserved and strengthened the institutional weapons in the war against antitrust enforcement. The so-called Reagan Revolution also created at least the appearance of an electoral mandate sufficient to chasten antitrust advocates in Congress.

Congressional interest in antitrust policy and professional sports in the 1980s reflected the conservative values of the day. In 1982, the Congress considered several bills to exempt professional sports leagues from exposure to antitrust law with regard to franchise relocation decisions. As the Oakland Raiders were entangled in litigation that would eventually result in the courts striking down the ability of sports leagues (other than baseball) to regulate individual owners' ability to relocate their teams, the Congress was considering alterations to antitrust law that would extend part of baseball's immunity to other sports.[92] Congressional support for exempting the ability of sports leagues to regulate franchise relocation from antitrust law was bipartisan, reflecting the changing attitudes about antitrust among policy elites.

Although the 1982 legislation died in committee, owing partly to the highly vocal opposition of the NFL players association and the forceful opposition in the Senate led by Senator Howard Metzenbaum (D–OH), the issue re-emerged in 1985 following the midnight escape of the Colts NFL franchise from Baltimore. Once again, both the House and the Senate considered legislation to protect communities from franchise relocations by exempting the NFL from exposure to antitrust law with regard to league control over franchise migration. The Senate considered three bills, while the House considered five measures. None of these proposed measures included the repeal of baseball's antitrust exemption; rather all sought to extend it partially to other sports in the interest of stabilizing franchise locations.[93] As was the case in 1982, the effort to provide antitrust immunity to the NFL was spearheaded in the Senate by Senators Arlen Specter (R–PA) and Dennis Deconcini (R–NM). These senators reintroduced bills which would exempt NFL regulation of franchise migration from exposure to antitrust law. Spector and Deconcini were spurred by the public outcry from communities such as Oakland, and Baltimore, that had been the victims of relocated professional football franchises. Once again the opposition to this effort was lead by Senator Howard Metzenbaum, who in a Senate hearing in 1985 argued:

I say, let the leagues fight it out. Repeal the baseball exemption; require the National and American Leagues to really compete with each other.... I don't kid myself. That is not going to happen; that is not the road we are going to go. I am not going to introduce any legislation, not because I do not think that it should pass, but because I am a realist.[94]

Metzenbaum's comments reflected the ascendant influence of opposition to antitrust policy in the 1980s. It was a time when attempts to repeal baseball's antitrust immunity were unrealistic and ill advised in Congress. While the issue of baseball's antitrust exemption was being debated on Capitol Hill, the question was whether to extend it to other sports not whether to repeal it. The proposals to extend antitrust immunity to the other sports, with regard to franchise relocation decisions, failed to get out of committee in both the House and the Senate.

The preservation of baseball's anomaly in the 1980s was aided by a paradox in the political environment. During the efficiency regime, organized baseball felt the wrath of disgruntled fans who were highly critical of its business practices, while at the same time it benefited from the institutional and rhetorical protection of the dominant faction in the elite public policy debate over state–economy relations. This contrasts sharply with the previous three regulatory regimes in which organized baseball capitalized upon its strong support among the American people, the fans, to fend off the imperatives of the dominant regulatory philosophy of government. With the rise of the Chicago school's view of antitrust policy in the 1980s, Major League Baseball's private self-government looked at times more like a harbinger of industrial policy than a threatened regulatory anomaly.

NOTES

1. Wilson, John, *Sport, Society, and the State: Playing by the Rules* (Detroit: Wayne State University Press, 1994), p. 147.

2. Eisner, Marc Allen, *Regulatory Politics in Transition* (Baltimore: The Johns Hopkins University Press, 1993), p. 118.

3. Eisner, p. 118.

4. For a comprehensive description of the "New Left" see Lindbeck, Assar, *The Political Economy of the New Left* (New York: Harper & Row Publishers, 1977) and Reich, Charles, *The Greening of America* (New York: Random House Publishing, 1970).

5. Eisner, p. 119.

6. Eisner's regulatory regime framework in general and his societal regime in particular find parallel expression in Harris, Richard and Sidney Milkis' *The Politics of Regulatory Change: A Tale of Two Agencies* (New York: Oxford University Press, 1989). Harris and Milkis call the regulatory regime of the late 1960s and 1970s the "public lobby regime."

7. Milkis, Sidney, "The Presidency, Policy Reform, and the Rise of Administrative Politics," in Harris and Milkis (eds.), *Remaking American Politics* (San Francisco: Westview Press, 1989), p. 164.

8. The "Class of '74" refers to the liberal Democratic freshman class of congressmen that year, who distinguished themselves as reformers of legislative and administrative processes. For a comprehensive discussion of New Left reforms see, Brand, Donald, "Reformers of the 1960s and 1970s," in Harris and Milkis (eds.), *Remaking American Politics* (San Francisco: Westview Press, 1989), p. 27–51.

9. See Inglehart, Ronald, *The Silent Revolution: Changing Values and Political Styles Among Western Publics* (Princeton: Princeton University Press, 1977). Inglehart's work, although seminal, is only one example of a wide literature on the shift from materialist to postmaterialist values in advanced industrial societies.

10. By implication this means that the people who grew up in the physical and economic insecurity of the first half of the twentieth century developed materialistic values and thus focused on lower order needs, which colored their social and political perceptions.

11. See Maslow, Abraham, *Motivation and Personality* (New York: Harper & Row Publishers, 1954).

12. Wilson, p.186–187.

13. Kelly, Alfred H., Winfred A. Harbison, and Herman Belz, *The American Constitution, Its Origins and Development, Vol. II* (New York: W. W. Norton & Co., 1991), p. 488.

14. Wilson, p. 187.

15. U.S. Congress. House, Select Committee on Professional Sports, *Final Report* (H.R. Rept. No. 1786, 94th Cong., 2d Sess., 1977), p. 458.

16. U.S. Congress, House, Select Committee on Professional Sports, *Final Report* (H.R. Rept. No. 1786, 94th Cong., 2d Sess., 1977), p. 458–461.

17. For a comprehensive treatment of the history of labor relations in baseball see David Voigt, "Serfs versus Magnates," in Paul Staudohar and James Mangan (eds.), *The Business of Professional Sports* (Chicago: University of Illinois Press, 1991), p. 95–114; Leo Lowenfish and Tony Lupien, *The Imperfect Diamond* (New York: Stein & Day, 1980).

18. Quoted in Korr, Charles P., "Marvin Miller and the New Unionism in Baseball," in Paul Staudohar and James Mangan (eds.), *The Business of Professional Sports* (Chicago: University of Illinois Press, 1991), p. 116.

19. Miller, James E., *The Baseball Business: Pursuing Pennants and Profits in Baltimore* (Chapel Hill: The University of North Carolina Press, 1990), p. 13–14.

20. Quoted in Korr, p. 116.

21. Miller, J., p. 141.

22. Quoted in Lowenfish and Lupien, p. 191; J. Miller, p. 142; Zimbalist, Andrew, *Baseball and Billions: A Probing Look Into the Big Business of our National Pastime* (New York: Basic Books, 1992), p. 17.

23. Miller, Marvin, *A Whole Different Ball Game: The Sport and Business of Baseball* (New York: Carol Publishing Group, 1991), p. 6.

24. For partisan descriptions of labor/management relations in baseball from the 1960s to the 1980s see Miller, Marvin, *A Whole Different Ballgame: The Sport and Business of Baseball* (New York: Carol Publishing Group, 1991) and Kuhn, Bowie, *Hardball: The Education of a Baseball Commissioner* (New York: Times Books, 1987).

25. Korr, p. 121–123, 133.

26. Rader, Benjamin, *Baseball: A History of America's Game* (Chicago: University of Illinois Press, 1992), p. 189.

27. Miller, J., p. 143.

28. For a detailed discussion of the owner's refusal to fund the MLBPA office as well as Miller's response, see Korr, p. 122–127.

29. Rader, p. 189–191; Miller, J., p. 142–144; Korr, p. 125–128.

30. Rader, p. 190.

31. Lowenfish and Lupien, p. 206–207; Zimbalist, p. 18–19.

32. The *Flood* case is discussed extensively in Miller, M., p. 169–202.

33. Koppett, Leonard, "Reserve Clause Could Aid Management, Veeck Says," *The Sporting News* (June 27, 1970), p. 30.

34. *Flood v. Kuhn*, 309 F. Supp. 793, 797 (1970).

35. *Flood v. Kuhn*, 443 F.2d 264 (1971).

36. *Flood v. Kuhn*, 443 F.2d 269 (1971).

37. This argument is made by David Curle in "On Higher Ground: Baseball and the Rule of *Flood v. Kuhn*," *Legal References Services Quarterly* 8 (1988), p. 29–62.

38. Broeg, Bob, "Just What Prompted Flood Lawsuit?" *The Sporting News* (February 7, 1970), p. 33.

39. Rader, p. 191.

40. Quirk, James, *Pay Dirt: The Business of Professional Team Sports* (Princeton: Princeton University Press, 1992), p. 194–195.

41. Quirk, p. 195.

42. Seitz had been an arbitrator between the NBA and the NBA Players Association in the late 1960s when he helped to clarify the NBA standard contract mak-

ing it clear that players were effectively free agents after playing out their option year without a contract. The reserve clause in NBA contracts was exactly the same as Major League Baseball contracts.

43. "Baseball Reserve Clause Dealt 3rd Loss in Row," The Japan Times (March 11, 1976), p. 10.

44. Hill, James R. and William Spellman, "Professional Baseball: The Reserve Clause and Salary Structure," Industrial Relations 22, no. 1 (Winter, 1983), p. 3.

45. Hill and Spellman, p. 5.

46. U.S. Congress, House, Select Committee on Professional Sports, Professional Sports and the Law, Study (94th Cong., 2d Sess., 1976), p. 1.

47. U.S. Congress, House, Select Committee on Professional Sports, Inquiry Into Professional Sports, Hearings (94th Cong., 2d Sess., 1976), p. 348–425.

48. U.S. Congress, House, Select Committee on Professional Sports, Inquiry Into Professional Sports, Hearings (94th Cong., 2d Sess., 1976), p. 110–191.

49. U.S. Congress, House, Select Committee on Professional Sports, Final Report (H.R. Rept. No. 1786, 94th Cong., 2d Sess., 1976), p. 4.

50. Professors Jesse Markham and Paul Teplitz of the Cambridge Research Institute conducted an extensive analysis of the economics of Major League Baseball in Baseball, Economics and Public Policy (Lexington, MA: D.C. Heath & Co., 1981).

51. Brady, Dave, "Congress Aims Anti-Trust Blow at Baseball," The Sporting News (August 28, 1976), p. 8.

52. For a detailed description of the events surrounding the 1981 strike see McCormick, Robert A., "Baseball's Third Strike: The Triumph of Collective Bargaining in Professional Baseball," Vanderbilt Law Review 35 (1982), p. 1131–1169. Also see Zimbalist, p. 20–21.

53. "Baseball's New Strike—By the Fans," U.S. News & World Report (Aug. 24, 1981), p. 8. This article is representative of the types of stories in the press following the 1981 strike.

54. In 1982, Marvin Miller resigned from the MLBPA. He was replaced by former federal mediator, Kenneth Moffitt. After just one year in office Moffitt was fired by the union for failing to take aggressive stands against management. Miller resumed control of the union until Donald Fehr, the union's general counsel, was named the new executive director in 1984.

55. Jennings, Kenneth, Balls and Strikes: The Money Game in Professional Baseball (New York: Praeger Publishers, 1990), p. 67.

56. Quirk, p. 193.

57. Cited in Quirk, p. 197.

58. United States v. National Football League, 116 F. Supp. 319 (Pa., 1953).

59. Radovich v. National Football League, 352 U.S. 445 (1957). The facts of this case are discussed in chapter two.

60. For a history of the reserve clause in football see, Garvey, Edward R., "From Chattle to Employee: The Athlete's Quest For Freedom and Dignity," Annals of the American Academy of Political and Social Science 445 (September, 1979), p. 92–95.

61. Staudahar, Paul, The Sports Industry and Collective Bargaining (Ithaca: ILR Press, 1989), p. 67–68.

62. United States v. National Football League, 196 F. Supp. 445 (SDNY, 1961).

63. Public Law 87–331, *The Sports Broadcasting Act of 1961* is discussed in detail in chapter two.

64. The merger fight in Congress is described in Wilson, p. 131–132.

65. *Mackey v. NFL*, 407 F. Supp. 1000 (Minn., 1975).

66. *Mackey v. NFL*, 543 F.2d 606 (8th Cir., 1976).

67. Harris, David, *The League: The Rise and Decline of the NFL* (New York: Bantam Books, 1986), p. 184.

68. Staudahar, p. 93.

69. Freedman, Warren, *Professional Sports and Antitrust* (Westport, CT: Greenwood Press, 1987), p. 78.

70. *Washington Professional Basketball Corp. v. NBA*, 147 F. Supp. 867 (SDNY, 1956).

71. *Haywood v. NBA*, 401 U.S. 1204 (1971).

72. U.S. Congress, Senate, Committee on the Judiciary, Subcommittee on Antitrust and Monopoly, *Professional Basketball, Hearings* (92d Cong., 1st Sess., 1971).

73. U.S. Congress, Senate, Committee on the Judiciary, Subcommittee on Antitrust and Monopoly, *Professional Basketball Hearings* (93rd Cong., 1st Sess., 1972), p. 241–245.

74. *Robertson v. National Basketball Association*, 389 F. Supp. 867 (SDNY, 1975).

75. For a detailed description of the terms of this agreement see Staudahar, p. 120.

76. *NBA v. SDC Basketball Club*, 815 F.2d 562 (1987).

77. Eisner, p. 172.

78. Harris and Milkis, p. 293.

79. Of particular importance to corporate lobbyists were the reforms in rule-making procedures which guaranteed access and input for interested private parties. With their superior resources such lobbyists are able to exert disproportionate influence on the regulatory process using the very reforms intended to end such advantages.

80. Edsall, Thomas Byrne, *The New Politics of Inequality* (New York: W. W. Norton & Co., 1984), p. 107.

81. Eisner, p. 176.

82. Eisner, p. 175.

83. Edsall, p. 117.

84. Adams, Walter and James W. Brock, *Antitrust Economics on Trial: A Dialogue on the New Laissez-Faire* (Princeton: Princeton University Press, 1991), p. xi.

85. Major League Baseball's Director of Government Relations acknowledged in an interview with the author that baseball's lawyers and lobbyists, beginning in the 1980s, consciously adopted the economic arguments which condemn antitrust policy as counterproductive. Interview with Gene Callahan, conducted on 8 January 1997.

86. Eisner, Marc Allen, *Antitrust and the Triumph of Economics* (Chapel Hill: University of North Carolina Press, 1991).

87. This term refers to the general consensus on economic policy that grew out of efforts to stabilize the economy after the Depression. Keynesian economics encompassed all attempts of the state to manage the economy through macroeconomic policy.

88. The Chicago school refers to a very conservative, laissez-faire view of state-economy relations. Free markets are understood to be self-regulating and efficiency producing. This school of thought has been vigorously advocated by scholars from the University of Chicago since the 1950s. Adherents to this philosophy are considered devotees of the Chicago school whether or not they are directly associated with the University of Chicago. Conservative economist Milton Friedman is often seen as the father of this school of thought.

89. Bork, Robert, *The Antitrust Paradox: A Policy at War with Itself* (New York: Maxwell Macmillan International Publishing, 1993), p. xi.

90. The traditional, and still dominant, scholarly view of antitrust adheres to monopoly power theory. This is the view that sees antitrust as means of preserving free and fair competition in the industrial market. The social and political assumptions of antitrust are spelled out well in Estes Kefauver's *In a Few Hands: Monopoly Power in America* (New York: Pantheon Books, 1965) and Earl Latham's *Political Theory of Monopoly Power* (College Park: University of Maryland Press, 1957). The economic theory of antitrust is explained in Thomas Karier's *Beyond Competition: The Economics of Mergers and Monopoly Power* (New York: M. E. Sharpe, Inc., 1993) and Hans Thorelli's *The Federal Antitrust Policy: Origination of an American Tradition* (Baltimore: The Johns Hopkins University Press, 1954).

91. This interpretation of the legislative history of antitrust is one of the main themes in Judge Bork's work.

92. U.S. Congress, Senate, Committee on the Judiciary, *Professional Sports Antitrust Immunity, Hearings on S. 2784 and S. 2821* (97th Cong, 2d Sess., 1982); U.S. Congress, House, Committee on the Judiciary, Subcommittee on Monopolies and Commercial Law, *Antitrust Policy and Professional Sports, Hearings on H.R. 823, H.R. 3287, and H.R. 6467* (97th Cong., 1st & 2d Sess., 1982).

93. U.S. Congress, Senate, Committee on Commerce, Science and Transportation, *Professional Sports Protection Act of 1985, Hearing* (99th Cong., 1st Sess., 1985).

94. U.S. Congress, Senate, Committee on the Judiciary, *Professional Sports Antitrust Immunity, Hearings* (99th Cong., 2d Sess., 1985), p. 32.

4

The Baseball Anomaly in the 1990s

Baseball's unregulated monopoly entered the 1990s without much pressure from Congress, despite continued conflict between Major League Baseball and both the players union and the minor leagues. Legislative proposals designed to repeal baseball's exemption from antitrust laws, which routinely accompanied labor disputes between the owners and the players, had since the late 1970s been overshadowed by the issues of cable television broadcasting and franchise migration in all professional sports.[1]

Work stoppages in baseball in 1981, 1985, and 1990 were greeted by legislative proposals to repeal baseball's exemption; however, none was given more than cursory consideration. The antigovernment atmosphere in the nation was redounding to the benefit of Major League Baseball's efforts to retain its unregulated monopoly. In February 1990, a Gallup poll asked, "If there is a strike, whose side do you favor, the owners or the players?" Fifty-seven percent responded that they would favor the owners, while only 22% would favor the players.[2] Another poll, conducted in April 1990, found that 70% of those surveyed felt that baseball players were overpaid, more overpaid than players in any other major sport.[3]

In 1994, however, Major League Baseball suffered its longest and most costly player strike in its history. The strike canceled both League Championship Series and the World Series, the latter for the first time since 1904. It also resulted in spring training games with replacement players and the cancellation of the early weeks of the 1995 season. On Capitol Hill, calls for the repeal of baseball's exemption were given more serious consideration than ever before. In the previous seventy years no bills affecting baseball's exemption had ever been voted out of committee in Congress. During the 1994–1995 strike two such bills were favorably reported out of committee. As the strike wore on, public sympathies for the owners faded. In March 1995, a Gallup poll found Americans almost evenly split on retaining the exemption, and support for the owners overall had declined significantly.[4] Gradually the public came to see both sides as culpable.

Though play resumed in 1995, the final resolution of the labor dispute that led to the 1994 strike did not come until the winter of 1996, when the owners and players finally signed a new labor agreement that will take baseball into the next century without further strikes.[5] Included in the agreement was a deal between the owners and players to seek congressional repeal of certain portions of the game's antitrust exemption.

BASEBALL AND ANTITRUST POLICY RE-EMERGE IN CONGRESS

During the 1980s, Congress addressed the issue of professional sports and antitrust policy more broadly than it had previously. The baseball anomaly was taken out of the spotlight. The hot topics in the 1980s were cable television deals with sports leagues and franchise relocations. In the 1970s, the advancing technology of television had collided with professional sports. Network television revenues in all major professional sports skyrocketed. The potential of paid television, such as cable and pay-per-view, was becoming more and more clear to the owners of professional sports teams. In the 1980s this profit potential produced political outrage. Members of Congress, for example, cried foul when the NFL signed a television contract with the cable TV sports channel ESPN. Many members of Congress felt that the proliferation of such deals would result in the inaccessibility of professional sports to those without the means to purchase paid television. Senator Howard Metzenbaum (D–OH), a vigorous antitrust advocate, foe of the baseball exemption, and then chairman of the Senate Subcommittee on Antitrust, Monopolies, and Business Rights, opened a hearing on the signing of the NFL–ESPN contract saying:

We know that the NFL–ESPN contract will put $153 million in the pockets of the club owners. The question I have here today is: Will that contract increase viewership, or will it instead limit the number of games available for viewing by those who cannot afford to subscribe to ESPN? Will it be in the interest of the viewing public, or is it the first step in an effort to reduce competition and make the public pay more?[6]

Senator Metzenbaum's comments captured the feelings of many in Congress, and also provided insight into the nexus among TV, antitrust, and professional sports. The importance of television in the maintenance of the baseball anomaly, as noted in the last chapter, was cemented in the *Sports Broadcasting Act of 1961*, which exempted pooled television contracts by professional sports leagues. The effect of this legislation on baseball was to defuse contentions that television made baseball unquestionably a matter of interstate commerce and therefore subject to antitrust law. In the 1980s, with the explosion of paid TV contracts such as the NFL–ESPN contract, Senator Metzenbaum and other antitrust advocates in Congress saw their opportunity to attack antitrust immunity in professional sports. A frontal assault on baseball's exemption was impossible in the political environment of the 1980s and early 1990s. However, the issue of sports broadcasting on cable television, to the exclusion of free television, gained political salience on Capitol Hill. Metzenbaum and others in Congress used this issue to get at the question of antitrust immunity in professional sports more broadly.

At issue was whether the *Sports Broadcasting Act of 1961* covered television contracts with paid television providers. The Act states that the exemption is for sponsored telecasting of sporting events. The question was whether cable TV is sponsored telecasting. Both the Justice Department's Antitrust Division and the Federal Trade Commission, in opinions provided to the Congress, stated their belief that the 1961 Act does not cover cable television deals. Both agencies, however, also found that existing league cable contracts did not warrant action by them. The agencies' opinions gave force to the threat of congressional action on the issue of cable television deals if the leagues crossed the line. While no legislation came out of congressional hearings on this issue in 1987, many in Congress hoped that the potential for such legislation would chasten the professional sports leagues in their dealings with paid television.

By 1989, sports league contracts with paid television had proliferated to the degree that Congress once again saw fit to scare the professional sports leagues. The Senate Judiciary Committee held hearings in the fall of 1989 to discuss the possibility of explicitly subjecting sports broadcasting deals with paid television providers to the antitrust laws. Senator Metzenbaum set the tone in his opening statement of the 1989 hearings. After chronicling the exodus of major sporting events from network TV to paid TV, the senator said:

Let me make one thing clear. As long as this Senator is around, that won't happen [i.e. sports not being accessible on free TV]. Congress has some leverage here, given the favorable antitrust treatment granted to sports leagues. We will use that leverage if need be, and I want to emphasize that. We are prepared to go back and reexamine the antitrust laws with respect to both football and baseball, if necessary.[7]

Metzenbaum's harsh warnings were not new. This was the type of threat that Major League Baseball had been hearing for forty years. Once again, no legislation was produced by these hearings, but the legislators made their point. The issue of cable television contracts with professional sports leagues constitutes the only area where the Congress considered applying

antitrust law to professional sports in the 1980s. The political atmosphere
was simply too poisoned against government regulation for antitrust advocates in Congress to succeed in applying antitrust law to baseball or any
other sport.

The issue of franchise migration, activated by the National Football League's Oakland Raiders move to Los Angeles and the Colts midnight ride
out of Baltimore, also produced continued concern in Congress. The difference, however, was that on this issue Congress considered granting antitrust immunity, not revoking it. In 1982 and again in 1985, the Congress
gave considerable scrutiny, in the form of extensive hearings, to proposals
to exempt from antitrust coverage any professional sports league rules that
limit a team's ability to relocate at will. In each session of Congress in the
1980s, bills were proposed to extend such an exemption to professional
football, basketball and hockey.[8]

This trend has continued during the 1990s. The moves of the Cleveland
Browns and others have kept the heat on for legislation to curb the destructive effects of franchise relocations on communities. The franchise relocation problems in football have provided ammunition to Major League
Baseball in its defense of the exemption. In addition, the fate of the minor
leagues if the exemption is lifted has become a growing concern in the
1990s, and this has redounded to the benefit of Major League Baseball's defense of the exemption.

Just one month after Bill Clinton's 1992 presidential election, Congress
once more began an investigation of baseball's continued exemption from
antitrust law. While bills to repeal the exemption had accompanied every
work stoppage in baseball since 1981, including the 1990 lockout of spring
training, no serious consideration, such as congressional hearings, had
been given to repealing baseball's exemption. Sensing the possibility of a
shift in political winds with the election of a Democratic President, the Senate Judiciary Committee, under Senator Metzenbaum, held hearings in December 1992. This was the first time since the 1976 Select Committee on
Professional Sports that congressional hearings addressed the specific issue of baseball's antitrust exemption.[9]

One of the key witnesses at these 1992 hearings was former Baseball
Commissioner Fay Vincent. Vincent had recently been forced out of baseball. His departure from the game was due to his involvement in the settlement of the 1990 labor dispute that followed an owners lockout of the
players during spring training. The owners, stung by the recent settlement
of the collusion cases which cost them $280 million, were determined to
bring revenue-sharing and a salary cap to baseball and used a spring training lockout to force the issue. The owners claimed that they were losing
money every year, while the union countered that the owners had cooked
the books.[10] The players' refusal to consider the cap resulted in the lockout,
which delayed the opening of spring training. Commissioner Vincent then

stepped into the negotiations and eventually took the salary cap and revenue-sharing off the table, which resulted in a deal with the players.[11]

Although they endorsed the deal at the time, it was widely reported that Allan "Bud" Selig, owner of the Milwaukee Brewers, and Jerry Reinsdorf, owner of the Chicago White Sox, were unhappy with Vincent. Over the next two years Selig and Reinsdorf quietly convinced other club owners that Vincent was too pro-player, not capable of representing the owners' interests in labor negotiations. Selig was quoted as saying, "There is no doubt in my mind that the commissioner and his entire office should never again participate in labor negotiations or even labor-related matters."[12] In May 1992, Selig and Reinsdorf asked Vincent to agree to remove himself from labor matters. Vincent's refusal allowed Selig and Reinsdorf to turn sixteen other owners against Vincent, who finally resigned under pressure in September 1992. The owners then chose Milwaukee owner, Bud Selig, to be acting commissioner until a replacement for Vincent could be found.[13]

As Senator Metzenbaum opened the December 1992 hearings, baseball was without a commissioner and the owners were restructuring the office of commissioner. Convinced that a strong, independent commissioner is the key to preserving public confidence in baseball and hoping that the election of President Clinton signaled a political shift in the country, Senator Metzenbaum called the hearings in order to pressure Major League Baseball into hiring a strong, independent commissioner. The traditional justification for the exemption offered by Major League Baseball had always been that a strong independent commissioner provided effective regulation of the game in the public interest and therefore government regulation was unnecessary. The firing of Fay Vincent severely weakened this argument.

At the 1992 Senate hearing Fay Vincent testified that the exemption "is not essential either to the economic health or the legal integrity of the game." He also said that "if the owners of baseball continue on their stated course of making baseball into their business, and at the same time insist that the commissioner is their CEO to be fired at will, I would no longer support the preservation of the exemption."[14] Despite these comments, Vincent stressed that the one utility of the exemption is the ability of Major League Baseball to control franchise migration.

Although Senator Metzenbaum made continued efforts to focus the hearing on the issue of a strong and independent commissioner, senator after senator shifted the focus to the franchise migration issue and defense of the exemption in this regard. The controversy over the proposed relocation of the San Francisco Giants to St. Petersburg was fresh on the minds of many senators. Senators Hank Brown (D–CO), Arlen Specter (R–PA), Diane Feinstein (D–CA), Paul Simon (D–IL) and even Senator-elect Barbara Boxer (D–CA) all expressed concerns about franchise migration. Each emphasized that changes to baseball's exemption must not jeopardize a league's ability to control franchise migration. Franchise migration and even cable television deals were resonating with the public, but no significant public support existed for lifting baseball's antitrust exemption. It was not until the 1994 strike that Senator Metzenbaum was able to begin to sway a significant number of his colleagues on the issue of the exemption.

The 1992 hearing produced no legislation. It did, however, lay out the various positions on the exemption issue. Those who favor repeal of baseball's exemption make one or all of the following arguments. First, the exemption underwrites the artificial scarcity of franchises by allowing baseball owners to control entry into the industry, both in terms of expansion and interleague competition. In addition, the owners' ability to maintain artificial values for their franchises gives them greater leverage with their local communities with which to extract lucrative and exploitative publicly-financed stadium deals. Second, the exemption provides owners with an unfair advantage in labor negotiations, especially if the commissioner is nothing more than the owners representative. Because baseball players do not have recourse to the courts, baseball's labor disputes have resulted in more work stoppages than in all the other major professional sports combined. These arguments have been advanced by the players union, as well as by members of Congress, academics, and local officials concerned with the escalating costs borne by local communities of keeping or obtaining professional baseball franchises.

Those who oppose the repeal of the exemption do so for one or all of the following reasons. The repeal of the exemption would result in destructive franchise relocations, an argument that is supported by pointing to football's recent and widespread troubles with franchise migration. Had the NFL been immune from antitrust law, Al Davis would not have prevailed in court, and thus the string of franchise relocations in football in the 1980s and 1990s would never have occurred. Others point to the destructive effects repeal would have on the minor leagues. Without the exemption big league clubs would not be able to reserve minor leaguers in the manner they currently do. This would have the effect of reducing the incentive of big league clubs to subsidize the minors. Without the ability to hold players for at least the six years from the date of initial signing, as minor leaguers are now reserved, the majors would not be willing to spend as much on player development. Without subsidies from major league clubs, many minor leagues might fold, unable to sustain profitable enterprises in small town, small market, areas. Another argument against repeal stresses its irrelevance to labor relations in baseball, which are covered by the nation's labor laws. Arguments for retaining the exemption are routinely accompanied by predictions of excessive and frivolous litigation that would be ever more injurious to the national pastime.

Opponents of the exemption's repeal have found that their predictions of doom for the minor leagues and of chaos from franchise relocation are the most potent arguments for the exemption. The minor leagues argument has been particularly successful on Capitol Hill, where around one hundred twenty-five members have minor league teams in their districts, a large enough number to warrant the creation of the Minor League Caucus in the House of Representatives in 1993. Rep. Sherwood Boehlert (R–NY), whose district includes Cooperstown and baseball's Hall of Fame, organized the caucus in cooperation with the National Association of Professional Baseball Leagues (NAPBL).[15] The primary purpose of the caucus was and is the promotion of the interests of minor league baseball and, although Rep. Boehlert denies it, this means opposing the repeal of the antitrust exemption.

In a letter to his congressional colleagues inviting them to join the caucus, Rep. Boehlert chronicles the recent threat to the minor leagues by noting that, "Congress may consider repealing baseball's antitrust exemption, a move that could have serious consequences for the minors." Boehlert implies that the exemption's repeal could put the minor leagues in real trouble. Despite a disclaimer in the letter assuring members that involvement in the caucus "doesn't commit you to a particular stand on the antitrust exemption issue," the message was clear.[16] Of the one hundred sixty-two members of Congress who belonged to the caucus in 1996, none has publicly supported the repeal of baseball's exemption. The caucus is clearly a vehicle for organizing opposition to repeal of the exemption.

The creation of the Minor League Caucus came in the wake of House hearings into baseball's exemption held in March 1993. While the 1992 Senate hearing had exposed all the various arguments for and against the exemption, the 1993 House hearings brought the question of the minor leagues into greater focus. The witness list was largely the same as the Senate hearing in 1992. Much of the testimony was also the same. One difference, however, was the presence of testimony from a representative of the NAPBL, the governing association of the minor leagues. In the 1992 hearing the only minor league representation was a former minor league player named Roric Harrison who testified that the antitrust exemption kept him from catching on with an expansion team and kept him stuck in the minors at the pinnacle of his career.[17] NAPBL Vice President Stanley Brand represented the minors at the 1993 House hearing, arguing that repeal of the exemption would crush the minors.

While the NAPBL has generally assisted Major League Baseball in the defense of its exemption, that assistance expanded considerably in the 1990s. The NAPBL became a more sophisticated lobbying organization. Before 1991, the Association had a small staff, a limited conception of its role and was not a very professional operation.[18] Operating from their offices in Florida, they played only a minor and inconsistent role in baseball's lobbying effort in Washington.[19] In fact, in 1990, several minor league owners took it upon themselves to come to Capitol Hill during their very tense negotiations with Major League Baseball over the Professional Baseball Agreement (PBA) which governs relations between the majors and minors, and in that instance they actually lobbied against the exemption.

Major League Baseball had decided that it needed to cut expenses. Having just lost $280 million in the resolution of the collusion cases, they wanted to cut corners and the minors seemed like a good place to start. Lower subsidies to their minor league clubs would help cushion the blow of the collusion payments. But, after minor league owners met with Senator Arlen Specter (R–PA), he began calling for immediate hearings into the matter. Under pressure of threatened congressional hearings and amidst a barrage of invectives in the press from minor league owners, an agreement between the majors and minors was reached.[20] While the threat of congressional scrutiny played a part in the hastening of a settlement, it is important to note that both sides were moving toward a sensible deal independently of the political pressure.

In 1991, Stanley Brand, newly elected Vice President of the NAPBL and former General Counsel to the House of Representatives, began from his Washington, DC law office what has been a steady and sophisticated campaign in support of baseball's exemption.[21] Brand's entrance onto the scene evinces a recognition of the importance of the minors in protecting the exemption in the 1990s, as well as the desire of Major League Baseball not to have to worry about minor league owners causing trouble on Capitol Hill.

In January 1993, Major League Baseball created the post of Director of Government Relations, headquartered in the Washington DC offices of the powerful and politically connected law firm, Baker and Hostetler, which has represented the American League since the 1920s. This made baseball the only major professional sport with a full-time office in Washington. The first incumbent of this newly created office was Eugene Callahan, a Washington insider who had spent ten years as an aid to Senator Allan Dixon (D–IL). Callahan, who had close personal relationships with numerous key legislators, was a well-known and respected figure on Capitol Hill until his retirement in early 1997. Callahan's experience in the Senate complimented Brand's experience in the House.

Together Brand, Callahan and the Congressional Minor League Caucus have maintained steady pressure on members of Congress since 1993, keeping the negative consequences for minor league baseball from the repeal of the exemption on the front burner. Numerous educational opportunities for members of Congress are routinely sponsored by the NAPBL, when minor and major league owners are brought to Capitol Hill for courtesy calls on legislators. The Minor League Caucus and NAPBL also co-sponsor social events several times a year where minor league owners can spend time with legislators.[22]

Increased sophistication and coordination of baseball's lobbying effort in Washington has become more important in the 1990s because, while the public continues to side with the owners more often than not, they also continue to register their growing disgust with the business of professional sports. As recently as the 1970s, baseball seemed able to exploit the cultural significance of the national pastime in their efforts to preserve the exemption, but that significance had eroded significantly by the 1990s and, with it, the strategy. Public opinion polls in the 1990s reveal that Americans now identify football as America's game as or more often than baseball.[23] This volatility in public sentiment increased the need for vigilance in baseball's courtship of Congress.

The creation of an official Major League Baseball lobbyist position in Washington, as well as the existence of a Washington based minor league lobbyist, both unprecedented, illustrates this increased vigilance. Prior to the 1990s baseball had no such permanent lobbying presence in Washington. In the 1990s, the tag team of Stan Brand and Gene Callahan has worked tirelessly and well to preserve baseball's antitrust exemption. The creation of the Congressional Minor League Caucus is also an example of the increased sophistication and professionalism in lobbying that Major League Baseball has deemed necessary for the protection of its antitrust exemption in the unstable political environment of the 1990s.[24]

The owners' increased firepower on Capitol Hill was also made necessary by their hard-line approach to labor relations in the 1990s. In December 1992, the owners, meeting in Louisville, Kentucky, voted 15–13 to reopen the part of the collective-bargaining agreement dealing with the game's economic system. In addition to reopening the sections on free agency, salary arbitration and the minimum salary, the owners passed a resolution requiring the assent of three-quarters of the owners to initiate a lockout. Armed with data from a recently released report by the Major League Baseball Economic Study Committee, which predicted economic hard times for baseball, the owners began planning for the 1994 labor negotiations.[25] By 1993, the owners had agreed among themselves on a revenue-sharing plan that would require the imposition of a salary cap on the players. During this same time period the owners were claiming poverty on Capitol Hill. In the 1992–1993 hearings, representatives of Major League Baseball defended their restructuring of the commissioner's office—the appointment of Bud Selig as acting commissioner—as a necessary step to save the game from financial ruin.

The economic study committee report, which the owners used to justify the reopening of the collective-bargaining agreement, was not the propaganda document the owners had hoped it would be. Although the whole committee did conclude that baseball faced many serious economic problems, one member of the committee attached a supplemental statement to the report in which he strongly condemned the broad conclusions of the report. Independent committee member Henry J. Aaron, of the Brookings Institution, did not agree that baseball had any significant economic troubles. He wrote:

Through the 9,000 words of text, however, the majority report leads readers up one blind alley and down another, suggesting that an industry whose companies are valued in the market at prices as high as, or higher than, ever before is on the brink of some vague sort of economic trouble.[26]

Aaron's statement went on to say that baseball's problems were political, not economic, caused by the game's lack of a strong, independent governing structure. Instead of a powerful, objective piece of evidence supporting the owners, the report produced a powerful piece of evidence for the players union. The report's majority conclusions were drowned out by Mr. Aaron's statement, which would be liberally referred to by the players union representatives on Capitol Hill.

The owners cries of pending economic collapse were given some support by continuing disclosures from CBS and ESPN of their declining revenues from baseball broadcasts. From 1990 through 1993, the television networks made public their large losses and indicated that, when broadcast contracts with baseball were reviewed in 1994, they would not be willing to pay nearly as much.[27] Going into the 1994 player negotiations, the owners pushed their revenue-sharing and salary cap plans, earlier versions of which had been rejected by the players in 1990. They argued that changes were needed to make up for the huge losses they claimed for the last several years as a result of escalating player salaries and because of additional losses expected from decreases in television revenue.

On January 18, 1994, the owners, meeting in Fort Lauderdale, Florida, adopted a revenue-sharing plan that would distribute $58 million to low-revenue teams. Implementation of the plan required the imposition of a player salary cap. The cap, however, would not be proposed to the players until June, six months later. By March 1994, a year and a half after forcing Fay Vincent from office, the owners had still not hired a new commissioner. Incensed by the owners' failure to find a new commissioner, as well as by the structural changes made in the powers of the commissioner's office, Senator Metzenbaum scheduled a Senate Judiciary Committee hearing for St. Petersburg, Florida, on March 21, 1994, to coincide with Major League Baseball's spring training. Metzenbaum opened the hearing saying:

Today's hearing will focus on major league baseball's decision not to name a new commissioner and to destroy—and I use the word destroy advisedly—to destroy the commissioner's power to police the business of major league baseball. By reason of the new restrictions on the commissioner, the commissioner doesn't become much more than a "lackey," working for baseball, rather than the independent commissioner that we have known over the years.[28]

The effort to repeal baseball's exemption was clearly picking up steam. The St. Petersburg hearing, which was considering a bill introduced by Senator Metzenbaum to repeal the exemption, brought attention, not only to the need for a commissioner, but also to baseball's slow expansion schedule and its failure to allow the relocation of the San Francisco Giants to St. Petersburg. This had led Florida Senators Connie Mack and Bob Graham to become advocates of the exemption's repeal. Throughout the summer and fall of 1994, Major League Baseball employed several public relations strategies to divert pressures. Periodically, they leaked names of possible replacements for Vincent, including the Majority Leader of the U.S. Senate, Democrat George Mitchell of Maine. They also used the veiled promise of expansion. Senator Connie Mack (R–FL) reported to a Florida newspaper that baseball owners had issued "veiled threats" to him that Florida would not get an expansion team unless he backed off the exemption issue.[29] In the months before the March hearing baseball formed an expansion committee to look into expansion sites. It seemed no coincidence that Florida topped the list.

THE 1994–1995 PLAYER STRIKE

The 1994 season opened in April amid threats of work stoppages. On June 14, the owners finally proposed the salary cap to the players. Their plan would split revenue fifty–fifty between owners and players in exchange for payroll limitations. The owners also proposed eliminating arbitration in exchange for lowering free agent eligibility from six to four years of service, with the provision that a player's former team could match any offer through the player's sixth year of service. On July 18, the players publicly rejected the cap proposal and countered with proposals to lower the tenure requirement for arbitration to two years, eliminate restrictions on repeat free agency, and raise the minimum salary.

With the back and forth maneuverings of the players and owners being widely reported in the press, the Small Business Committee of the U.S. House of Representatives began to inquire into the business of minor league baseball. The House hearing, held July 20, 1994, was to investigate the possible negative effects that the repeal of baseball's antitrust exemption would have for the minor leagues. That such a hearing was held was a victory for Major League Baseball, because the uncertainty around the impact of the exemption's repeal on the minor leagues has in the 1990s become the most important political weapon in Major League Baseball's arsenal.

The network of minor league teams across the country has since 1993 made unprecedented efforts in support of baseball's antitrust immunity. While it is true that baseball has long enjoyed a lobbying advantage in Congress due to its vertically integrated governance structure, which makes all of the one hundred seventy minor league owners and local officials de facto baseball lobbyists, the game had never utilized this advantage in such a co-ordinated and professional way.[30] In the past, the minor league advantage remained in the background, while baseball justified its privileged legal status by citing the special nature and cultural significance of America's national pastime. Baseball's owners were able to exploit the cultural significance of the game, as well as the uncertainty of applying antitrust laws to Major League Baseball. With the erosion of baseball's special cultural significance and the rise of the players association, which dismantled the reserve clause, much of what the exemption had arguably protected had been lost. This left Major League Baseball with only two significant arguments for its exemption: to prevent franchise migration and protect to the minor leagues.

At the House hearings in July 1994, several witnesses testified about the negative effects of repealing the exemption. Stanley Brand gave what had by then become a well-worn speech. In fact, Brand, Selig, and all the other exemption defenders who had testified in Congress since 1991 were literally reading from the same script. A document entitled "Talking Points Regarding Baseball's Antitrust Exemption" had been distributed to all of Major League Baseball's defenders, including several members of Congress.[31]

The document includes six subheadings: franchise stability, preservation of the minors, governance, labor relations, expansion, and the inappropriateness of applying the antitrust laws to baseball. The script prompts baseball advocates to argue that, without the exemption:

- the Oakland Raiders precedent would become the norm in baseball;
- the minor leagues would crumble without big league subsidies for player development.

The script further prompts the reader to mention that:

- the commissioner search committee is "now actively working to identify a strong leader of unquestioned integrity";
- the exemption is irrelevant to player relations because those relations are governed by the labor laws, and the players union in baseball has gotten more than any other players union at the bargaining table;
- baseball expansion is on a par with nonexempted sports because baseball has the same number of teams as the NFL and more than the NBA and NHL; and, antitrust laws are inappropriate because sports leagues are joint ventures, single entities, whose internal rules and regulations are wholly appropriate.

Attention to the arguments of baseball's officials, lobbyists, and congressional allies makes it clear that everybody is following the same script.

The transcript of the House minor league baseball hearing in July, 1994, chaired by Rep. John Lafalce (D–NY), himself an active member of the Minor League Caucus, revealed a decided bias on the part of the committee members. In an opening statement, the chairman of the Minor League Caucus, New York Republican Rep. Sherwood Boehlert, passionately defended baseball's exemption and drew praise from many committee members—even a standing ovation from one member, California Republican, Michael Huffington. The hearing appeared to be almost a public relations event staged by the Minor League Caucus.[32]

The House hearing illustrates well the institutional advantage of Major League Baseball in defending its exemption from legislative repeal. While the Senate became embroiled in the substantive policy debate on the exemption, the House remained firmly in the grip of baseball's lobbyists, who because of the great number of minor league teams maintain much greater leverage with members in the House. U.S. Representatives also must face the voters every two years and run in districts rather than in statewide elections. This enables local interests, including minor league teams and their local supporters, to exert a greater influence in House elections than in Senate elections. This institutional advantage is further illustrated by the fact that no member of the House who has a minor league team in his district has publicly opposed the exemption.

Meanwhile, on July 27, 1994, the owners rejected the players latest proposals and, the next day, the executive committee of the players union voted unanimously to strike beginning August 12. On August 1, 1994, the owners, not happy with the players rejection of the salary cap, refused to make a scheduled payment of $7.8 million to the players' pension plan. The owners' failure to make the payment resulted in charges of unfair labor practices being filed by the players with the National Labor Relations Board (NLRB). On August 12, the strike began.

At the heart of the strike was the disagreement between the owners and players about the financial health of Major League Baseball. The owners claimed that they were losing money because player salaries were out of control due to free agency bidding wars. The competitive balance on the field was also said to be jeopardized by the continued escalation of these wars. Smaller market teams, the owners argued, were disadvantaged because they could not attract huge television deals. The players responded that the owners were lying about revenue losses, that television revenues, among other things, evinced huge profits in baseball, and that even the smaller market teams were profitable. The players union argued that revenues were in fact rising at twice the rate of player salaries.

The owners refused to open their books to public scrutiny and relied on the report of their Economic Study Commission to make the case that the game's financial health was threatened by escalating player salaries. The players, whose incomes are made public by the union, countered the owners' references to the Economic Study Committee Report with the supplemental statement of committee member Henry Aaron of the Brookings Institution. The players augmented their rhetorical weaponry in August

1994, when a study, commissioned by the Players Association, was released. Conducted by economist Roger Noll, this study found that baseball was financially healthy and that poor management, not declining viability of small market teams and decreased value of TV contracts, was to blame for its troubles.[33] Major League Baseball responded to the Noll Report with a statement that simply cited the counter conclusions of their Economic Study Committee Report. It was a standoff between the experts on both sides.[34]

As the players strike got under way in August 1994, opinion polls revealed the precarious nature of baseball in the hearts and minds of Americans. A Gallup poll conducted just days before the strike began revealed the danger of continued labor unrest in baseball. The poll found Americans disgusted with the greed of the players and the dishonesty of the owners. Two-thirds of those polled supported a cap on player salaries, and 45% to 27% said that the term "greedy" applied more to players than to owners. Half of those surveyed felt that the players' demands were unreasonable, while only 29% felt the owners demands were unreasonable. The owners, however, were not immune to public disgust. The poll also found that half of the people surveyed felt that the players were honest, while only 16% thought the owners were. In addition, the poll found that most Americans believed the players, not the owners, were bargaining in good faith. More alarming perhaps for baseball was what the poll said about Americans love of the national pastime: Less than half of those surveyed indicated that they would miss baseball at all during the strike.[35]

Selective results of this poll, as well as internal polls regularly commissioned by Major League Baseball, were publicly trumpeted by organized baseball as showing support for the owners' position on baseball's exemption. Privately, Major League Baseball was aware of the volatility of public opinion. Just days before the House Judiciary Subcommittee on Economic and Commercial Law, chaired by Democrat Jack Brooks of Texas, opened hearings on baseball's antitrust exemption in September 1994, Major League Baseball released the results of an internal poll that they would claim indicated, among other things, public support for baseball's antitrust immunity.

The September 19 press release was entitled, "Baseball Fans Reject Government Role in Players Strike." Conducted by the polling firm of Penn & Schoen, the poll found that 80% of those surveyed saw no role for government in resolving the strike. When asked if Congress should become more involved in the management of baseball, 89% of the people polled said, "no." On the question of blame for the strike, 31% found the players culpable, while only 19% blamed the owners. The poll also found strong support for the owners' proposed salary cap and revenue sharing plan. Conspicuously absent from the poll's reported results was a direct question about the antitrust exemption. Nevertheless, the poll would be marshaled by Major League Baseball in defending the exemption.[36]

When Chairman Jack Brooks opened the September 22, 1994, hearing into baseball's antitrust exemption, the labor dispute between the players and owners was being fought out in the press and the World Series had already been canceled. Brooks, a longtime foe of baseball's antitrust immunity, began with a passionate statement about the cultural significance of baseball in America. He spoke of the game's contributions in helping the nation cope with hard times and then declared that with the ongoing strike "the fabric of our national life was torn asunder." He went on to say that "the lords of the game will have to reap their bitter harvest."[37] Brooks' outrage illustrated the changing mood even in the House. Prior to the strike, baseball's exemption faced significant challenges only in the Senate. The House had been tightly controlled by baseball lobbyists.

Numerous bills repealing all or part of baseball's exemption were taken under consideration in the House in the wake of the strike. Before the strike began only two bills affecting baseball's exemption had been considered in the 103rd Congress. A bill to exclude baseball from the benefits of the *Sports Broadcasting Act*, which exempts pooled television contracting by professional sports leagues, was introduced by Republican Rep. Michael Bilirakis of Florida in March, 1993. This limited proposal for repealing baseball's exemption followed an earlier more ambitious effort in January 1993 by Bilirakis and others that had aimed at total repeal of the exemption. Neither bill was reported out of the Judiciary Committee.

After the players strike began in August 1994, however, there was a flurry of bills introduced in the House calling for the limited repeal of baseball's exemption. These included the "Baseball Fans Protection Act of 1994" (H.R. 4965), the "Baseball Fans and Community Protection Act of 1994" (H.R. 4994), and the "Major League Play Ball Act" (H.R. 5095). H.R. 4965, introduced by Democrat Rep. Major Owens of New York, called for the application of antitrust law to any term or condition unilaterally imposed by either party in the baseball labor dispute. This limited repeal was greeted with disdain on all sides. Those opposed to the exemption felt that it was not enough, while defenders of the exemption felt that acceptance of this limited repeal would jeopardize the remaining immunity in the future. Exemption opponents in the House, led by Rep. Bilirakis, introduced H.R. 4994 a week later, calling for the complete repeal of the exemption. However, while the strike had stirred up opposition to the exemption, the complete repeal was still unlikely given the activities of the Minor League Caucus in the House.

In light of this political reality, Bilirakis and the others who sponsored H.R. 4994, including baseball Hall of Famer, Republican Rep. Jim Bunning of Kentucky, amended H.R. 4994, bringing it into line with the more limited proposals for repeal.[38] At the same time in the Senate, Republican Dennis Deconcini of New Mexico introduced a bill to create a regulatory commission to oversee professional baseball and resolve disputes such as the strike. Deconcini's bill was never given serious consideration, but it did indicate the atmosphere in the Senate, where baseball's exemption was seriously threatened even before the strike.

The September 1994 hearings into baseball's antitrust immunity did not go well for Major League Baseball.[39] Members of the House Judiciary Subcommittee on Economic and Commercial Law grilled acting commissioner Bud Selig on the propriety of the exemption. Rep. Michael Synar, a principle sponsor of a bill for partial repeal of the exemption, very nearly called Selig a liar. Congressman Synar asked the acting commissioner, "Why should anyone believe what you say?" He lectured Selig for reneging on his two-year-old promise to appoint a strong commissioner.[40] There were no diversions to other issues such as franchise migration at this hearing. Players Association chief, Donald Fehr, told the committee that if Congress passed the limited repeal presently under consideration the players would return to work and fight it out in the courts.[41]

The witness list at this hearing evidenced a shift in the balance of power. Until the 1994 strike, the players union had stood alone among interest groups in advocating a repeal of the exemption.[42] Although there was plenty of expert testimony against the exemption from economists, legal scholars and political scientists, antitrust advocates such as Metzenbaum and Republican Orrin Hatch of Utah were hard pressed to generate support in Congress for repealing the exemption. Once the strike began, however, the players union was more vigorous in its campaign to end the exemption, and other groups joined in the effort for repeal.

Small organized groups of disgruntled fans began appearing in the fall of 1994, the most notable being "Sports Fans Unlimited," whose founder, Adam Kolton, accompanied by Frank Sullivan of "Fans First" and Bradley Stillman of the Consumer Federation of America, testified at the September House hearing. In cooperation with the Consumer Federation of America, which claims to represent over fifty million consumers, Kolton's and Sullivan's groups, joined also by over a dozen other fan groups across the country, conducted a national petition campaign to end the antitrust exemption. The appearance of grass roots lobbying against baseball's exemption was indicative of the increasingly precarious position of baseball's unregulated monopoly in the fall of 1994. Despite their polls showing public approval of the owners' positions, Major League Baseball was quite aware of the damage being caused by the strike.

The September 1994 hearing ended with Acting Commissioner Selig trying to object to a comment by union chief Donald Fehr. Chairman Brooks cut him off and closed the hearing with a scathing indictment of Major League Baseball. He made it clear that, when Congress reconvened in 1995, if the strike were not settled, Congress would surely act.[43] One week after the hearing, the Subcommittee on Economic and Commercial Law became the first congressional panel to vote for the repeal of part of baseball's antitrust immunity. The subcommittee's action was followed the next day by the full House Judiciary Committee, which, by voice vote, passed H.R. 4994, that would apply antitrust law to baseball's labor relations.[44]

While it appeared that both public and congressional sentiment was moving toward support for at least a partial repeal of the exemption, several factors involved in the committee approval of H.R. 4994 weighed against such an outcome. The bill passed through the Judiciary Committee by voice vote, which meant that committee members were unwilling to go on the record in support of repeal. In addition, the version of the bill voted out of committee had been considerably weakened. While it would apply antitrust laws to labor disputes, it did not include a provision, as in the original that would provide an automatic injunction against a salary cap until the settlement of any pending lawsuits. The bill approved by the committee left it to the courts to decide whether the union would have to decertify before an antitrust suit could be heard.[45] The committee action thus seemed more symbolic—a threat to Major League Baseball—and, indeed, players union chief Donald Fehr announced that his promise to return to work for the passage of legislation did not apply to this bill.[46]

The interest of the 103rd Congress in baseball's exemption was not exhausted by the House Judiciary Committee vote. Representative Pat Williams, Chairman of the House Education and Labor Subcommittee on Labor-Management Relations, who had introduced a bill that would impose binding arbitration on owners and players if no agreement were reached by February 1, 1995, held a hearing on his bill on September 29, 1994. He opened the hearing saying, "I intend, although I don't like binding arbitration, to raise legislative hell between now and spring training to see that the 1995 season goes on as scheduled."[47] Williams' hearing revealed no new information, other than that most of his colleagues were also not fans of binding arbitration. The bill was never reported out of committee.

In mid-October, after the Congress had gone home to campaign for reelection, President Bill Clinton called Bud Selig and Donald Fehr to the White House. On the same day Secretary of Labor Robert Reich appointed former Secretary of Labor W. J. Usery to mediate the dispute between the players and owners.[48] Secretary Reich called Usery the "Mr. October" of labor negotiations and predicted that the highly respected mediator would bring the two sides in baseball back together. For his part, Usery sounded a cautious tone saying that resolution of the dispute would be very difficult.[49]

Since the strike began, there had been calls for President Clinton to intervene to stop it. Fan groups, as well as some legislators, urged Clinton in September to use his executive powers, as he had in a recent railroad strike and the American Airlines flight attendant strike, in order to save the 1994 baseball season. It was hoped than Clinton would issue a sixty-day back to work order, which might salvage the World Series.[50]

Just days before the historic 1994 midterm elections, on the same day Major League Baseball was meeting in Chicago to consider proposals from groups hoping to win expansion franchises, a small band of baseball entrepreneurs headed by famed player attorney and agent Richard Moss announced the creation of the United League (UL). The UL was the first attempt to create a new league since the Continental League in 1960, which had prompted Major League Baseball's expansion. Organizers of the new league, which operated out of a Manhattan real estate office, included Moss, former Congressman from New York, Robert Mrazek, and then current member of Congress John Bryant, Democrat of Texas. Also listed among the officers of the new league was Curt Flood, whose challenge to baseball's reserve clause in 1970 was instrumental in eventually gaining free agency for the players. On November 1, 1994, the group announced six charter cities where UL teams would play: Washington, Los Angeles, New Orleans, New York, Vancouver, and San Juan, Puerto Rico. The new league was to begin play with a 156–game schedule in March 1997.[51]

It quickly became apparent that the UL, organized entirely by people with serious connections to the MLBPA, was an attempt by advocates and friends of the players association to pressure the owners into a settlement. Nevertheless, the new league regularly reported ambitious plans and received endorsements from economists, including Andrew Zimbalist, who said that it could be viable.[52] The UL organizers kept the league idea alive through the 1995 season and into the 1996 season, only folding their tent, according to organizers, after TV and stadium deals fell through in April 1996.[53] Representatives of Major League Baseball claim that the UL was never considered anything more than a bargaining tactic by the players union.

Other than the announcements coming from the UL, November 1994 in Washington was consumed with aftershocks from the congressional elections. The 1994 midterm elections transformed the partisan makeup of the House of Representatives and the Senate, both of which were captured by the Republicans, ending forty years of Democratic rule in the House. One of the victims of the Republican sweep was Texas Democratic Rep. Jack Brooks, the leading foe of baseball's exemption in the House.[54] In addition, Democrat Michael Synar of Oklahoma, a principle sponsor of H.R. 4994 was defeated for re-election. In the Senate, the retirement of Senator Howard Metzenbaum removed a principle opponent of baseball's exemption as well. Toward the end of the 103rd Congress, Senator Metzenbaum had been preoccupied with getting the Brady handgun waiting period bill passed, which he had long considered his first priority, and had not been as involved with baseball issues.

Despite these setbacks for the advocates of repealing the exemption, the election seemed to provide encouragement to both sides. With the new Republican majorities, Major League Baseball's hope of appointing Democratic Senator George Mitchell of Maine became less viable. In the Senate,

Orrin Hatch, who replaced Metzenbaum as chairman of the Senate Judiciary Committee, would himself propose a limited repeal of the exemption, but the Republican takeover put Henry Hyde of Illinois in charge of the House Judiciary Committee, and Hyde was an opponent of the exemption's repeal. He would turn back the momentum for repeal in the House Judiciary Committee that had been built up by that panel's vote in the previous Congress to lift the exemption in labor matters.[55]

During the winter of 1994, the players and owners had several negotiating sessions with Bill Usery, but no agreement was reached. On December 14, the NLRB issued a complaint against the owners for their failure to make the pension plan contribution in August. A week later, the owners declared an impasse and unilaterally imposed their final offer, a complicated system of payroll taxes and revenue-sharing that had the effect of a salary cap. On December 27, both sides filed unfair labor practices charges with the NLRB. When the NLRB made it clear that it was going to issue a complaint against the owners, alleging that the salary cap had been imposed illegally, the owners rescinded the economic system they had imposed.

Frustrated with the lack of progress, President Clinton ordered talks to resume and set a deadline of February 6 for progress on an agreement. The deadline came without progress. The President extended it by one day and called both sides to the White House for a summit of sorts. At the February 7 White House meeting, the President asked both sides to accept binding arbitration. The owners refused. Both the President's and Mr. Usery's attempts to mediate the strike were rebuffed by both sides. The President thereupon sent a proposal for binding arbitration to Congress where it was dead on arrival.

During the winter, Major League Baseball felt that it was winning the public relations war. In November, just two days before the first negotiating session with Usery as mediator, MLB put out a full page ad in *USA Today* intended to win fans over to their side.[56] Their internal polling was telling them that the players were getting the brunt of public disgust. Oakland A's General Manager, Sandy Aldersom, suggested that the union was acting with "the same institutional arrogance that proved the downfall of the owners in the '70s."[57] The objective of the owners was to break the union by bringing in replacement players for the 1995 season. Internal Major League Baseball public opinion polls at the time indicated that fans were willing to support replacement players, a conclusion backed up by independent polling data.[58]

Meanwhile, the 104th Congress, when not consumed with "Contract with America" legislation, was considering several bills aimed at either the complete or partial repeal of baseball's exemption. On the first day of the 104th Congress, Senator Daniel Patrick Moynihan, a New York Democrat, introduced a bill to repeal the exemption entirely.[59] Two weeks later, Moynihan backed off his bill and cosponsored one proposed by the new chairman of the Senate Judiciary Committee, Republican Orrin Hatch, which was a more limited repeal of the exemption to apply only to labor matters. Another bill, sponsored by Democratic Senator Patrick Leahy of Vermont and South Carolina Republican Strom Thurmond, was also proposed in the opening days of the 104th Congress and would have removed the exemption only in labor matters. It was these measures that were under consideration when the Senate Judiciary Subcommittee on Antitrust held hearings in February 1995.[60] These hearings, chaired by Senator Thurmond, provided a sounding board for frustrations with the ongoing strike. Both bills under consideration, while lifting the exemption in labor matters, would have left the exemption intact with regard to the minor leagues and franchise relocation decisions. Several senators expressed concerns that these bills would have unintended consequences.

Senator Nancy Kassebaum, Republican of Kansas, quoted a section of one of the pending bills out of context and claimed that it would alter current labor law and give an unfair advantage to the players union. Senator Arlen Specter repeatedly questioned the bill's sponsor, Hatch, about whether his bill would pertain to the current strike. Specter obstinately insisted that because no unilateral terms were imposed in the current conflict, a bill to extend antitrust coverage to such impositions was irrelevant.[61] Despite repeated reminders from Senator Hatch and Democrat Bob Graham of Florida that the owners had in the past and would likely in the future impose such unilateral terms, Senator Specter continued to assail the bill.[62]

The contrast between this hearing in the 104th Congress, where senators openly argued with each other about the merits of these limited repeals of the exemption, and similar sessions held in the previous Congress, where such bills had passed out of committee in the House, is both striking and telling. The concerns expressed by senators Specter and Kassebaum had not been raised in the 103rd Congress. Ironically, their doubts about this limited repeal came after the release of a study by the Congressional Research Service (CRS), a nonpartisan organization within the Library of Congress, which contravened nearly all of the owners arguments for retaining the exemption.

The CRS report found that baseball's exemption allows owners to declare an impasse in collective bargaining and to impose employment terms that differ from any in prior labor agreements including those that do not qualify for the narrow nonstatutory labor antitrust exemption which covers the collective bargaining process. The report further found that the owners' contention that a salary cap and revenue-sharing were the only ways to correct the problems created by inequality of resources among teams was questionable. The salary cap and revenue-sharing were said to be one option among many to solve the problem. The report also concluded that these measures imposed the "greatest share of costs on the players" and that other options would distribute the costs more evenly. The report recommended, among other things, expanding the number of franchises in large-revenue markets and using the new franchise fees to compensate the present owners for their losses. This would restore competitive balance without unfairly burdening either the players or owners.[63]

Major League Baseball responded to the report with a press release entitled, "The Fallacies of the CRS Report for Congress of January 13, 1995." The release was a hastily prepared document filled with disparaging comments about the CRS report, as well as the qualifications of its authors. While the arguments in the press release were generally without merit, they nonetheless convinced the right people. Senators Specter and Kassebaum's criticisms of Senator Hatch's bill evidenced familiarity with the arguments of Major League Baseball contained in the press release.

Enthusiasm for repealing the exemption eroded significantly with the election of the 104th Congress. Despite the fact that members from both parties can be found on both sides of this issue, it is clear that the political atmosphere was recharged with antigovernment intervention sentiment as a result of the Republican takeover of both houses of Congress. It is also clear that this sentiment, as it had throughout the 1980s, redounded to the benefit of Major League Baseball.

When the President suggested that the Congress consider legislation to subject the two sides in baseball to binding arbitration, Senate Majority Leader Robert Dole and House Speaker Newt Gingrich jointly responded, saying "[t]he President has apparently thrown the ball into Congress' court. We maintain our view that Congress is ill-suited to resolving private labor disputes."[64] This statement indicated the view of the new majority that government intervention was to be avoided wherever possible, including antitrust issues. Although the members of the Senate Judiciary Committee would vote narrowly on August 3, 1995, to approve a bill to lift baseball's exemption in labor matters while retaining it with regard to the minor leagues and franchise relocation, they did so knowing full well that the majority leader had no intention of bringing it to the floor.[65]

The suddenly sour mood toward repealing the exemption, illustrated by Senators Specter and Kassebaum, may also have been inspired by the work of Major League Baseball. From the start of the 104th Congress, Major League Baseball lobbyists stormed Capitol Hill in numbers heretofore unseen. Major League Baseball's chief lobbyist, Gene Callahan, speaking of the lobbying effort in the 104th Congress predicted that, "before our effort is over, every member of Congress will be contacted by baseball people."[66] Aided by Stan Brand and the NAPBL and an array of high priced lobbyists, many of whom were former staffers to key members of Congress, Callahan conducted a massive campaign in the first two months of the 104th Congress to save the exemption.

The success of this effort cannot be measured easily, but one member frankly admitted that he had withdrawn his support for a repeal of the exemption in return for a promise of an expansion team from Major League Baseball. In a *Washington Post* article, an aide to Virginia Senator John Warner was quoted as saying, "we were kind of bought off, if you will." The aide went on to say that Boston Red Sox owner and expansion committee chairman John Harrington had promised Warner a team in return for his withdrawal of support for repealing the exemption. The same article went on to say that Warner had joined "several Northern Virginia Members of Congress who see the baseball players' strike as a chance to score points with the owners."[67]

In March 1995, the pressure on Congress to act was diminished by the actions of the NLRB and a federal district court judge in New York. On March 27, the NLRB filed for an injunction to restore the rules of the expired labor agreement. Four days later, U.S. District Court Judge Sonia Sotomayor ruled in favor of the players and issued an injunction to restore the terms of the expired agreement. The next day the players association voted to return to work immediately.[68] The owners, disappointed by the ruling, decided that a lockout would be a public relations nightmare and allowed the players back. With the court decision, the owners released the replacement players who were poised to play in the big leagues and postponed opening day to April 26. The 1995 schedule had to be cut from 162 games to 144 games.

THE AFTERMATH OF THE STRIKE

With the return of baseball following the strike, even before the new labor agreement in which the owners and players agreed to lobby Congress for a limited repeal of the antitrust exemption in labor matters, the politics of the exemption had changed dramatically. It was the strike and the resulting loss of baseball that had fueled attempts to repeal the exemption. With the return of baseball, despite the agreement, the labor dispute lost urgency and political salience. Indeed, for the remainder of the 104th Congress there were no more hearings on the exemption's repeal and, as it had in the 1980s, attention shifted to the issue of franchise relocation in all professional sports.

In November 1995, the Senate Judiciary Subcommittee on Antitrust held a hearing on franchise relocations following the NFL's Cleveland Browns move to Baltimore, the moves of two Los Angeles teams, the Raiders and Rams, to Oakland and St. Louis respectively, and the announcement that Houston's NFL team would move to Nashville, as well as rumors of several other possible moves throughout the NFL. The NHL was also experiencing a wave of relocations, with the Quebec team moving to Denver and Minnesota to Dallas. Once again, as in the 1980s, talk of removing baseball's exemption was replaced by talk of granting limited exemptions to all sports.[69]

In January 1996, the full Senate Judiciary Committee held hearings on professional sports. While the Committee was ostensibly looking into antitrust issues and professional sports, the hearing consisted of brief references by Senator Hatch to the destructive effects of baseball's exemption amid the overwhelming concern of most members of the committee that professional sports needed a limited exemption to prevent what California Senator Diane Feinstein called franchise musical chairs. Feinstein, whose hometown San Francisco Giants were blocked by Major League Baseball in their attempt to move to Florida, told the hearing, "this game of franchise musical chairs is why I strongly believe that Major League Baseball's exemption from the antitrust laws should not be repealed and why I favor extending baseball's antitrust exemption to other major professional sports.[70] Her views were shared by the majority of the committee. Even Senator Hatch endorsed the idea of providing professional sports with antitrust protection regarding league rules on franchise migration.

Two weeks after the Senate hearing, the House Judiciary Committee held a hearing on franchise relocation legislation. As in the Senate hearing, the voices speaking out against baseball's exemption were drowned out by those calling for exemptions to prevent franchise migration in all sports. Rep. John Conyers of Michigan, spoke in vain at the hearing about his bill to remove baseball's exemption in labor matters. In an opening statement, he sarcastically reminded the members of the committee that his baseball bill, on which the committee had failed to act, was also within the jurisdiction of the committee.[71] In June, following the hearing, a bill regarding franchise migration was reported out of the House Judiciary Committee.[72]

Despite the reprieve granted by the return of the players, Major League Baseball lobbyists kept the heat on in the 104th Congress. *Roll Call*, a Capitol Hill newspaper, reported that Major League Baseball spent $630,000 lobbying Congress in the first six months of 1996, which dwarfed the efforts of the Players Association during the same time period. The MLBPA reportedly spent $196,000 during the same period.[73] Despite the continued efforts of lobbyists on all sides, the politics of the exemption in Congress was undergoing some change, much of which could be attributed to the changing fate of the exemption in the courts.

THE IMPACT OF RECENT COURT DECISIONS ON THE BASEBALL ANOMALY

Settlement of the most destructive labor strike in baseball came without a single piece of legislation being enacted into law. Indeed, only two bills affecting baseball's exemption were even voted out of committee in the 104th Congress. In the 1990s, as had been the case in the previous seven decades, it appeared that the judicial branch would have the greatest impact on the baseball anomaly. Several court decisions changed the terms of the exemption debate and contributed to Major League Baseball's eventual decision to settle the labor dispute, as well as to support a partial repeal of the exemption in labor matters.

Three decisions in the 1990s signaled the increasingly precarious position of the exemption in the courts. In *Postema v. National League*, a female umpire named Pamela Postema sued Major League Baseball after she was fired as a minor league umpire. She charged Major League Baseball with restraint of trade. In its decision, a U.S. District Court in New York ruled that, while Major League Baseball's antitrust exemption "immunizes baseball from antitrust challenges to its league structure and its reserve system," it "does not provide baseball with a blanket immunity for anticompetitive behavior in every context in which it operates."[74]

In the cases of *Piazza v. Major League Baseball* and *Butterworth v. National League of Professional Baseball Clubs*, the court decisions seemed to further limit the reach of baseball's antitrust exemption. Both of these cases resulted from an aborted sale of the San Francisco Giants. In *Piazza*, a group of investors from Tampa Bay, Florida, sought to purchase the Giants from the club's owner Bob Lurie, who decided to sell the franchise due to personal financial trouble. The two key members of the investors group were Vince Piazza and Vincent Tirendi. Piazza, the father of professional baseball player, Mike Piazza, and Tirendi are self-made millionaires from Philadelphia. Before the deal was closed Major League Baseball canceled the sale, citing the questionable character of the two principle buyers. Fred Kuhlmann, chairman of the baseball ownership committee, announced on September 10, 1992, that Piazza and Tirendi were being turned down because of the results of background checks conducted by Major League Baseball.[75]

Piazza and Tirendi sued Major League Baseball claiming that it acted illegally in frustrating their efforts to buy the Giants and move the team to Florida. They claimed that Major League Baseball had not evaluated their application to purchase the Giants in good faith and, further, that Major League Baseball had violated antitrust laws by disallowing the relocation of the Giants to Florida. Major League Baseball, in arguing for a summary judgment, claimed immunity for their decision to cancel the sale based on the game's blanket antitrust exemption. U.S. District Court Judge John R. Padova disagreed, ruling that baseball's antitrust immunity applies only to the reserve clause, not to issues of relocation.[76]

If the logic of Judge Padova's decision is broadly accepted by the legal community, then baseball's exemption is one case away from extinction. Padova's opinion held that the three historic baseball decisions, *Federal Baseball*, *Toolson*, and *Flood*, all involved attempts to obtain relief from the anticompetitive effects of baseball's reserve clause and that, therefore, the exemption is limited to the reserve clause. Major League Baseball had argued that these decisions involve broader issues and provide an exemption for the business of baseball, which includes much more than the reserve clause.

Padova relied on *Flood* in holding that the claim for a broader exemption had been eroded. Justice Harry Blackmun's opinion in *Flood* supported Padova's argument that the reserve clause was the subject of all three of these pivotal cases. Blackmun wrote, "For the third time in fifty years, the Court is asked specifically to rule that professional baseball's reserve clause is within the reach of the federal antitrust laws."[77] Judge Padova held that, even if *Federal Baseball* and *Toolson* granted a wider interpretation of the exemption, Blackmun's majority opinion in *Flood* took away any precedential value these earlier cases may have had over and above the issue of the reserve clause. Prior to *Flood*, according to Padova, lower courts were bound by "stare decisis"[78] to follow the rule and result of *Federal Baseball* and *Toolson*. In *Flood*, the court invalidated the rule of these earlier cases when it ruled that baseball was indeed interstate commerce, but upheld the results of these cases by ruling that the reserve clause is beyond the reach of federal antitrust laws. Therefore, Padova concluded that the only decisional precedent was to be found in *Flood*, and *Flood* was unquestionably limited to the reserve clause.[79]

Major League Baseball had backed up its contention that the exemption covered more than the reserve clause by citing the opinion of the Federal Appeals Court for the Seventh Circuit in the case of *Finley & Co. v. Kuhn*. In that case, the court found invalid Finley's claim that the exemption did not protect Major League Baseball from his suit challenging the commissioner's actions voiding trades of several of his players. The court ruled that "the Supreme Court intended to exempt the business of baseball, not any particular facet of that business, from federal antitrust laws."[80] Judge Padova did not share this view. In his opinion, he argued that the Seventh Circuit had misunderstood the extent to which *Flood* centered on the reserve clause.

Major League Baseball avoided the possible damage this decision could do to its unregulated monopoly by appealing it to a higher court and then settling the case out of court. The terms of the settlement are secret, but Piazza and Tirendi have stated that they were quite pleased with the deal. This, however, did not end the judicial threat to Major League Baseball's exemption, as Padova's bold interpretation was adopted by another court.

In the case of *Butterworth v. National League*, the Florida Attorney General, Robert Butterworth, pursuant to Florida antitrust law, issued antitrust civil investigatory demands against the National League in the aftermath of the aborted move of the San Francisco Giants to Florida. The Florida charges alleged that Major League Baseball had combined or conspired to restrain trade in connection with the sale and purchase of the San Francisco Giants baseball franchise.

The Florida Supreme Court ruled, in a 5–1 decision, that baseball's antitrust exemption covers only matters related to the reserve system and does not cover decisions involving the sale or location of franchises. In its ruling, which allowed the Florida attorney general to proceed with his investigation, the Florida court agreed with the court in *Piazza* that the decisions in *Federal Baseball*, *Toolson*, and *Flood* do not extend the exemption beyond the facts of those cases.[81] If *Butterworth* were appealed and heard by the Supreme Court, it may well result in the repeal of the exemption. Consequently, no appeals have been filed by Major League Baseball.

In addition to these direct assaults on the exemption, several court decisions involving labor law have had an important impact upon the exemption debate. The 1994–1995 player strike caused the most serious effort on Capitol Hill to date to repeal, at least partially, baseball's exemption from antitrust law. In the debates over these partial exemptions, opponents of even a partial repeal rebutted attempts to repeal the exemption in labor matters with claims that labor negotiations were already granted both a statutory and a court-imposed antitrust exemption, which made the repeal of baseball's exemption in labor matters irrelevant.

The statutory exemption refers to a provision of the Clayton Antitrust Act of 1914 by which the unilateral activities of labor unions were granted immunity from antitrust challenge. The provision was intended to clarify the Sherman Act, which was not intended to be used against unions. The Supreme Court extended the statutory labor exemption to qualifying terms of collective bargaining agreements in the cases of *Allen Bradley Co. v. Local Union 13, IBEW, UMW v. Pennington & Local Union 189*, and *Amalgamated Meat Cutters v. Jewel Tea Co.*[82]

In these cases the Court determined that, without extending the labor exemption to some bilateral agreements, unions would be exposed to antitrust actions in certain circumstances. Before the Court created this nonstatutory labor exemption, unions were protected from antitrust liability in their unilateral activities to achieve their demands vis-à-vis management, but they lost that protection if management agreed to their demands. That is to say, when terms went from unilateral demands to labor–management agreements, these demands were no longer unilateral union activities and therefore became subject to antitrust liability. The Court-imposed nonstatutory exemption was intended to correct this unintended result.[83]

The Court-imposed, or nonstatutory, labor exemption was first applied to professional sports in the case of *Philadelphia World Hockey Club, Inc. v. Philadelphia Hockey Club, Inc.* in 1972.[84] In this case, the World Hockey League sued the National Hockey League (NHL) for restraint of trade, arguing that the NHL reserve clause resulted in a monopoly in the hockey player market. The NHL defended its reserve clause as a product of collective bargaining and thus immune from antitrust challenge by the nonstatutory labor exemption. The application of the nonstatutory exemption required that the agreement in question be the result of union self-interest and the product of good faith bargaining. That is to say, an agreement can only be protected from antitrust challenge if it is good for the labor union and resulted from a negotiation in which both sides had meaningful input. The Court ruled that this standard had not been met in the *World Hockey League* case. Three years later, in *Robertson v. NBA*,[85] the Court struck down basketball's reserve clause, ruling that it was not entitled to the nonstatutory labor exemption for the same reasons.

In the 1976 case of *Mackey v. NFL*, a Federal Appeals Court clearly defined how the nonstatutory labor exemption applied to professional sports. In *Mackey*, the court constructed a three-part standard for applying the nonstatutory antitrust exemption for labor: (1) the provision being challenged must affect only the parties to the collective bargaining agreement; (2) the challenged provision must pertain to a mandatory subject of collective bargaining; and (3) the challenged provision must have been the result of "bona fide arm's-length bargaining."[86]

In the 1990s, three court cases were particularly important to Major League Baseball. The cases of *Powell v. NFL*,[87] *NBA v. Williams*,[88] and *Brown v. Pro Football, Inc.*[89] all dealt with the scope of the nonstatutory labor exemption; and, in all three, Federal Appeals Courts held that the imposition of terms by employers after an impasse in collective bargaining has been reached is immune from antitrust liability so long as a collective bargaining relationship between employers and a union exists. These cases essentially made baseball's antitrust exemption in labor negotiations irrelevant. By ruling that the nonstatutory labor exemption applies so widely, the courts diminished Major League Baseball's need for its exemption in labor matters, allowing them to offer it up in labor negotiations and thereby co-opt the most potent foe of the exemption, the players.

In *Powell*, the U.S. Court of Appeals for the Eighth Circuit reversed a lower court ruling that the nonstatutory labor exemption continues only until an impasse is reached. The case involved a challenge to the unilateral imposition of player restraints by the NFL after collective bargaining with the football players association broke down. The court held that this unilateral action was entitled to antitrust immunity, despite the bargaining impasse, because it still satisfied the three-part test established in *Mackey*. It affected only the owners and players in the NFL; it concerned mandatory subjects of collective bargaining; and it had resulted from bona fide arm's length bargaining.

The players association claimed that the player restrictions in question were not in compliance with the third part of the test. They were not the result of bona fide arm's length bargaining. However, the court found that, because all the player restraints imposed had been included in the 1982 collective bargaining agreement signed by both parties, they did comply with the third part of the test; and thus the restrictions were entitled to antitrust immunity so long as a collective bargaining relationship existed between the players and owners in the NFL.

In *Williams*, the U.S. Court of Appeals for the Second Circuit affirmed a lower court ruling that the nonstatutory labor exemption continues after impasse as long as a collective bargaining relationship exists between the relevant parties. The case involved the unilateral imposition of a player draft and a salary cap by the NBA after collective bargaining broke down with the basketball players association. The court found that the test for applying the nonstatutory labor exemption had been satisfied by the employment terms in this case. The salary cap and the player draft were terms previously agreed to by the players in the expired labor agreement.

Both *Williams* and *Powell* held that the exemption extends beyond impasse and that unions must decertify prior to mounting an antitrust challenge against management. Both of these cases, however, involved the unilateral imposition of terms contained in previous collective bargaining agreements. In the absence of its general antitrust exemption, Major League Baseball's unilateral imposition of a salary cap, a term that had not been a part of any previous agreement, may well have been beyond the protection of the nonstatutory labor exemption in 1995 when Congress was debating a partial repeal of the exemption in labor matters.

Brown grew out of negotiations between the NFL and the Football Players Association following the expiration of the football collective bargaining agreement in 1987. During the negotiations the NFL adopted a plan to permit each club to establish a developmental squad made up of first year players who had not been picked up by other teams. The plan required teams to pay developmental players $1,000 a week, no more, no less. The union rejected the plan and eventually an impasse was reached on the issue of the developmental squad. The NFL, then, unilaterally imposed the plan on the teams, resulting in a antitrust lawsuit filed by 235 developmental squad players against the NFL and its member teams.

The results of the *Brown* case, however, have shielded Major League Baseball's imposition of a salary cap from antitrust liability because in this case the court ruled that the nonstatutory labor exemption both extends beyond an impasse in collective bargaining and applies to the unilateral imposition of any good faith offer by either side, regardless whether that offer had been contained in a prior agreement.[90]

The effect of *Brown* on baseball's exemption is significant. *Brown* clarified that unilateral terms imposed by management need not have been included in prior labor agreements in order to be protected from antitrust challenge by the nonstatutory labor exemption. Knowing this, Major League Baseball's agreement with the players to lobby Congress for the repeal of the exemption as it relates to labor matters becomes much more understandable. The limited exemption passed in the Curt Flood Act of 1998, which both players and owners agreed to in the wake of the 1994–1995 strike, only put baseball players in the same position vis-à-vis antitrust law and labor negotiations as football, basketball and hockey players. With the *Brown* decision, all professional athletes are in a relatively weak position in this regard. With the new labor agreement, Major League Baseball has reduced the political salience of the exemption from antitrust law and, by agreeing to support a partial repeal, made all but irrelevant by the *Brown* decision, Major League Baseball co-opted the most potent force opposing its continued unregulated monopoly—namely, the players.

THE BASEBALL ANOMALY IN THE 105th CONGRESS

In the 105th Congress, in the wake of a new labor agreement that will take baseball into the twenty-first century, numerous bills were considered that would partially repeal baseball's exemption. The new labor agreement included a memorandum of understanding between the players and owners that expressed the willingness of both parties to accede to the repeal of the exemption by Congress as it pertains to labor matters. Both sides agreed to forego any lobbying efforts on Capitol Hill regarding the exemption, with the exception of support for the limited repeal, throughout the life of the new contract that expires in the year 2000 or 2001.

As the 105th Congress opened, baseball's new labor agreement had been reached in principle. While the Republicans held onto both houses of Congress, Democrat Bill Clinton was re-elected President. Most pundits agree that Clinton retained the White House by moving to the right, co-opting the Republican's smaller government theme, but his re-election nonetheless represented a retreat from the intensely antigovernment rhetoric of the previous two years.

In politics, the antigovernment mood was dampened by the shutdown of the federal government, for which the public blamed the congressional Republicans who had apparently thought that no one would miss it. In baseball, the cancellation of the World Series and the continued war of words between the owners and players softened the antigovernment bias that had led most Americans to favor keeping Congress out of baseball's governance. Increasingly, fans were receptive to government intervention.

Despite the softening of the antigovernment mood in the nation, there were few political incentives for members of Congress to repeal baseball's exemption. With the exception of the Major League Players Association, no one would be upset at continued congressional inaction.[91] Congressional zealots like Senator Howard Metzenbaum and Reps. Mike Synar and Jack Brooks were gone, and while Senator Orrin Hatch and Reps. Jim Bunning and John Conyers continued the fight, they were outnumbered and had no issue, such as a player strike, around which to rally support. The players would have no real leverage until the year 2000, when they have the power to opt out of the final year of the agreement and begin bargaining all over again. Advocates of repeal, however, saw the exit of former Senate Majority Leader Robert Dole as helping them in the 105th Congress. Dole had been instrumental in keeping the partial repeal bill, passed by the Senate Judiciary Committee in the 104th Congress, from making it to the floor. But, Dole's replacement, Trent Lott also failed to bring the bill to the floor, despite his earlier support for it.[92]

Indeed, the political equation at the outset of the 105th Congress favored Major League Baseball and inaction on the exemption issue. Although the players and owners had agreed to limit their lobbying efforts to the support of a partial repeal of the exemption in labor matters, the minor leagues were not a party to this agreement. The minor leagues have a large stake in the retention of the antitrust exemption as it relates to the control of minor league players. Without the exemption, major league teams would be unable to strictly control minor leaguers. This would reduce their incentive to subsidize minor league teams, which would result in severe economic hardships for many minor league clubs.

The minor leagues, therefore, were in the driver's seat in the 105th Congress. Their considerable lobbying muscle, represented by Stanley Brand's NAPBL and the Congressional Minor League Caucus, would enable them to control the destiny of the exemption in Congress. This gave Major League Baseball a decided advantage over the players association for two reasons. First, the minors would never support legislation that could possibly alter their subsidiary relationship with Major League Baseball; and second, the *Brown* decision had already emasculated the proposed repeal in labor matters. Therefore, as long as Major League Baseball had good relations with the minors, the activities of Stanley Brand and the NAPBL could only be helpful to Major League Baseball. The minors would either prevent any legislation or support legislation which poses no conceivable threat to the most important aspects of the exemption, namely franchise migration decisions, control of the minor leagues, and broadcasting and licensing rights.

With the end of the 1997 baseball season, the Professional Baseball Agreement (PBA) between the major and minor leagues expired. At that time the minors would seek a better deal with their senior partners. This was an important test of the relationship between Major League Baseball and the minors. The last PBA negotiations in 1990, before the arrival of Stanley Brand to the NAPBL, were not colored by the politics of the exemption. In the 1990 PBA negotiations, most observers agree, the minor leagues got a poorer deal than they already had. During the 1990 negotiations on the PBA, Major League Baseball threatened to end its affiliation with the minor leagues.[93] Knowing that without big league subsidies most of the minor league clubs would not survive, the minors had little leverage with which to oppose this, although they used the threat of lobbying against the exemption to some effect.[94]

In 1997 things were different. The NAPBL, which oversees the operation of the minor leagues, led by a new president, Mike Moore, had modernized its operations. Following the 1990 PBA negotiations with the majors, it had reformed its governance structure and reorganized its central office, expanding its activities, adding more professional staff, establishing a continuous relationship with the majors, and giving itself both the time and resources to plan. The position of vice-president occupied by Stanley Brand was created as part of this, and the highly professional lobbying association he constructed was one dimension of the general overhaul of the NAPBL. The growing political influence of the NAPBL and the Minor League Caucus in Congress had, by 1997, placed them in the position of controlling the fate of the exemption in the national legislature. The result was that the minors went into the 1997 PBA negotiations with a much stronger economic and political position than they had seven years earlier.

As the 1997 PBA negotiations drew closer, rumors circulated that Major League Baseball intended to impose a five-affiliate limit on all major league teams, resulting in the loss of many single A farm teams across the country. Representatives of Major League Baseball, as well as the Major League Players Association, have in the past complained that too much money is spent on player development. The rumored proposal did not surface in the 1997 PBA negotiations. No doubt the improved negotiating position of the minor leagues was a factor. The activities of Stanley Brand and the NAPBL, as well as the Congressional Minor League Caucus, made it very clear to Major League Baseball that an equitable PBA was in their best interests. In speaking of the 1997 PBA, Stanley Brand indicated that the new agreement would be mutually beneficial to both Minor League and Major League Baseball. Brand made clear that both sides in the 1997 PBA recognized the benefits of cooperation between the majors and the minors. Major League Baseball realized that it had a very powerful business partner in the NAPBL.[95]

The increased economic viability of independent minor leagues also factored into the bargaining position of the minors. Since 1990, independent minor leagues throughout the country have sprung up and are proving that such ventures can be profitable even in small rural markets. The most well-known of these is the Northern League whose member club the St. Paul Saints had Darryl Strawberry before selling him to the New York Yankees. These independent leagues and teams were a response to the 1990 negotiations over the PBA. The agreement mandated that every minor league team affiliated with the major leagues had to bring its stadium up to a national standard with regard to seating and facilities. The requirements were extensive and even the most minute detail was scrutinized. One requirement, for example, was that every ladies room had to have a purse rack in each stall.

These requirements proved expensive. Many communities were unable to afford them and lost their teams. Independent leagues moved into many of these communities replacing NAPBL teams, but keeping the local team names. In Elmira, New York, for example, Major League Baseball removed its affiliate because the community failed to bring the stadium up to requirements. An independent league came in and replaced the Elmira team. The team has prospered despite the loss of subsidies from Major League Baseball. These independent leagues, which include the Northern League, the Texas-Louisiana League, and as many as nine others are proving that minor league baseball can survive without the majors. A key figure in the creation of the Northern League, Mike Veeck, commenting on the economic viability of independent minor leagues said, "minor league baseball could survive without the majors, although it would require improved business management of most clubs." He went on to say, "independent leagues are very viable."[96]

Major League Baseball is aware of this increased economic viability and has taken steps to limit the ability of the minors to compete with the majors for fan dollars. Several aspects of the 1990 PBA, such as the stadium requirements, may be interpreted as attempts to limit the profitability of the minors.[97] In 1995, Major League Baseball enacted new rules allowing all professional teams to expand the territory they control. This maneuver was motivated by "the decade long growth of the minor leagues, which are attracting sell out crowds in new suburban markets."[98]

The expanded territories will limit the ability of the minors to expand when the majors expand. Speaking of the new rules, the owner of the Phillies farm club in Reading, Pennsylvania, said, "[t]here are a lot of major league owners who feel they don't want to have the competition, and there's no downside to eliminating that competition."[99] Mike Veeck, commenting on the behavior of Major League Baseball toward the minors, said, "They constantly muscle you and control your every move." When asked about specific examples of behavior by Major League Baseball intended to limit the ability of the minors to compete with big league clubs for fan dollars, Veeck said, "it's like trying to catch mercury, everything they do is subtle. They don't let us play to win."[100] In the 1997 PBA, Major League Baseball clearly recognized the importance of good relations with the minor leagues. The improved political and economic clout of the minor leagues played an important part in shaping the 1997 PBA.

Unquestionably the fate of the antitrust exemption in Congress, at least as it relates to labor negotiations, rested in the hands of the minor leagues. Their opening position, as espoused by Stanley Brand and the NAPBL, was to oppose any legislation affecting the exemption. This dogmatic stand was motivated by substantial legal concerns. Any bill crafted to end the exemption in labor matters, if not carefully written, could provide grounds for minor leaguers to challenge the exemption. Brand and his organization, recognizing their leverage initially chose the safe route of total opposition.

The agreement between the players and owners that helped end the 1994–1995 strike, which was to eliminate the exemption as it relates to labor relations between the owners and the major league players, was crafted into bill form by Senator Orrin Hatch (R–UT) and dubbed the Curt Flood Act of 1997. A companion bill in the House was proposed by Rep. John Conyers (D–MI). Hatch had attempted to craft a bill that would be acceptable to all sides, a bill worded in a way that would protect franchise migration, the minors, as well as the exemptions created in the Sports Broadcasting Act. Nevertheless, the initial language of the Curt Flood Act was unacceptable to Brand and the NAPBL. The Commissioner's office also expressed concern just days after it had approved the legislative language. In a letter from Bud Selig to Chairman Hatch, the Acting Commissioner wrote that "although the owners' Executive Council had formally approved the legislative language . . . their support was tempered by the fact that [their] business partner, the National Association of Professional Baseball Leagues (NAPBL) has concerns as to whether the proposed legislation adequately protects their interests." [101]

On June 17, 1997, just one day after Hatch received the letter from the Commissioner's office, the Senate Judiciary Committee held a hearing on the proposed Curt Flood Act. The witnesses at the hearing included Donald Fehr, executive director of the MLBPA, and a former minor league player named Dan Peltier. Stanley Brand and the NAPBL were invited to testify, but they were not informed of the hearing until just days before. Brand chose not to attend. In the absence of the minor leagues' governing association in the negotiations, the outlook for the Curt Flood Act was bleak. Until Brand and the minors could be assured that the language would suit them, no bill had a chance in the House of Representatives.

Brand and the NAPBL did counter Hatch's initial attempts to satisfy them with legislative language that would have positively carved out a statutory exemption for the minor leagues, franchise relocation, control of expansion, and even areas as obscure as umpire development. In addition, the NAPBL proposed language that would reaffirm the licensing exemptions created in the Sports Broadcasting Act. This language was, however, in the words of one of the players' lobbyists, a "nonstarter."[102] Congressional opponents to the exemption in both houses, but particularly the Senate, found this language completely unacceptable. While statutory exemptions may have had a chance in the House, where the Minor League Caucus holds sway, the Senate, whose members represent wider and more diverse constituencies, had no appetite for such legislation. Carving out these statutory exemptions was problematic for two reasons. First, there is a strong sentiment among governors and other state officials that the antitrust exemption negatively affects their ability to attract major league teams to their states. In addition, they feel that the exemption puts them at a bargaining disadvantage both with existing teams and potential teams for their states. Second, creating statutory exemptions for baseball would create great pressure to carve out similar protections for the other major sports leagues.

While statutory exemptions for a wide range of activities was a nonstarter, there was overwhelming agreement that the Curt Flood Act should place Major League Baseball players in the same labor negotiating position vis-à-vis management as other professional athletes. There was also broad agreement that the bill should in no way affect the current state of the law in the areas of franchise migration, control of expansion, the minor leagues, and broadcasting and licensing rights.

In the area of licensing rights the language of the bill was particularly controversial because of an ongoing antitrust lawsuit filed by George Steinbrenner and the New York Yankees. Steinbrenner sued Major League Baseball for restraint of trade. The Yankee, owner had made an independent marketing agreement with the sports apparel manufacturer *Adidas*. The ten-year deal was worth more than $90 million. In the negotiations over the Curt Flood Act all sides wanted to prevent creating an advantage for one side or the other in the pending *Adidas* litigation.

The sticking points in the negotiations over the bill were purely matters of wording. The minor leagues and their business partner, Major League Baseball, needed to be absolutely sure that the language of the bill did not unintentionally create a cause of action for minor league players under the antitrust laws. Any word vulnerable to misinterpretation by the courts was thoroughly vetted by attorneys on all sides. One particular phrase raised a red flag in the mind of House Judiciary General Counsel, Alan Coffey. Coffey believed that the language of the bill, which was intended to lift the exemption in labor matters but leave it with regard to franchise relocations and the minor leagues, was unclear and may in fact have jeopardized league rules on franchise relocations as well as the minor leagues.[103]

At issue for Coffey was the phrase "applicability or nonapplicability." In both the Senate and House versions of the bill, the following language was meant to exclude issues relating to franchise relocation, the minor leagues, and licensing agreements from the effects of the legislation:

Nothing in this section shall be construed to affect—(1) the **applicability or nonapplicability** of the antitrust laws to professional baseball's amateur draft, the minor league reserve clause, the professional baseball agreement, or any other matter relating to the minor leagues; (2) the **applicability or nonapplicability** of the antitrust laws to any restraint by professional baseball on franchise relocation; or (3) the application of Public Law 87–331 (commonly known as the Sports Broadcasting Act of 1961) (emphasis in original).[104]

Coffey contended that this phrase is subject to interpretation by the courts and that it could be interpreted to include subjecting franchise relocation and the minor leagues to antitrust liability. The sponsors of this language contended that the phrase in fact protected against the very interpretation about which Coffey was worried. Leaving aside the merits of Coffey's argument, it is clear that his doubts fueled the fire being ignited on Capitol Hill by minor league baseball lobbyists in their efforts to avoid legislation that would threaten their economic wellbeing.

This problematic phrase was finally removed in the fifth and final version of the Curt Flood Act and replaced with explicit, unambiguous language stating that the Act would have NO impact on the current state of the law in these vital areas. Another demand of the minor leagues was a more limited definition of "standing" than the one provided for in current antitrust law. This was important to Brand and the NAPBL because under the default standing clause many believe that there was room for minor league players to file an antitrust suit.

The Curt Flood Act of 1998 was signed into law by President Clinton just days before the 1998 midterm congressional elections. The players, owners, and the minor leagues were all quite happy with the finished product. The players believe that the availability of antitrust lawsuits, despite the need for the players union to decertify to take advantage of it, will enhance the players' bargaining position in the next labor negotiations. The owners are satisfied because they are convinced that the *Brown* case makes the threat of antitrust litigation in labor matters all but mute. In addition, the owners benefit from the settlement by effectively co-opting their most potent foes on the antitrust issue, the players. Without opposition from the players or the minor leagues, the two most politically powerful threats to Major League Baseball's unique regulatory status are neutralized.

Despite its apparently secure political position, Major League Baseball's monopoly faces uncertainty in the courts where jurists are increasingly articulating limits on the game's special privileges. In addition, it is not at all clear that the nation is willing to view baseball as the national pastime any more. Most polls indicate that the NFL occupies the most cherished place in the hearts of American sports fans today. In other words, while the barons of baseball are succeeding in the political defense of their terrain, they are losing ground on the institutional and ideological fronts where the courts, the Congress, and the country are increasingly willing to reconsider their situation.

NOTES

1. Only a handful of bills were proposed in the 1980s which would have repealed baseball's antitrust immunity. None of these was ever given serious consideration.

2. Hueber, Graham, "Majority Expects Baseball Strike and Would Side with Owners," *The Gallup Poll Monthly* (February 1990), p. 37.

3. Newport, Frank and Linda DeStefano, "Football Top Sport Among Fans; Basketball Gains Support," *The Gallup Poll Monthly* (April 1990), p. 19.

4. Moore, David, "Most Fans Support Replacement Players," *The Gallup Poll Monthly* (March 1995), p. 39–48.

5. The strike actually ended on March 31, 1995, when the terms of the previous labor agreement were reinstated by a court injunction. However, the new labor pact was not agreed to until January, 1997.

6. U.S. Congress, Senate, Committee on the Judiciary, Subcommittee on Antitrust, Monopolies, and Business Rights, *Antitrust Implications of the recent NFL Television Contract, Hearings* (100th Cong., 1st Sess., 1987), p. 2.

7. U.S. Congress, Senate, Committee on the Judiciary, Subcommittee on Antitrust, Monopolies, and Business Rights, *Sports Programming and Cable Television, Hearings* (101st Cong., 1st Sess., 1989), p. 3.

8. Congressional interest in franchise relocations in the 1980s are discussed in chapter two.

9. U.S. Congress, Senate, Committee on the Judiciary, Subcommittee on Antitrust, Monopolies, and Business Rights, *Baseball's Antitrust Immunity, Hearings* (102nd Cong., 2d Sess., 1992).

10. Chass, Murray, "Chill of Labor Impasse Threatens Baseball's Spring," *The New York Times* (Feb. 9, 1990), p. A1, A26; "Myths Surround Negotiations," *The New York Times* (Feb. 12, 1990), p. C2.

11. Staudohar, Paul D., "Baseball Labor Relations: The Lockout of 1990," *Monthly Labor Review* (October, 1990), p. 32–36.

12. Chass, Murray, "Diamond Business," *Athlon Baseball* (1995), p. 76.

13. Selig was officially the chairman of the executive council, but was for all practical purposes "acting" commissioner. Selig became the commissioner officially on July 9, 1998.

14. U.S. Congress, Senate, Committee on the Judiciary, Subcommittee on Antitrust, Monopolies, and Business Rights, *Baseball's Antitrust Immunity, Hearings* (102nd Cong., 2d Sess., 1992), p. 4–5.

15. Boehlert's up-state New York district includes three minor league teams as well as the Baseball Hall of Fame.

16. The quotations come from a "Dear Colleague" letter to Members of the House dated Feb. 1, 1995.

17. U.S. Congress, Senate, Committee on the Judiciary, Subcommittee on Antitrust, Monopolies, and Business Rights, *Baseball's Antitrust Immunity, Hearings* (102nd Cong., 2d Sess., 1992), p. 405–408.

18. Shapiro, Paul W., "Monopsony Means Never Having To Say You're Sorry—A Look At Baseball's Minor Leagues," *Journal of Contemporary Law* 4 (1978), p. 191–209.

19. The NAPBL was founded in 1901 as the governing body of the affiliated minor leagues. The association's headquarters have moved periodically. Initially the NAPBL offices were in Auburn, New York. In 1932, the offices moved to Durham, North Carolina. In 1947, the offices moved to Columbus, Ohio and in 1973 the NAPBL offices moved to their present city, St. Petersburg, Florida.

20. The 1990 PBA negotiations are discussed in Zimbalist, Andrew, *Baseball and Billions* (New York: Basic Books, 1992), p. 113–116. The lobbying efforts of the NAPBL are discussed in a document prepared by the Major League Baseball Players Association entitled "Baseball's Antitrust Exemption—A Resource Book" (1992), p. 22–23; Madden, Bill, "Baseball; Grass Roots Chaos," *The Sporting News* (Dec. 3, 1990), p. 44.

21. It is noteworthy that Brand was not affiliated with the NAPBL in 1990 when several minor league owners challenged the exemption. Of that effort Brand simply says that they were a small number of recalcitrant owners acting without NAPBL approval.

22. Interview with Stanley Brand, Vice President, National Association of Professional Baseball Leagues, 8 January 1997.

23. Gallup, George Jr. and Frank Newport, "Football Remains America's Number One Spectator Sport," *The Gallup Poll Monthly* (October 1992), p. 36–38.

24. Interview with Eugene Callahan, Major League Baseball (MLB) Director of Government Relations, 9 January 1997. Mr. Callahan retired from this position February 1, 1997. As of this writing no replacement has been named.

25. The Economic Study Committee was commissioned during the 1990 collective bargaining process. In the labor agreement of 1990, the committee was created to determine the actual financial heath of baseball, in order that the exaggerated claims of both sides would be minimized in the next labor agreement negotiations. See also Baldo, Anthony et al., "Secrets of the Front Office: What America's Pro Teams are Worth," *Financial World* (July 9, 1991), p. 28–43.

26. Statement of Henry J. Aaron, attached to the Major League Baseball Economic Study Committee Report issued December 3, 1992, p.10.

27. Many commentators argue that the networks' claims of huge losses are nothing more than posturing designed to elicit more favorable deals in the future. See Zimbalist, p. 160–162.

28. U.S. Congress, Senate, Committee on the Judiciary, Subcommittee on Antitrust, Monopolies, and Business Rights, *Professional Baseball Teams and the Antitrust Laws, Hearings* (103rd Cong., 2d Sess., 1994), p. 1.

29. Dahl, David, "Baseball Owners Dealt Blow By Panel," *St. Petersburg Times* (September 30, 1994), p. 1C.

30. Discussion of baseball's lobbying advantage resulting from its vertically integrated governance structure can be found in Ellig, Jerome R., "Law, Economics, and Organized Baseball: Analysis of a Cooperative Venture" (Ph.D. Dissertation, George Mason University, 1987), p. 41–62.

31. The author was provided with copies of these "talking points" by Stanley Brand (NAPBL), Gene Callahan (MLB), and Congressman Sherwood Boehlert (R–NY).

32. U.S. Congress, House, Committee on Small Business, *The Key Issues Confronting Minor League Baseball, Hearings* (103rd Cong., 2d Sess., 1994).

33. Noll, Roger, "Baseball Economics in the 1990s: A Report to the Major League Baseball Players Association" (August 1994).

34. A copy of a document entitled "Response Prepared by MLB to Roger Noll Analysis" was provided to the author by the Congressional Research Service (CRS). The document's author was not cited, and it was undated.

35. McAneny, Leslie and Lydia Saad, "With Popularity on the Upswing, Baseball Strikes Out," *The Gallup Poll Monthly* (August 1994), p. 28–31.

36. The Penn & Schoen poll was conducted on September 13–14, 1994. The results were included in a September 19, 1994, press release of Major League Baseball. The author made repeated attempts to obtain this and other poll data directly from Penn & Schoen, but access to the data was not provided.

37. U.S. Congress, House. Committee on the Judiciary, Subcommittee on Economic and Commercial Law, *Baseball's Antitrust Exemption (Part 2), Hearings* (103rd Cong., 2d Sess., 1994), p. 1.

38. Michael Synar (D–OK) and Major Owens (D–NY) were the other cosponsors of H.R 4994.

39. Vecsey, George, "The Owners Strike Out On Hill, Too," *The New York Times* (September 23, 1994), p. B9.

40. Hosansky, David, "Baseball's Antitrust Exemption Draws Fire in Congress," *Congressional Quarterly Weekly Report* (September 24, 1994), p. 2673.

41. U.S. Congress, Senate, Committee on the Judiciary, Subcommittee on Economic and Commercial Law, *Baseball's Antitrust Exemption (Part 2), Hearings* (103rd Cong. 2d Sess., 1994), p. 172–174.

42. The exception was the brief time in 1990, when a small group of minor league owners were temporarily against the exemption.

43. U.S. Congress, Senate, Committee on the Judiciary, Subcommittee on Economic and Commercial Law, *Baseball's Antitrust Exemption (Part 2), Hearings* (103rd Cong. 2d Sess., 1994), p. 177–178.

44. Dahl, David, "Baseball Owners Dealt Blow By Panel," *St. Petersburg Times* (September 30, 1994), p. 1C, 4C.

45. Decertification means that a labor union disqualifies itself from acting as a collective bargaining agent for its members. In effect, it constitutes the elimination of the union. To decertify, a union must file a petition with the NLRB, then hold a decertification election among its members. Decertification requires that a majority of union members vote to dissolve the union.

46. Thomas, Jennifer, "Subcommittee Backs Anti-exemption Bill," *St. Petersburg Times* (September 28, 1994), p. 9C.

47. U.S. Congress, House, Committee on Education and Labor, Subcommittee on Labor–Management Relations, *The Impact on Collective Bargaining of the Antitrust Exemption: H.R. 5095, Major League Play Ball Act of 1995, Hearings* (103rd Cong., 2d Sess., 1994), p. 2.

48. Usery had served as the Secretary of Labor in the Ford Administration.

49. Neikirk, William and James Warren, "Labor's 'Mr. October' new hope for baseball," *Chicago Tribune* (October 15, 1994), p. 2.

50. Johnson, Chuck, "Fans ask Clinton to help save season," *USA Today* (September 8, 1994), p. 12C.

51. Loverto, Thorn, "United, it waits: New baseball league passes on the 1996 season, plans for 1997," *The Washington Times* (February 29, 1996), p. C1.

52. Shapiro, Leonard, "New Baseball League Still Lacking Owners, Players, Stadiums," *The Washington Post* (May 23, 1995), p. E1, E6.

53. Shuster, Rachel, "League Folds," *USA Today* (April 12, 1996), p. B1.

54. Brooks' defeat cannot be attributed to his position on baseball's exemption. There is no record of his opponent raising the exemption issue during the campaign.

55. Dodd, Mike, "Election results encourage both sides on antitrust issue," *USA Today* (November 11, 1994), p. 7C.

56. "Baseball in the Twenty-First Century: Still Accessible, Affordable, and Competitive," *USA Today* (November 9, 1994), p. 9C.

57. Gammons, Peter, "The big picture escapes small minds," *The Boston Sunday Globe* (February 12, 1995), p. 83.

58. Moore, David W., "Most Baseball Fans Support Replacement Players," *The Gallup Poll Monthly* (March 1995), p. 39–41.

59. *National Pastime Preservation Act of 1995*, S. 15 (104th Cong., 1st Sess., 1995).

60. U.S. Congress, Senate, Committee on the Judiciary, Subcommittee on Antitrust, Business Rights, and Competition, *The Court-Imposed Major League Baseball Antitrust Exemption, Hearings* (104th Cong., 1st Sess., 1995).

61. Senator Hatch's proposed bill, S. 415, would have allowed the players to file antitrust suits if the owners unilaterally imposed conditions other than those of the expired labor agreement.

62. U.S. Congress, Senate, Committee on the Judiciary, Subcommittee on Antitrust, Business Rights, and Competition, *The Court-Imposed Major League Baseball Antitrust Exemption, Hearings* (104th Cong., 1st Sess., 1995), p. 6, 11–14.

63. Zimmerman, Dennis and William Cox, "The Baseball Strike and Federal Policy: An Economic Analysis," *CRS Report for Congress* (January 13, 1995), p. 20–21.

64. Quoted in Guarisco, John W., "Buy Me Some Peanuts And Crackerjacks, But You Can't Buy The Team: The Scope And Future Of Baseball's Antitrust Exemption," *University of Illinois Law Review* 1994:3 (1994), p. 682.

65. U.S. Congress, Senate, Committee on the Judiciary, *Major League Baseball Reform Act of 1995* (Rept. No. 104–231, 104th Cong., 2d Sess., 1996), p. 4.

66. Chass, Murray, "Halls of Congress Fill With New Lobbyists," *The New York Times* (January 8, 1995), p. 10.

67. Lipton, Eric and Mark Maske, "Aide Says Warner Cut Deal for Baseball Team," *The Washington Post* (February 23, 1995), p. B1.

68. Whiteside, Larry, "After injunction, major leaguers vote to play ball," *The Boston Globe* (April 1, 1995), p. 1.

69. U.S. Congress, Senate, Committee on the Judiciary, Subcommittee on Antitrust, Business Rights, and Competition, *Antitrust Issues In Relocation of Professional Sports Franchises, Hearings* (104th Cong., 1st Sess., 1995).

70. U.S. Congress, Senate, Committee on the Judiciary, *Professional Sports: The Challenges Facing the Future of the Industry, Hearings* (104th Cong., 2d Sess., 1996), p. 9.

71. U.S. Congress, House, Committee on the Judiciary, *Professional Sports Franchise Relocation: Antitrust Implications, Hearings* (104th Cong., 2d Sess., 1996), p. 3.

72. U.S. Congress, House, Committee on the Judiciary, *Fan Freedom and Community Protection Act of 1996* (H.R. Rept. No. 104–656, 104th Cong., 2d Sess., 1996).

73. Henry, Ed, "Baseball Lobbying Hits Major League on Hill," *Roll Call* (October 21, 1996), p. 15.

74. *Postema v. National League of Professional Baseball Clubs*, 799 F. Supp. 1475 (S.D.N.Y. 1992).

75. Vick, Karl, "Vince Piazza still trying to make a name for himself in baseball," *St. Petersburg Times* (March 20, 1994), p. 8A.

76. *Piazza v. Major League Baseball*, 831 F. Supp. 420 (E.D. Pa. 1993).

77. *Flood v. Kuhn*, 407 U.S. 258 (1972).

78. Latin for "let the decision stand," this term refers to the judiciary's policy of relying on precedent whenever possible. By so doing the court's legitimacy is enhanced by the law's predictability.

79. Gould, Mark T. "Baseball's Antitrust Exemption: The Pitch Gets Closer and Closer," *Seton Hall Journal of Sport Law* 5 (1995), p. 273–289.

80. Quoted in Guarisco, John W., "Buy Me Some Peanuts And Crackerjacks, But You Can't Buy The Team: The Scope And Future Of Baseball's Antitrust Exemption," *University of Illinois Law Review* 1994:3 (1994), p. 659.

81. *Butterworth v. National League of Professional Baseball Clubs*, 644 So. 2d 1021 (Fla. 1994). See also *Morsani v. Major League Baseball*, 1995 Fla. App. Lexis 10391 (Fla. 2d DCA 1995). This court followed the rationale of *Butterworth* in reinstating

state antitrust claims. But see *New Orleans Pelicans Baseball, Inc. v. NAPBL*, No. 93–253, 1994 WL 631144 (U.S.D.C., E.D. La. Mar. 1, 1994). This court rejected *Piazza*, granting summary judgment based on the existence of the antitrust exemption.

82. *Allen Bradley Co. v. Local Union 13, IBEW*, 325 U.S. 797 (1945); *UMW v. Pennington & Local Union 189*, 381 U.S. 657 (1965); *Amalgamated Meat Cutters v. Jewel Tea Co.*, 381 U.S. 676 (1965).

83. Closius, Philip J., "Professional Sports and Antitrust Law: The Ground Rules of Immunity, Exemption, and Liability," in Johnson, Arthur T. and James Frey's (eds.), *Government and Sport: The Public Policy Issues* (USA: Rowman & Allanheld Publishers, 1985), p. 140–158.

84. *Philadelphia World Hockey Club, Inc. v. Philadelphia Hockey Club, Inc.*, 351 F. Supp. 462 (E.D. Pa. 1972).

85. *Robertson v. NBA*, 389 F. Supp. 867 (S.D.N.Y. 1975).

86. Quoted in Closius, p. 144.

87. *Powell v. NFL*, 678 F. Supp. 777, 788–89 (D. Minn. 1988), rev'd, 930 F. 2d 1293 (8th Cir. 1989), cert. denied, 498 U.S. 1040 (1991).

88. *NBA v. Williams*, 857 F. Supp. 1069 (S.D.N.Y. 1994), aff'd, 45 F. 3d 684 (2d Cir. 1995).

89. *Brown v. Pro Football, Inc.*, 787 F. Supp. 125, 130 (D.D.C. 1991), rev'd 50 F. 3d 1041 (D.C. Cir. 1995), 518 U.S. 231 (1996).

90. The judgment of whether the term in question is indeed a "good faith" offer is subject to adjudication by the NLRB and ultimately the courts.

91. During the strike numerous fan groups formed to protest the ongoing strike. These groups became vigorous supporters of the repeal of the antitrust exemption. However, with the settlement of the strike, these groups have lost most of their momentum and do not figure to be prominent in the congressional debates on the partial repeal of the exemption in the 105th Congress.

92. Henry, Ed, "Baseball Lobbying Hits Major League on Hill," *Roll Call* (October, 1996), p. 1, 15.

93. Chass, Murray, "With the Minors," *The New York Times* (December 3, 1990), p. C2.

94. Smith, Claire, "Major-Minor Rift Going Legal Route," *The New York Times* (November 26, 1990), p. C2.

95. Interview with Stanley Brand on October 31, 1998.

96. Telephone Interview with Mike Veeck, Owner, Charleston River Dogs Minor League Baseball Team, 19 March 1997.

97. It is only fair to note that this interpretation of the 1990 PBA is not universally shared. Many argue that while the effect of measures such as stadium upgrading was to limit profitability, the intention was to improve facilities for both players and fans. Furthermore, the 1990 PBA allowed Major League Baseball to market minor league merchandise, which expanded profits, as well as visibility, for the minors.

98. Fatsis, Stefan, "Major Leagues Keep Minors at a Distance," *The Wall Street Journal* (November 9, 1995), p. B1, B9.

99. Fatsis, p. B1.

100. Telephone interview with Mike Veeck, Owner, Charleston River Dogs Minor League Baseball Team, 19 March 1997.

101. Quoted in Senate Judiciary Committee Report 118–105.

102. Telephone interview with Marken Erickson of McGuiness & Holch, lobbyists for the Players Association. (December 2, 1998).

103. Telephone Interview with Alan Coffey, General Counsel to the House Judiciary Committee, 16 January 1997.

104. H.R. 21, "The Baseball Fans and Community Protection Act of 1997" was introduced by Rep. John Conyers on January 6, 1997.

Conclusion—The Future of the Baseball Anomaly

Major League Baseball's singular enjoyment of freedom from government regulation cannot be attributed to isolated causal factors. The persistence of baseball's unregulated monopoly is not a mere historical accident originating in judicial sentimentality and persisting due to the rules of precedent. Nor can baseball's paradoxical status be explained as simply the result of interest group politics as usual. However, while the cultural significance of the national pastime has surely played a large part in its unusual treatment by the government, the mere evolution of the game in the minds of Americans is not in itself sufficient to explain this regulatory anomaly. The unique place of the business of baseball in America—its regulatory anomaly—is a function of the game's historical development as encased in the interplay of institutions and ideas, as well as politics. This anomaly has been maintained through a succession of political environments with distinct institutional, ideological, and political characteristics, and a fuller understanding of it is gained by focusing on these changing regulatory regimes.

The developing national institutions of the Progressive Era together with Victorian values, gave birth to the baseball anomaly. The Depression and World War II brought with them a distinct regulatory environment with which baseball's anomaly at first seemed consistent, only to be ignored later amid more pressing concerns. The 1960s and 1970s brought dissensus to American regulatory politics, but baseball's unregulated monopoly weathered the period, albeit with difficulty. The 1980s and early 1990s were a period of antigovernment politics. Governmental excesses of previous decades were decried and actions taken to reduce the size of the public sector. A conservative politics, with a laissez-faire attitude about government regulation, provided Major League Baseball with some respite from the assault on its unregulated monopoly.

The player strike of 1994–1995 signaled the end of baseball's reign as America's national pastime. Public disgust with the business of baseball reached unprecedented levels as a consequence of the game's ninth work stoppage in twenty years. Numerous surveys illustrated Americans' disgust with the game as the cultural pedestal on which baseball had rested for a century toppled. The political and legal ground beneath baseball's anomaly was crumbling as well. The Congress finally eliminated a piece of the exemption and the courts have also shown increasing willingness to threaten the exemption. In addition, the advent of the twenty-first century and the Information Age is transforming industry worldwide, and the globalization of markets promises to have a profound impact on American industrial policy, including antitrust policy. As the century draws to a close antitrust law is being put to the test by several megamergers, as well as an antitrust action against the world's largest computer software company, Microsoft. While the outcome of the Microsoft case is still in question, it is fair to say that antitrust policy faces extreme challenges in the dawning Information Age.

THE BASEBALL ANOMALY IN THE
TWENTY-FIRST CENTURY

One of the most salient features of the coming century will undoubtedly be the globalization of economic markets of all kinds. Baseball will not be an exception to this. The internationalization of baseball is already under way. In North America, Major League Baseball has expanded to Canada and there is talk about expansion teams from Latin America joining the big leagues. Professional baseball exists in numerous foreign countries such as Mexico, Venezuela, the Dominican Republic, Australia, as well as the Far East. The popularity of baseball in the Far East rivals that in the United States. Professional baseball leagues exist in Japan, Korea and Taiwan.

It is unclear how the internationalization of baseball will affect the unregulated monopoly of Major League Baseball. However, the recent controversy over the signing of foreign free agents not subject to the draft is certainly one example of the type of issues baseball will face in the coming years. The popularity of baseball worldwide means that players are increasingly recruited from other countries. The problem with this is that the player draft only includes players from the United States and Puerto Rico. If the draft is not expanded to international talent, then wealthy owners could clean up on the international free agent market. The result would be an even further erosion of competitiveness in Major League Baseball.

The issue of antitrust law becomes severely muddled when the world economy is considered. The assault in the United States on antitrust policy by devotees of the Chicago school approach to economic regulation could cut both ways in an increasingly global economy. Conservative commentators argue that American industries must be allowed to cooperate in order to compete with foreign companies that are not hamstrung by domestic antitrust laws. On the other hand, the advantage of foreign competitors is often the result of government subsidies and state-sponsored monopolies intended to bolster the national economy. The existence of state-sponsored monopolies in Japan and elsewhere may push American trade policy in the opposite direction. Instead of merely unburdening businesses from antitrust law, a return to the associationalism of the 1920s might be in order for the purpose of steering American industry through the maze of international competition.

The issue of worldwide antitrust and trade policy is one of the most hotly debated topics in international relations today.[1] In the United States, the conflict between internal fairness and external competitiveness in the global market continues to be a dilemma. In baseball, the most likely potential international competitor for Major League Baseball is Japan, where baseball has become a national obsession, if not the national pastime. But several recent developments in Japanese baseball indicate that they will not be able to exploit non-western trade policy in order to cut into the American baseball market.

Antitrust policy is a western invention that does not fit easily with Asian social and cultural norms. In Japan, antitrust law was imposed on the country by its American occupiers after World War II. The imperial government of prewar Japan had a long history of state control of the economy. Traditionally, the Japanese government promoted and managed key industries and then turned them over to private firms to run. This practice was seen as necessary in order to protect the viability of Japanese businesses. Because the tiny island nation lacks the natural resources to be self-sufficient, it has been forced to rely on international trade in order to provide its citizens with basic necessities.

This external reliance has traditionally prompted the Japanese government to prop up its industries through government subsidies and state-sponsored monopolies. The imposition of western concepts of antitrust conflicted with this established practice, and although Japan continues to have antitrust laws on the books, enforcement is selective at best. Japan continues to exempt certain industries from the antitrust laws in order to assist Japanese industries in being competitive on the global market.

Professional baseball in Japan has operated free from the strictures of antitrust regulation since its inception in the 1930s. The Japanese government has never enforced the antitrust laws against the two professional baseball leagues in the country. Japan's Central and Pacific Leagues operate very much like the American and National Leagues with respect to policies that might be considered restraints of trade. The freedom of Japanese baseball owners to skirt antitrust laws in Japan seems to indicate that Japanese baseball could in the future cut into the American baseball market by utilizing its competitive advantages, especially with government subsidies. Recent developments in Japanese baseball, however, might mitigate against this scenario.[2]

Although Japanese culture leads players to subordinate themselves to the needs and good of the team, the ability of Japanese baseball owners to use this cultural affinity to run a disciplined cartel has diminished in recent years. Japan is often recognized as a nation that has been successful in importing American technologies and industrial methods without allowing American cultural and social norms to erode Japanese traditions. In fact, their ability to import western methods while retaining Japanese philosophies of individual subordination have been crucial to Japan's ability to become a major player in international trade. Baseball, however, has been a bit different.

To bolster the business of baseball, the Japanese imported more than the game. They also brought over many of the players. American players in Japan have greatly raised the profile of baseball in that country and they have also raised the level of play. One of the unintended consequences of importing American players, however, has been an erosion of traditional Japanese attitudes about the balance between individualism and team play. Japanese players, seeing the Americans come to Japan and earn five times the salary of Japanese players, are becoming more concerned with getting their fair share. The storied Japanese work ethic is being eroded by the example of the "Gaijin," who rarely engage in the rigorous training of the Japanese players.[3]

The influence of American ideas in Japanese baseball has been evident in the last several years. In 1985, "the importance of the team over the individual, at least in the area of player contracts, may have . . . become a thing of the past in Japanese baseball."[4] That was the year when Japanese players formed a union. The Japanese players union has since become a force to be reckoned with in collective bargaining. In 1993, the union succeeded in obtaining a system of free agency, increasing both player salaries and the movement of players between teams.

The advent of the Japanese players union may well have the same effect on the Japanese owners' unregulated monopoly as the American Players Association is having on Major League Baseball's monopoly. In both countries, the rise of labor to positions of parity, so far as negotiations are concerned, may well bring the game of baseball within the strictures of antitrust law in both countries. If that happens, international antitrust regulation of baseball would become viable. In fact, the uniquely favorable position of professional athletes in labor negotiations may make an internationally recognized antitrust policy in professional sports more viable than such a policy would be in more conventional industries.

The future of Major League Baseball's anomaly is far from certain. In the short run, it appears that assaults on the key elements of the exemption have been adroitly diffused by Major League Baseball. In addition, Major League Baseball continues to benefit from the regulatory atmosphere of the 1980s and 1990s, which has seen the ascendance of the Chicago school's laissez-faire approach to antitrust law. The 1990s have been the era of the megamerger with giant firms combining forces. Many of these mergers have passed antitrust scrutiny. Nonetheless, support for vigorous enforcement of the nation's antitrust laws is low. As this book went to press Bill Gates and Microsoft were in the middle of antitrust litigation. The outcome of the Microsoft suit may be an important indicator of the status of antitrust law as we enter the twenty-first century.

On the other hand, the disparity between the regulatory status of baseball and the other major professional sports continues to be a salient issue. Furthermore, baseball no longer enjoys national pastime status. The peculiar nexus between baseball and American culture is considerably weaker than it was just a decade ago. The politics of franchise migration and publicly subsidized stadiums are issue areas that could produce future challenges to the exemption. Even the owners themselves are not immune from internal coups on the exemption front. George Steinbrenner's suit against Major League Baseball over his marketing agreement with Adidas is significant in this regard.[5]

Baseball's freedom from antitrust regulation has truly been anomalous in the Industrial Age. As we enter the so-called Information Age, will the business of baseball continue to be an anomaly or will it be a harbinger of American regulatory policy in the new age? For whom is baseball a good example, the advocates of vigorous antirust policy or those who believe antitrust law is a relic of the Industrial Age no more compatible with the Information Age than the hierarchical bureaucratic organization? These larger questions remain unanswered, but it is clear that baseball's monopoly is not what it used to be. The institutions, ideas and interests of the new century are sure to create a new environment for the business of baseball.

With the return of economic prosperity to the United States and the apparent slaying of the deficit dragon, it may be that the public's appetite for government regulation will increase. If baseball is unable to recover its position as the national pastime and if the owners fail to sustain their precarious alliance with the players, as well as with the minor leagues, it is likely that baseball's monopoly will not survive. The direction of the courts in sports-related antitrust cases is obviously disheartening for Major League Baseball. If the courts continue to narrow baseball's exemption, Major League Baseball will have to push for statutory protections, which not only require the cultivation of the interests of the players and the minors, but also the interests of the other major professional sports.

As it has throughout its history, baseball's regulatory status will be determined by the coming regulatory regime. The configuration of institutions, interests, and ideas will determine the fate of the baseball anomaly as the new century dawns. As this century closes, baseball has lost its cultural advantage. It is carefully juggling the relevant competing interests, and the judiciary is moving closer to eliminating the game's greatest institutional advantage.

NOTES

1. See Fox Eleanor M., "Toward World Antitrust and Market Access," *American Journal of International Law* 91:1 (January 1997), p. 1–25.

2. See Braver, Andrew F., "Baseball or Besoburo: The Implications of Antitrust Law on Baseball in America and Japan," *New York Law School Journal of International and Comparative Law* 16 (1996).

3. This term refers to foreign born players, which in most cases means American born players.

4. Braver, p. 451.

5. New York Yankee owner George Steinbrenner sued Major League Baseball's commissioner for interfering with his exclusive marketing agreement with Adidas. As this book went to press the case was still pending.

Selected Bibliography

BOOKS AND ARTICLES

Abrams, Richard. (ed.). *The Issue of Federal Regulation in the Progressive Era*. Chicago: Rand McNally & Co., 1989.

Abramson, Dan. "Baseball & the Court." *Constitution* 4, no. 3 (Fall 1992), p. 68–75.

Adams, Walter, and James W. Brock. *Antitrust Economics on Trial: A Dialogue on the New Laissez-Faire*. Princeton: Princeton University Press, 1991.

Alexander, Charles C. *Our Game: An American Baseball History*. New York: Henry Holt & Co., 1991.

Armentano, D. T. *Antitrust Policy: The Case for Repeal*. Washington, DC: The Cato Institute, 1986.

Asch, Peter. *Industrial Organization and Antitrust Policy*. New York: John Wiley & Sons, 1983.

Baldo, Anthony. "Secrets of the Front Office: What America's Pro Teams are Worth." *Financial World* (July 9, 1991), p. 28–42.

"Baseball in the Twenty-First Century: Still Accessible, Affordable, and Competitive." *USA Today* (November 9, 1994), p. 9C.

"Baseball's New Strike—By the Fans." *U.S. News & World Report* (August 24, 1981), p. 8.

"Baseball's Reserve Clause Dealt 3rd Loss in Row." *The Japan Times* (March 11, 1976), p. 10.

Bauer, Joseph P. "Antitrust and Sports: Must Competition on the Field Displace Competition in the Marketplace?" *Tennessee Law Review* 60 (1993), p. 263–294.

Bellamy, Robert V. "Impact of Television Marketplace on the Structure of Major League Baseball." *Journal of Broadcasting & Electric Media* 32, no. 1 (Winter 1988), p. 73–87.

Berger, Robert G. "After the Strikes: A Reexamination of Professional Baseball's Exemption from the Antitrust Laws." *University of Pittsburgh Law Review* 45 (1983), p. 209–226.

Berry, Robert and Glenn Wong. *Law and Business of the Sports Industries*. Vols. I & II. London: Auburn House Publishing Co., 1986.

Bork, Robert. *The Antitrust Paradox*. New York: Maxwell Macmillan International, 1993.

Brady, Dave. "Congress Aims Anti-Trust Blow at Baseball." *The Sporting News* (August 28, 1976), p. 8.

Braver, Andrew F. "Baseball or Besoburo: The Implications of Antitrust Law on Baseball in America and Japan." *New York Law School Journal of International and Comparative Law* 16, no. 3 (1996), p. 421– 454.

Bryce, Philip R. "The Sherman Act and Professional Team Sports: The NFL Rozelle Rule Invalid Under the Rule of Reason: *Mackey v. National Football League*, 543 F.2d 606 (8th Cir. 1976)," *Connecticut Law Review* 9 (1977), p. 336–345.

Burns, James MacGregor. *Roosevelt: The Lion and the Fox*. New York: Harcourt Brace Publishers, 1956.

Chass, Murray. "Chill of Labor Impasse Threatens Baseball's Spring." *The New York Times* (February 9, 1990), p. A1, A26.

———. "Myths Surround Negotiations." *The New York Times* (February 12, 1990), p. C2.

———. "With the Minors." *The New York Times* (December 3, 1990), p. C2.

———. "Diamond Business." *Athlon Baseball* (1995), p. 76.

———. "Halls of Congress Fill with New Lobbyists." *The New York Times* (January 8, 1995), p. 10.

Clary, Jack. "Who's on First . . . World Series or Superbowl?" *The Saturday Evening Post* (January/February 1982), p. 44–46.

Closius, Philip J. "Professional Sports and Antitrust Law: The Ground Rules of Immunity, Exemption, and Liability." In Johnson, Arthur T. and James Frey (eds.). *Government and Sport: The Public Policy Issues*. USA: Rowman & Allanheld Publishers, 1985, p. 140–158.

Crepeau, Richard C. *Baseball, America's Diamond Mind: 1919–1941*. Orlando: University Presses of Florida, 1980.

Croly, Herbert. *Progressive Democracy*. New York: Macmillan Publishing, 1914.

Curle, David. "On Higher Ground: Baseball and the Rule of *Flood vs. Kuhn*." *Legal References Services Quarterly* 8 (1988), p. 29–62.

Dahl, David. "Baseball Owners Dealt Blow By Panel." *St. Petersburg Times* (September 30, 1994), p. 1C.

DeBonis, J. Nicholas, Robert S. Kahan, J. David Pincus, Edgar P. Trotter, and Stephen C. Wood. "The Baseball Commissioner's Public Communication Role: A Test of Leadership." in Noll, Roger (ed.). *Government and the Sports Business*. Washington, DC: The Brookings Institute, 1974, p. 187–211.

Derthick, Martha, and Paul Quirk. *The Politics of Deregulation*. Washington, DC: The Brookings Institute, 1985.

Dewey, Donald. *The Antitrust Experiment in America*. New York: Columbia University Press, 1990.

Dodd, Mike. "Election results encourage both sides on antitrust issue." *USA Today* (November 11, 1994), p. 7C.

Dodge, John. "Regulating the Baseball Monopoly: One Suggestion for Governing the Game." *Seton Hall Journal of Sport Law* 5 (1995), p. 35–67.

Dunn, Scott A. "The Effect of Collective Bargaining on the Baseball Antitrust Exemption." *Fordham Urban Law Journal* 12 (1984), p. 807–839.

Edsall, Thomas Byrne. *The New Politics of Inequality*. New York: W. W. Norton & Company, 1984.

Eisenach, Eldon J. *The Lost Promise of Progressivism*. Lawrence: University Press of Kansas, 1994.

Eisner, Marc Allen. *Antitrust and the Triumph of Economics: Institutions, Expertise, and Policy Change*. Chapel Hill: University of North Carolina Press, 1991.

———. "Institutional History and Policy Change: Exploring the Origins of the New Antitrust." *Journal of Policy History* 1, no. 3 (1990), p. 261–287.

———. *Regulatory Politics in Transition*. Baltimore: The Johns Hopkins University Press, 1993.

Ellig, Jerome R. "Law, Economics, and Organized Baseball: Analysis of a Cooperative Venture." Ph.D. Dissertation, George Mason University, 1987.

Euchner, Charles C. *Playing the Field: Why Sports Teams Move and Cities Fight to Keep Them*. Baltimore: The Johns Hopkins University Press, 1993.

Fatsis, Stefan. "Major Leagues Keep Minors at a Distance." *The Wall Street Journal* (November 9, 1995), p. B1, B9.

———. *Wild and Outside*. New York: Walker & Co., 1995.

Feinstein, John. *Play Ball: The Life and Troubled Times of Major League Baseball*. New York: Villard Books, 1993.

Feller, Bob. "Then and Now: Why I Still Love the Game of Baseball." *Baseball Digest* (March 1995), p. 78–83.

Flint, William C., and D. Stanley Eitzen. "Professional Sports Team Ownership and Entrepreneurial Capitalism." *Sociology of Sport Journal* 4 (1987), p. 17–27.

Fox, Eleanor M. "Toward World Antitrust and Market Access." *American Journal of International Law* 91, no. 1 (January 1997), p. 1–25.

Freedman, Warren. *Professional Sports and Antitrust*. Westport, CT: Greenwood Press, 1987.

Gallup, George Jr., and Frank Newport. "Football Remains America's Number One Spectator Sport." *The Gallup Poll Monthly* (October 1992), p. 36–38.

Gammons, Peter. "The big picture escapes small minds." *The Boston Sunday Globe* (February 12, 1995), p. 83.

Garvey, Edward R. "From Chattle to Employee: The Athlete's Quest for Freedom and Dignity." *Annals of the American Academy of Political and Social Sciences* 445 (September 1979), p. 92–95.

Gattuso, James. "Congress and Rule-Making." *Society* 23, no. 4 (May/June 1986), p. 6–10.

Glastris, Paul, and Greg Ferguson. "A Bronx Cheer for Baseball." *U.S. News & World Report* 117 (August 22, 1994), p. 24–28.

Goldstein, Warren. *Playing for Keeps: A History of Early Baseball*. Ithaca: Cornell University Press, 1989.

Gould, Mark T. "Baseball's Antitrust Exemption: The Pitch Gets Closer and Closer." *Seton Hall Journal of Sport Law* 5 (1995), p. 273–289.

Gray, John A., and Stephen J. K. Walters. "Is The NFL an Illegal Monopoly?" *University of Detroit Law Review* 66 (1988), p. 5–32.

Gray, Paul. "Egghead at the Plate." *Time* (September 26, 1988), p. 72–74.

Gregory, Robert. *Diz: The Story of Dizzy Dean and Baseball During the Great Depression.* New York: Penguin Books USA Inc., 1992.

Grobani, Anton. (ed.). *Guide to Baseball Literature.* Detroit: Gale Research Co., 1975.

Guarisco, John W. "Buy Me Some Peanuts and Cracker Jack, But You Can't Buy the Team: The Scope and Future of Baseball's Antitrust Exemption." *University of Illinois Law Review* 3 (1994), p. 651–682.

Guttmann, Allen. *A Whole New Ball Game: An Interpretation of American Sports.* Chapel Hill: University of North Carolina Press, 1988.

Harris, David. *The League: The Rise and Decline of the NFL.* New York: Bantam Books, 1986.

Harris, Mark. *Diamond.* New York: Donald I. Fine, Inc., 1994.

Harris, Richard A., and Sidney M. Milkis. *The Politics of Regulatory Reform: A Tale of Two Agencies.* New York: Oxford University Press, 1989.

Harris, Richard A., and Sidney M. Milkis. (eds.). *Remaking American Politics.* San Francisco: Westview Press, 1989.

Heidt, Robert H. "Don't Talk of Fairness: The Chicago School's Approach Toward Disciplining Professional Athletes." *Indiana Law Journal* 61 (1985), p. 53–64.

Helvar, John. *Lords of the Realm: The Real History of Baseball.* New York: Villard Books, 1994.

Henry, Ed. "Baseball Lobbying Hits Major League on Hill." *Roll Call* (October 21, 1996), p. 15.

High, Jack C., and Wayne Gable. (eds.). *A Century of the Sherman Act: American Economic Opinion, 1890–1990.* Fairfax, VA: George Mason University Press, 1992.

Hill, James Richard, and William Spellman. "Professional Baseball: The Reserve Clause and Salary Structure." *Industrial Relations* 22, no. 1 (Winter 1983), p. 1–19.

Hofmann, Dale, and Martin J. Greenberg. *SPORT$BIZ: An Irreverent Look at Big Business in Pro Sports.* Champaign, IL: Leisure Press, 1989.

Holahan, William L. "The Long-Run Effects of Abolishing the Baseball Player Reserve System." *Journal of Legal Studies* 7 (1978), p. 129–138.

Holtzman, Jerome. (ed.). *No Cheering in the Press Box.* New York: Henry Holt, 1995.

Hosansky, David. "Baseball's Antitrust Exemption Draws Fire in Congress." *Congressional Quarterly Weekly Report* (September 24, 1994), p. 2673.

Hueber, Graham. "Majority Expects Baseball Strike and Would Side with Owners," *The Gallup Poll Monthly* (February 1990), p. 37–49.

Inglehart, Ronald. *The Silent Revolution: Changing Values and Political Styles Among Western Publics.* Princeton: Princeton University Press, 1977.

Irwin, Richard L. "A Historical Review of Litigation in Baseball." *Marquette Sports Law Journal* 1, no. 2 (1991), p. 283–300.

Jacobs, Michael S. "Professional Sports Leagues, Antitrust, and the Single-Entity Theory: A Defense of the Status Quo." *Indiana Law Journal* 67 (1991), p. 25–58.

Jennings, Kenneth M. *Balls & Strikes: The Money Game in Professional Baseball*. New York: Praeger Publishing, 1990.

Johnson, Arthur T. "Public Sports Policy." *American Behavioral Scientist* 21, no. 3 (January/February 1978), p. 319–344.

———. "Congress and Professional Sports: 1951–1978." *The Annals of the American Academy of Political and Social Sciences* 445 (September 1979), p. 102–115.

———. *Minor League Baseball and Local Economic Development*. Chicago: University of Illinois Press, 1993.

Johnson, Arthur T., and James H. Frey. *Government and Sport: The Public Policy Issues*. Totowa, NJ: Rowman & Allanheld, 1985.

Johnson, Chuck. "Fans ask Clinton to help save season." *USA Today* (September 8, 1994), p. 12C.

Juarez, Michael H. "Baseball's Antitrust Exemption." *Hastings Communication and Entertainment Law Journal* 17 (1995), p. 737–762.

Kahn, Roger. *The Era, 1947–1957: When the Yankees, the Giants, and the Dodgers Ruled the World*. New York: Tickner & Fields, 1993.

Karier, Thomas. *Beyond Competition: The Economics of Mergers and Monopoly Power*. New York: M. E. Sharpe, Inc., 1993.

Karl, Barry D. *The Uneasy State: The United States From 1915–1945*. Chicago: University of Chicago Press, 1983.

Kefauver, Estes. *In A Few Hands: Monopoly Power in America*. New York: Pantheon Books, 1965.

Keller, Morton. *Regulating a New Economy: Public Policy and Economic Change in America, 1900–1933*. Cambridge: Harvard University Press, 1990.

Kelly, Alfred H., Winfred A. Harbison, and Herman Belz. *The American Constitution, Its Origins and Development*. Vol. II. New York: W. W. Norton & Co., 1991.

Kirsch, George B. *The Creation of American Team Sports: Baseball and Cricket, 1838–1872*. Chicago: University of Illinois Press, 1989.

Koppett, Leonard. "Reserve Clause Could Aid Management, Veeck Says." *The Sporting News* (June 27, 1970), p. 30.

Kuhn, Bowie. *Hardball: The Education of a Baseball Commissioner*. New York: Times Books, 1987.

Latham, Earl. *Political Theory of Monopoly Power*. College Park: University of Maryland Press, 1957.

Lazaroff, Daniel E. "The Antitrust Implications of Franchise Relocation Restrictions in Professional Sports." *Fordham Law Review* 53 (1984), p. 157–220.

Lindbeck, Assar. *The Political Economy of the New Left: An Outsider's View*. New York: Harper & Row Publishers, 1977.

Lipton, Eric, and Mark Maske. "Aide Says Warner Cut Deal for Baseball Team." *The Washington Post* (February 23, 1995), p. B1.

Lovento, Thorn. "United it waits: New baseball league passes on the 1996 season, plans for 1997." *The Washington Post* (February 29, 1996), p. C1.

Lowenfish, Leo, and Tony Lupien. *The Imperfect Diamond*. New York: Stein & Day Publishers, 1980.

Lundquist, Carl. "From Landis to Kuhn: Memories of Baseball's Commissioners." *Baseball Digest* (February 1986), p. 33–37.

MacPhail, Lee. *My 9 Innings: An Autobiography of 50 Years in Baseball.* Westport, CT: Meckler Books, 1989.

Madden, Bill. "Baseball: Grass Roots Chaos." *The Sporting News* (December 3, 1990), p. 44.

Markham, Jesse W., and Paul Teplitz. *Baseball Economics and Public Policy.* Lexington, MA: D. C. Heath and Co., 1981.

Maslow, Abraham. *Motivation and Personality.* New York: Harper & Row Publishers, 1954.

McAneny, Leslie, and Lydia Saad. "With Popularity on the Upswing, Baseball Strikes Out." *The Gallup Poll Monthly* (August 1994), p. 28–31.

McChesney, Fred S., and William F. Shughart II. *The Causes and Consequences of Antitrust: The Public Choice Perspective.* Chicago: University of Chicago Press, 1995.

McCormick, Robert A. "Baseball's Third Strike: The Triumph of Collective Bargaining in Professional Baseball." *Vanderbilt Law Review* 35 (1982), p. 1131–1169.

Mead, William B., and Paul Dickson. "The President's Game." *The Diamond* (January/February 1994), p. 14–19.

Meggyesy, David. "The National Football League Monopoly." *Society* 23, no. 4 (May/June 1986), p. 16–21.

Mileur, Jerome M. (ed.). *The Liberal Tradition in Crisis: American Politics in the Sixties.* Lexington, MA: D. C. Heath & Co., 1974.

Milkis, Sidney M. *The President and the Parties: The Transformation of the American Party System Since the New Deal.* New York: Oxford University Press, 1993.

Miller, James Edward. *The Baseball Business: Pursuing Pennants and Profits in Baltimore.* Chapel Hill: University of North Carolina Press, 1990.

Miller, Marvin. *A Whole Different Ball Game: The Sport and Business of Baseball.* New York: Birch Lane Press, 1991.

Milton, David. *The Politics of U.S. Labor: From the Great Depression to the New Deal.* New York: Monthly Review Press, 1982.

Moore, David. "Most Fans Support Replacement Players." *The Gallup Poll Monthly* (March 1995), p. 39–41.

Morris, John P. "In the Wake of the Flood." *Law and Contemporary Problems* 38 (1973), p. 85–98.

Murdock, Eugene C. *Ban Johnson: Czar of Baseball.* Westport, CT: Greenwood Press, 1982.

Neale, Walter. "The Peculiar Economics of Professional Sports Teams." *Quarterly Journal of Economics* 78 (February 1964), p. 1–14.

Neikirk, William, and James Warren. "Labor's 'Mr. October' new hope for baseball." *Chicago Tribune* (October 15, 1994), p. 2.

Newport, Frank, and Linda DeStephano. "Football Top Sport Among Fans; Basketball Gains Support." The Gallup Poll Monthly (April 1990), p. 19–21.

Noll, Roger. (ed.). *Government and the Sports Business.* Washington, DC: The Brookings Inst., 1974.

Pearson, Daniel M. *Baseball in 1889: Players vs. Owners*. Bowling Green, OH: Bowling Green State University Popular Press, 1993.

Quinn, Hal. "They Staged a Strike and Nobody Struck." *Maclean's* 93 (June 2, 1980), p. 53–54.

Quirk, James P. *Pay Dirt: The Business of Professional Team Sports*. Princeton: Princeton University Press, 1992.

Rader, Benjamin G. *Baseball: A History of America's Game*. Chicago: University of Illinois Press, 1992.

Reich, Charles. *The Greening of America*. New York: Random House Publishing, 1970.

Reilly, Rick. "Glory to the Gridiron: Baseball Strikes Out With Football Aficionado." *Sports Illustrated* 69 (August 29, 1988), p. 140.

Riess, Stephen A. *Touching Base: Professional Baseball and American Culture in the Progressive Era*. Westport, CT: Greenwood Press, 1980.

Roberts, Barry S., and Brian A. Powers. "Defining the Relationship Between Antitrust Law and Labor Law: Professional Sports and the Current Legal Battleground." *William and Mary Law Review* 19, no. 3 (Spring 1978), p. 395–467.

Roberts, Gary. "On The Scope and Effect of Baseball's Antitrust Exclusion." *Seton Hall Journal of Sport Law* 4 (1994), p. 321–336.

Roberts, Gary R. "Sports Leagues and the Sherman Act: The Use and Abuse of Section 1 to Regulate Restraints on Intraleague Rivalry." *UCLA Law Review* 32 (1984), p. 219–307.

Rogers, C. Paul. "Judicial Reinterpretation of Statutes: The Example of Baseball and the Antitrust Laws." *Houston Law Review* 14, no. 3 (1977), p. 611–634.

Rosenbaum, Thane N. "The Antitrust Implications of Professional Sports Leagues Revisited: Emerging Trends in the Modern Era." *University of Miami Law Review* 41, no. 4 (March 1987), p. 729–822.

Rosenberg, Edwin. "Simple Problems, Simple Solutions." *Society* 23, no. 4 (May/June, 1986), p. 24–27.

Ross, Stephen F. "Monopoly Sports Leagues." *Minnesota Law Review* 73, no. 3 (February 1989), p. 643–761.

Samborn, Randell. "Baseball's Lawyer." *The National Law Journal* 16, no. 7 (October 18, 1993), p. 1, 48–49.

Sands, Jack, and Peter Gammons. *Coming Apart at the Seams: How Baseball Owners, Players, and Television Executives Have Led Our National Pastime to the Brink of Disaster*. New York: Macmillan Publishing Co., 1993.

Seymour, Harold. *Baseball: The Golden Age*. New York: Oxford University Press, 1971.

Shapiro, Leonard. "New Baseball League Still Lacking Owners, Players, Stadiums." *The Washington Post* (May 23, 1995), p. E1, E6.

Shapiro, Paul W. "Monopsony Means Never Having to Say You're Sorry—A Look at Baseball's Minor Leagues." *Journal of Contemporary Law* 4 (1978), p. 191–209.

Shughart, William F. *Antitrust Policy and Interest Group Politics*. New York: Quorum Books, 1990.

Shuster, Rachel. "League Folds." *USA Today* (April 12, 1996), p. B1.

Skolnik, Richard. *Baseball and the Pursuit of Innocence: A Fresh Look at the Old Ball Game*. College Station, TX: Texas A&M University Press, 1994.

Skowronek, Stephen. *Building a New American State: The Expansion of National Administrative Capacities, 1877–1920*. New York: Cambridge University Press, 1982.

Smith, Claire. "Major-Minor Rift Going Legal Route." *The New York Times* (November 26, 1990), p. C2.

Smith, Myron J. *Baseball: A Comprehensive Bibliography*. Jefferson, NC: McFarland & Co., 1986.

Spink, J. G. Taylor. *Judge Landis and Twenty-Five Years of Baseball*. New York: Thomas Y. Crowell Co., 1947.

Staudohar, Paul D. *The Sports Industry and Collective Bargaining*. Ithaca: ILR Press, 1986.

———. "Baseball's Labor Relations: The Lockout of 1990." *Monthly Labor Review* (October 1990), p. 32–36.

Story, Ronald. "The Country of the Young." In Noll, Roger (ed.). *Government and the Sports Business*. Washington, DC: The Brookings Institute, 1974, p. 324–342.

———. "The Black Sox Scandal." In Graebner, William (ed.). *True Stories from the American Past*. New York: McGraw-Hill, 1993, p. 107–125.

Sullivan, E. Thomas, and Jeffrey L. Harrison. *Understanding Antitrust and its Economic Implications*. New York: Matthew Bender & Co., 1994.

Taft, William Howard. *The Antitrust Act and the Supreme Court*. New York: Harper & Brothers Publishers, 1914.

Taylor, Stephanie L. "Baseball as an Anomaly: American Major League Baseball Antitrust Exemption—Is the Australian Model a Solution?" *Seton Hall Journal of Sport Law* 5, no. 2 (1995), p. 359–388.

Thomas, Jennifer. "Subcommittee Backs Anti-exemption Bill." *St. Petersburg Times* (September 28, 1994), p. 9C.

Thorelli, Hans B. *The Federal Antitrust Policy: Origination of an American Tradition*. Baltimore: The Johns Hopkins Press, 1955.

Topkis, J. H. "The Super Bowl and the Sherman Act: Professional Team Sports and the Antitrust Laws." *Harvard Law Review* 81 (1967), p. 418–434.

Turland, Kathleen L. "Major League Baseball and Antitrust: Bottom of the Ninth, Bases Loaded, Two Outs, Full Count and Congress Takes a Swing." *Syracuse Law Review* 45 (1995), p. 1330–1391.

Vecsey, George. "The Owners Strike Out On Hill, Too." *The New York Times* (September 23, 1994), p. B9.

Vick, Karl. "Vince Piazza still trying to make a name for himself in baseball." *St. Petersburg Times* (March 20, 1994), p. 8A.

Vincent, Ted. *The Rise and Fall of American Sport*. Lincoln: University of Nebraska Press, 1981.

Voigt, David Q. *American Baseball: From Gentleman's Sport to the Commissioner System*. Norman: University of Oklahoma Press, 1966.

———. *American Baseball: From the Commissioners to Continental Expansion*. Vol. II. Norman: University of Oklahoma Press, 1970.

———. *America Through Baseball*. Chicago: Nelson-Hall Publishing, 1976.

———. *American Baseball: From Postwar Expansion to the Electronic Age*. University Park: The Pennsylvania State University Press, 1983.

Waller, Spencer W., Neil B. Cohen, and Paul Finkelman. (eds.). *Baseball and the American Legal Mind*. New York: Garland Publishing, Inc., 1995.

Wecter, Dixon. *The Age of the Great Depression: 1929–1941*. New York: The Macmillan Co., 1948.

Weistart, John C. "Player Discipline in Professional Sports: The Antitrust Issues." *William and Mary Law Review* 18 (Summer 1977), p. 703–739.

———. "League Control of Market Opportunities: A Perspective on Competition and Cooperation in the Sports Industry." *Duke Law Journal* 6 (December 1984), p. 1013–1070.

White, G. Edward. *Creating the National Pastime: Baseball Transforms Itself, 1903–1953*. Princeton: Princeton University Press, 1996.

Whiteside, Larry. "After injunction, major leaguers vote to play ball." *The Boston Globe* (April 1, 1995), p. 1.

Whitford, David. *Playing Hardball: The High-Stakes Battle for Baseball's New Franchises*. New York: Doubleday Publishers, 1993.

Wilson, John. *Sport, Society and the State: Playing by the Rules*. Detroit: Wayne State University Press, 1994.

Zimbalist, Andrew. *Baseball and Billions: A Probing Look Into the Big Business of Our National Pastime*. New York: Basic Books, 1992.

CONGRESSIONAL HEARINGS AND REPORTS

U.S. Congress. House. Committee on the Judiciary, Subcommittee on Monopolies and Commercial Law. *Organized Baseball, Hearings*. 82nd Cong., 1st Sess. 1951.

U.S. Congress. House. Committee on the Judiciary, Subcommittee on the Study of Monopoly Power. *Organized Baseball*. H.R. Rept. No. 2002, 82nd Cong., 2d Sess. 1952.

U.S. Congress. Senate. Committee on Interstate and Foreign Commerce, Subcommittee on Televising Baseball Games. *Broadcasting and Television Baseball Games, Hearings*. 83rd Cong., 1st Sess. 1953.

U.S. Congress. Senate. Committee on the Judiciary, Subcommittee on Antitrust and Monopoly. *Subjecting Professional Baseball Clubs to the Antitrust Laws, Hearings*. 83rd Cong., 2d Sess. 1954.

U.S. Congress. House. Committee on the Judiciary, Subcommittee on Antitrust. *Organized Professional Sports Teams, Hearings*. 85th Cong., 1st Sess. 1957.

U.S. Congress. House. Committee on the Judiciary. *Applicability of Antitrust Laws to Organized Professional Team Sports*. H.R. Rept. No. 1720, 85th Cong., 2d Sess. 1958.

U.S. Congress. Senate. Committee on the Judiciary, Subcommittee on Antitrust and Monopoly Power. *Organized Professional Team Sports, Hearings*. 85th Cong., 2d Sess. 1958.

U.S. Congress. Senate. Committee on the Judiciary, Subcommittee on Antitrust and Monopoly Power. *Organized Professional Team Sports, Hearings*. 86th Cong., 1st Sess. 1959.

U.S. Congress. Senate. Committee on the Judiciary, Subcommittee on Antitrust and Monopoly Power. *Organized Professional Team Sports, Hearings*. 86th Cong., 2d Sess. 1960.

U.S. Congress. House. Committee on the Judiciary, Subcommittee on Antitrust. *Telecasting of Professional Sports Contests, Hearings*. 87th Cong., 2d Sess. 1961.

U.S. Congress. Senate. Committee on the Judiciary. *Applicability of the Antitrust Laws to Certain Aspects of Designated Organized Professional Team Sports*. S. Rept. No. 1303, 88th Cong., 2d Sess. 1964.

U.S. Congress. Senate. Committee on the Judiciary, Subcommittee on Antitrust and Monopoly Power. *Professional Sports Antitrust Bill—1964, Hearings*. 88th Cong., 2d Sess. 1964.

U.S. Congress. Senate. Committee on the Judiciary, Subcommittee on Antitrust, Monopolies and Business Rights. *Professional Sports Antitrust, Hearings*. 88th Cong., 2d Sess. 1964.

U.S. Congress. Senate. Committee on the Judiciary. *Professional Sports Act of 1965*. S. Rept. No. 462, 89th Cong., 1st Sess. 1965.

U.S. Congress. House. Committee on the Judiciary, Subcommittee on Antitrust. *Hearings on the Professional Football League Merger*. 89th Cong., 2d Sess. 1966.

U.S. Congress. Senate. Committee on the Judiciary, Subcommittee on Antitrust and Monopoly Power. *Professional Basketball, Hearings*. 92nd Cong., 1st Sess. 1971.

U.S. Congress. House. Committee on the Judiciary, Subcommittee No. 5. *Antitrust Laws and Organized Professional Team Sports Including Consideration of the Proposed Merger of the American and National Basketball Associations, Hearings*. 92nd Cong., 2d Sess. 1972.

U.S. Congress. Senate. Committee on the Judiciary. *Federal Sports Act of 1972, Hearings*. 92nd Cong., 2d Sess. 1972.

U.S. Congress. Senate. Committee on Commerce. *Federal Sports Act of 1972, Hearings*. 93rd Cong., 2d Sess. 1972.

U.S. Congress. Senate. Committee on Commerce, Subcommittee on Communications. *Hearings on TV Blackouts of Sporting Events*. 92nd Cong., 2d Sess. 1972.

U.S. Congress. House. Committee on the Judiciary, Subcommittee on Antitrust. *The Antitrust Laws and Organized Professional Team Sports, Hearings*. 92nd Cong., 2d Sess. 1972.

U.S. Congress. House. Committee on Interstate and Foreign Commerce, Subcommittee on Communications and Power. *Professional Sports Blackouts, Hearings*. 93rd Cong., 1st Sess. 1973.

U.S. Congress. House. Committee on the Judiciary, Subcommittee on Monopolies and Commercial Law. *Rights of Professional Athletes, Hearings*. 94th Cong., 1st Sess. 1975.

U.S. Congress. House. Select Committee on Professional Sports. *Professional Sports and the Law*. 94th Cong., 2d Sess. 1976.

U.S. Congress. House. Select Committee on Professional Sports. *Inquiry into Professional Sports, Hearings*. 94th Cong., 2d Sess. 1976.

U.S. Congress. House. Select Committee on Professional Sports. *Inquiry into Profes-sional Sports*. H.R. Rept. No. 1786, 94th Cong., 2d Sess. 1976.

U.S. Congress. House. Committee on the Judiciary, Subcommittee on Monopolies and Commercial Law. *Rights of Professional Athletes, Hearings*. 95th Cong., 1st Sess. 1977.

U.S. Congress. House. Committee on Interstate and Foreign Commerce, Subcom-mittee on Communications. *Sports Anti-blackout Legislation, Hearings*. 95th Cong., 2d Sess. 1978.

U.S. Congress. House. Committee on Interstate and Foreign Commerce, Subcom-mittee on Communications and Power. *Sports Anti-blackout Legislation, Hearings*. 96th Cong., 1st Sess. 1979.

U.S. Congress. House. Committee on the Judiciary, Subcommittee on Monopolies and Commercial Law. *Antitrust Policy and Professional Sports, Hearings*. 97th Cong., 1st & 2d Sess. 1981.

U.S. Congress. House. Committee on the Judiciary, Subcommittee on Monopolies and Commercial Law. *Antitrust Policy and Professional Sports, Hearings*. 97th Cong., 1st & 2d Sess. 1982.

U.S. Congress. Senate. Committee on the Judiciary. *Professional Sports Antitrust Im-munity, Hearings*. 97th Cong., 2d Sess. 1982.

U.S. Congress. Senate. Committee on the Judiciary. *Professional Sports Antitrust Im-munity, Hearings*. 98th Cong., 1st Sess. 1983.

U.S. Congress. House. Committee on Energy and Commerce, Subcommittee on Commerce, Transportation, and Tourism. *Professional Sports Team Com-munity Protection Act, Hearings*. 98th Cong., 2d Sess. 1984.

U.S. Congress. Senate. Committee on Commerce, Science, and Transportation. *Professional Sports Team Community Protection Act, Hearings*. 98th Cong., 2d Sess. 1984.

U.S. Congress. House. Committee on Energy and Commerce, Subcommittee on Commerce, Transportation, and Tourism. *Professional Sports, Hearings*. 99th Cong., 1st Sess. 1985.

U.S. Congress. Senate. Committee on the Judiciary. *Professional Sports Antitrust Im-munity, Hearings*. 99th Cong., 1st Sess. 1985.

U.S. Congress. Senate. Committee on Commerce, Science, and Transportation. *Professional Sports Community Protection Act of 1985, Hearings*. 99th Cong., 1st Sess. 1985.

U.S. Congress. Senate. Committee on the Judiciary. *Professional Sports Antitrust Im-munity, Hearings*. 99th Cong., 2d Sess. 1986.

U.S. Congress. Senate. Committee on the Judiciary, Subcommittee on Antitrust, Monopolies, and Business Rights. *Antitrust Implications of the Recent NFL Television Contract, Hearings*. 100th Cong., 1st Sess. 1987.

U.S. Congress. Senate. Committee on the Judiciary, Subcommittee on Antitrust, Monopolies, and Business Rights. *Professional Sports Antitrust Immunity, Hearings*. 100th Cong., 2d Sess. 1988.

U.S. Congress. Senate. Committee on the Judiciary, Subcommittee on Antitrust, Monopolies, and Business Rights. *Competitive Issues in the Cable Television Industry, Hearings*. 100th Cong., 2d Sess. 1988.

U.S. Congress. Senate. Committee on the Judiciary, Subcommittee on Antitrust, Monopolies, and Business Rights. *Sports Programming and Cable Television, Hearings.* 101st Cong., 1st Sess. 1989.

U.S. Congress. Senate. Committee on the Judiciary, Subcommittee on Antitrust, Monopolies, and Business Rights. *Competitive Problems in the Cable Television Industry.* 101st Cong., 1st Sess. 1990.

U.S. Congress. House. Committee on Energy and Commerce, Subcommittee on Telecommunications and Finance. *Cable Television Regulation (Part 2), Hearings.* 101st Cong., 2d Sess. 1990.

U.S. Congress. Senate. Committee on the Judiciary, Subcommittee on Antitrust, Monopolies, and Business Rights. *Sports Programming and Cable Television, Hearings.* 101st Cong., 2d Sess. 1991.

U.S. Congress. Senate. Committee on the Judiciary, Subcommittee on Patents, Copyrights, and Trademarks. *Prohibiting State-Sanctioned Sports Gambling, Hearings.* 102nd Cong., 1st Sess. 1991.

U.S. Congress. Senate. Committee on the Judiciary, Subcommittee on Antitrust, Monopolies, and Business Rights. *Baseball's Antitrust Immunity, Hearings.* 102nd Cong., 2d Sess. 1992.

U.S. Congress. House. Committee on the Judiciary, Subcommittee on Economic and Commercial Law. *Baseball's Antitrust Immunity, Hearings.* 103rd Cong., 1st Sess. 1993.

U.S. Congress. House Committee on Small Business. *Key Issues Confronting Minor League Baseball, Hearings.* 103rd Cong., 2d Sess. 1994.

U.S. Congress. House. Committee on the Judiciary, Subcommittee on Ecomonic and Commercial Law. *Baseball's Antitrust Exemption (Part 2), Hearings.* 103rd Cong., 2d Sess. 1994.

U.S. Congress. House. Committee on Education and Labor, Subcommittee on Labor-Management Relations. *Impact on Collective Bargaining of the Antitrust Exemption, H.R. 5095, Major League Play Ball Act of 1995, Hearings.* 103rd Cong., 2d Sess. 1994.

U.S. Congress. House. Committee on the Judiciary. *Baseball Fans and Community Protection Act of 1994.* H.R. Rept. No. 103–871, 103rd Cong., 2d Sess. 1994.

U.S. Congress. Senate. Committee on the Judiciary, Subcommittee on Antitrust, Monopolies, and Business Rights. *Professional Baseball Teams and the Antitrust Laws, Hearings.* 103rd Cong., 2d Sess. 1994.

U.S. Congress. Senate. Committee on the Judiciary, Subcommittee on Antitrust, Business Rights, and Competition. *The Court-Imposed Major League Baseball Antitrust Exemption, Hearings.* 104th Cong., 1st Sess. 1995.

U.S. Congress. Senate. Committee on the Judiciary, Subcommittee on Antitrust, Business Rights, and Competition. *Antitrust Issues in Relocation of Professional Sports Franchises, Hearings.* 104th Cong., 1st Sess. 1995.

U.S. Congress. House. Committee on the Judiciary. *Professional Sports Franchise Relocation: Antitrust Implications, Hearings.* 104th Cong., 2d Sess. 1996.

U.S. Congress. House. Committee on the Judiciary. *Fan Freedom and Community Protection Act of 1996.* H.R. Rept. No. 104–656, 104th Cong., 2d Sess. 1996.

U.S. Congress. Senate. Committee on the Judiciary. *Professional Sports: The Challenges Facing the Future of the Industry, Hearings.* 104th Cong., 2d Sess. 1996.

U.S. Congress. Senate. Committee on the Judiciary. *Major League Baseball Reform Act of 1995*. S. Rept. No. 104–231, 104th Cong., 2d Sess. 1996.

COURT CASES

Addyston Pipe & Steel Co. v. U.S., 175 U.S. 211 (1899).

Allen Bradley Co. v. Local Union 13, IBEW, 325 U.S. 797 (1945).

Amalgamated Meat Cutters v. Jewel Tea Co., 381 U.S. 676 (1965).

American League Baseball Club of Chicago v. Chase, 149 N.Y.S. 6 (1914).

American League Baseball Club of New York, Inc. v. Pasquel, 63 N.Y.S. 2d 537 (1946).

Brown v. Pro Football, Inc., 787 F. Supp. 125 (D.D.C. 1991); rev'd 50 F. 3d 1041 (D.C. Cir. 1995); 518 U.S. 231 (1996).

Butterworth v. National League of Professional Baseball Clubs, 644 So. 2d 1021 (Fla. 1994).

Charles O. Finley & Co. v. Kuhn, 569 F.2d 527 (7th Cir. 1978).

Federal Baseball Club of Baltimore, Inc. v. National League, 259 U.S. 200 (1922).

Flood v. Kuhn, 309 F. Supp. 793 (1970); 443 F.2d 264 (1971); 407 U.S. 258 (1972).

Gardella v. Chandler, 172 F.2d 402 (2d Cir. 1946).

Hart v. Keith Vaudeville Exchange, 262 U.S. 271 (1923).

Haywood v. National Basketball Association, 401 U.S. 1204 (1971).

Hooper v. California, 155 U.S. 648 (1894).

L.A. Memorial Coleseum v. NFL, 726 F.2d 1381 (9th Cir. 1984); cert denied, 469 U.S. 990 (1984).

Mackey v. NFL, 407 F. Supp. 100 (Minn. 1975); 543 F.2d 606 (8th Cir., 1976): cert dismissed, 434 U.S. 801 (1977).

Metropolitan Exhibition Co. v. Ewing, 42 F. Supp. 198 (S.D.N.Y. 1890).

Metropolitan Exhibition Co. v. Ward, 9 N.Y.S. 779 (1890).

Mid-South Grizzlies v. NFL, 720 F.2d 772 (3d Cir. 1983).

Morsani v. Major League Baseball, 1995 Fla. App. Lexis 10391 (Fla. 2d DCA 1995).

NBA v. SDC Basketball Club, 815 F.2d 562 (1987).

NBA v. Williams, 857 F. Supp. 1069 (S.D.N.Y. 1994); aff'd, 45 F.3d 684 (2d Cir. 1995).

New Orleans Pelicans v. National Assoc. of Professional Baseball Leagues, Inc., 93–253, 1994 WL 631144 (U.S.D.C., E.D. La. 1994).

Northern Securities Co. v. U.S., 193 U.S. 197 (1904).

Paul v. Virginia, 8 Wall. 168 (1869).

Philadelphia Ball Club v. Lajoie, 202 Pa. 210, 51 A. 973 (1902).

Philadelphia World Hockey Club, Inc. v. Philadelphia Hockey Club, Inc., 351 F. Supp. 462 (E.D. Pa. 1972).

Piazza v. Major League Baseball, 831 F. Supp. 420 (E.D. Pa. 1993).

Postema v. National League of Professional Baseball Clubs, 799 F. Supp. 1475 (S.D.N.Y. 1992).

Powell v. National Football League, 678 F. Supp. 777 (D. Minn. 1988); rev'd, 930 F. 2d 1293 (8th Cir. 1989); cert. denied, 498 U.S. 1040 (1991).

Radovich v. National Football League, 352 U.S. 445 (1957).

Robertson v. National Basketball Association, 389 F. Supp. 867 (S.D.N.Y. 1975).

Schecter v. U.S., 295 U.S. 495 (1935).

Silverman v. Major League Baseball Player Relations Committee, 880 F. Supp. 246 (S.D.N.Y. 1995); aff'd, 67 F.3d 1054 (2d Cir. 1995).

Toolson v. New York Yankees, Inc., 346 U.S. 356 (1953).
UMW v. Pennington & Local Union 189, 381 U.S. 657 (1965).
U.S. v. E.C. Knight, 156 U.S. (1895).
U.S. v. International Boxing Club of New York, Inc., 150 F. Supp. 397 (1957).
U.S. v. National Football League, 196 F. Supp. 445 (S.D.N.Y. 1961).
U.S. v. Shubert, 348 U.S. 222 (1955).
Washington Professional Basketball Corp. v. NBA, 147 F. Supp. 154 (S.D.N.Y. 1956).
West Coast Hotel Co. v. Parrish, 300 U.S. 379 (1937).

INTERVIEWS

Brand, Stanley. Vice President, National Association of Professional Baseball Leagues. 8 January 1997.
Callahan, Eugene. Director of Government Relations, Office of the Commissioner of Major League Baseball. 9 January 1997.
Coffey, Allen. General Counsel, U.S. House of Representatives, Committee on the Judiciary. 16 January 1997.
Erickson, Markem. Associate, McGuiness & Holch. 2 December 1998.
Hanley, Cassandra. Legislative Assistant to U.S. Senator Daniel Patrick Moynihan (D–NY). 14 January 1997.
Veeck, Mike. General Manager, Charleston River Dogs Minor League Baseball Team. 19 March 1997.

MISCELLANEOUS DOCUMENTS

Boehlert, Sherwood L. "Dear Colleague Letter." (February 1, 1995).
Letter by Franklin D. Roosevelt. On file at the National Baseball Hall of Fame Library. Cooperstown, NY. (January 15, 1942).
Major League Baseball Players Association. "Baseball's Antitrust Exemption—A Resource Book." (1992).
Noll, Roger. "Baseball Economics in the 1990s: A Report to the Major League Baseball Players Association." (August 1994).
O'Brien, John Lord. "Proposed Legislative Program." Confidential Memorandum sent to Baseball Commissioner A. B. Chandler. (November 30, 1949).
Zimmerman, Dennis and William Cox. "The Baseball Strike and Federal Policy: An Economic Analysis." *CRS Report for Congress*. (January 13, 1995).

Index

About the Author

JEROLD J. DUQUETTE is Assistant Professor of Government and Politics at George Mason University. Professor Duquette has worked as a congressional staffer on Capitol Hill as well as in the U.S. Environmental Protection Agency.

ISBN 0-275-96535-X

EAN

HARDCOVER BAR CODE